The ...... world
...... t
...... praise of
BusinessSpeak

★

"Wow . . . a thorough guide to the language of today's
business world. If you don't know what people are talking
about at work these days, read this book. It may be the best
'foreign language' guide yet to help you in your career."
—**Charles C. Manz, Professor of Management at Arizona
State University, author of *Mastering Self-Leadership***

★

"A practical sourcebook that will help make some sense of
the jargon used in business . . . an easy-to-use resource . . .
with just the right amount of whimsy. . . . I definitely plan on
making this a part of the corporate library."
—**Wanda J. Breeden, Corporate Director of
Organizational Development, Quebecor Printing**

★

"In any organization, common understanding of terms is
essential. This work provides the basis for such
understanding for both the novice and the experienced
business person."
—**John B. Knauff, Director of MBA program,
University of St. Thomas**

★

"A valuable addition to any business library."
—**Seth Godin, editor,
*The Information Please Business Almanac***

DICK SCHAAF and MARGARET KAETER's diverse talents, experience, and activities expose them to the jargon most used by today's business professionals. Both have risen from blue-collar roots to the white-collar world, enabling them to gain a unique perspective on the challenges of making the transition to corporate America.

DICK SCHAAF is the co-author of *The Service Edge: 101 Companies That Profit from Customer Care*, the critically acclaimed book that shares the secrets of the 101 best service companies in America. His other books include *Taking Care of Business* and (with Margaret Kaeter) *Pursuing Total Quality*; he frequently conducts seminars and workshops for small business owners on the tenets of service quality.

MARGARET KAETER has written to niche markets such as agriculture, engineering, and training in her career as a public relations professional, business writer, and magazine writer. Former editor of a magazine for small business retailers, she writes and speaks frequently on business subjects.

BUSINESSSPEAK

4,000
BUSINESS TERMS,
BUZZWORDS, ACRONYMS,
AND TECHNICAL WORDS:
All You Need to Say
to Get Ahead in
Corporate America

DICK SCHAAF and MARGARET KAETER

WARNER BOOKS

A Time Warner Company

WARNER BOOKS EDITION

Cover design by Diane Luger

Warner Books, Inc.
1271 Avenue of the Americas
New York, NY 10020

 A Time Warner Company

Printed in the United States of America

First Printing: February, 1994

10 9 8 7 6 5 4 3 2 1

BUSINESS SPEAK

A Few Words Before We Get to the Words

Writers are packrats. We collect things—people, ideas, odd facts, stray thoughts . . . .and words to explain them to other people. Working separately and together, we've been writing about business in all its various forms since the late 1960s, in the process using literally thousands of terms, from the simple to the arcane, to describe what we found going on. We didn't invent them. Truth be told, we didn't always understand them. But we collected them and used them and watched them change to take on new meanings as people in business needed new ways to explain what they were doing. You'll find a lot of those words in the following pages.

The *way* you'll find them defined deserves a brief explanation, however. We've joked for years that what we do is "vernacular engineering," but the label is apt: the vernacular is the informal, commonly used side of a language, usually the way it's spoken; engineering is an organized way of putting things together. The written form of our language tends to have a lot more structure and rules, while the vernacular takes on new meanings and styles virtually every day. Most dictionaries, including a number of very good business dictionaries, define the former. Our objective here is to translate the latter.

Yes, we'll tell you what words and phrases like *debenture, material requirement planning,* and *P/E ratio* mean. But we'll also try to help you understand what's involved in a *limbo contest,* the purpose of a *dawn patrol,* and the tremendous power available to you if you're the only one in the room who knows the meaning of *insegrevious.* We won't pretend that our definitions are all-encompassing. We've deliberately left out a lot of formal dictionary features such as pronunciation guides and

1

parts of speech. But we hope you'll find the listings readily understandable—and even a little fun. That's why we've included not only meanings but occasional parenthetical notes on context or origins.

We've also tried to anticipate your needs as you thumb through the listings. Where two words occasionally confuse (*anecdote* and *antidote*, or *biannual* and *biennial*, for example), we've referenced each in the other's definition. If we felt a word borders on jargony, we said so—and made a point of noting the simpler alternative as well (case in point: *utilize* and *use*). When we've come across words and phrases borrowed from other languages (*ad valorem, Karoshi*), we've tried to include both the meaning and the point of origin. And we've opted not to sanitize our listings for anyone's protection—terms like *anal retentive, bimbo* and *open kimono* are valid and valuable parts of the business lexicon. If treating them frankly fails to meet your standards of what's *politically correct*, we're sorry. For you.

In building our list, we tried to cover the most common terms from accounting, finance, investing and administration—professions that deal with money. We've thrown in some common forms of "bureaucrat-speak" along with specialized jargon from such diverse fields as agriculture, medicine, marketing, management, training, the quality movement, and the media. We've also provided three appendices to help you decipher the special complexities involved in acronyms and abbreviations, computer terms, and sports jargon used in business conversation.

Undoubtedly, we've left something out or given something a different twist than somebody else might have. That's what makes the English language so much fun to use (not to mention so much work to master): It changes all the time. If your experience doesn't match ours, or you come across something really new and different that you'd like to share, please feel free to drop us a line, c/o P.O. Box 1332, Burnsville, MN 55337.

We couldn't have done all of this by ourselves, obviously. There's no way to acknowledge everyone we've learned something from over the years, but thank you Jonathan Adams, Kristin Anderson, Susan Clark, Tom Cothran, Connie Crane, Diane Dimaggio, Debra Dinnocenzo, Barbara Dixon, Cheryl Gapinski, Georgia Gould, Carter Hedberg, Denny Jackson, Tom Kaeter, Jaimie Kiefer, Susan B. Levy Haskell, Connie Loetterle,

John McCain, Michael Olesen, Don Picard, Susan Quint, Gerry Richman, Karen Ross-Brown, Mike Schaaf, Joe Stone, Ron Wright—and especially Carter McNamara, our designated computer guru. Our special thanks to Colleen Kapklein, our patient and supportive editor at Warner Books—who stuck with us through some very trying circumstances—and Jeannie Hanson, our agent, who brought us the idea for *BusinessSpeak* in the first place.

Whether you're just entering the workforce or have been out there longer than we have, whether you're doing the same old thing or preparing for new challenges, we think you'll agree that words are the building blocks of basic, everyday commercial commerce—and conversation. In any business today, you need to be able to "speak the language." Here's what everybody is talking about.

—Dick Schaaf
—Margaret Kaeter
—July 8, 1993

A

a la carte agency—creative services agency that provides its services piece by piece rather than under a packaged arrangement or retainer.

a priori statement—judgment or conclusion that is reached without facts and cannot be proved or disproved.

A&P mix—advertising and promotion: the various amounts of different types of advertising, public relations, and other marketing communications activities being used to meet a specific goal.

AB roll—direct video-signal transfer from tape A to tape B.

ABC analysis—decision-making tool that puts items into categories (A, B, C) based on their significance.

abandonment—voluntarily eliminating a fixed asset from use; deciding not to offer a product for sale anymore.

abandonment stage—final stage in a product's life cycle, at which point production is discontinued.

abate—to cancel all or part of an amount due, such as rents or taxes.

aberration—significant departure from the norm; informally, an event or circumstance with negative consequences that wasn't anticipated.

ability—skill or talent for doing something (different from, and difficult to predict from, knowledge alone).

above the line—amounts of tax return deducted from gross income to determine adjusted gross income.

abrogate—to end or annul.

absenteeism—the rate at which an individual or group fails to show up for work.

absolute advantage—capability of one organization to produce a product using fewer resources than any other organization.

absorb—to soak up; to understand completely; a securities issue that has been completely sold out; business costs not added to the final cost of a product or service; in finance, an account that is merged with another account, in the process losing its own identity.

abstain—to purposely not do something, such as vote.

accelerated cost recovery system (ACRS)—1981 tax code modification allowing faster depreciation of assets put into service after 1980; modified again in 1986.

accept—to receive; agree; approve for use.

acceptable quality level (AQL)—minimum percentage of parts that must meet quality standards; allowing a certain percentage of mistakes, errors, or substandard parts is understandable, but can contribute to being content with poor quality (the level set becomes a self-fulfilling prophecy); in quality theory, the only acceptable quality level is 100%.

acceptance sampling—testing a batch of product or data for defects to determine if the entire batch should be accepted or rejected.

access code—individualized numbers and/or letters used to enter an electronic system, such as a computer, an electronic funds account, or a building security system.

access time—time taken by a computer to locate data and make it available to the user, often measured in milliseconds (thousandths of a second).

accessory equipment—industrial goods that are not part of a physical product and are used repeatedly, such as installation equipment.

accommodation paper—cosigned note that allows another person to obtain credit.

accord and satisfaction—settlement of a claim when the person filing the claim accepts something other than what was originally sought.

account—in finance, any category to which income and expenses are assigned; in business, the client in a relationship; in meetings, a story about something that happened; when reporting to a superior, to explain what happened before you get in trouble.

account assistant—low-level support person who performs clerical, research, administrative, and other less-important activities for an account. Often used as an apprenticeship or entry-level training ground for future account executives.

account executive (AE)—someone in an advertising, public relations, brokerage, accounting, or other service firm who oversees a specific account, coordinates activities for the account, and is the principal contact person with the account. Several account executives may work on one account; one account executive may handle several accounts. In a brokerage firm, the account executive also has the legal powers of an agent.

account number—number assigned to any entity (customer, supplier, lender, etc.) with whom a company does business for record-keeping convenience. Account numbers are often coded with information on location, size, and status of the account.

account statement—record of all transactions and their effects on the balance of an account during a specific time period.

account supervisor—senior contact person for an account, often a vice president of the organization. Account executives report to the account supervisor when conducting business for that account.

accountability—responsibility for a project; implies that the person responsible reports to someone higher in the organization or directly to the client.

accountant—person who balances business and individual financial accounts and files tax returns (not all accountants are Certified Public Accountants, or CPAs).

accountant's report—a formal, written document from an independent certified public accountant that explains how an organization's financial records were examined. The most common opinions are: clean, qualified, adverse, disclaimer.

accounting—the process of recording and reporting an entity's financial position.

accounting cycle—procedures beginning with the first entry of a fiscal year and ending with the closing entry.

accounting error—unintentional, inaccurate representation of a financial item.

accounting period—time covered by an income statement, usually a quarter, six months, or one year.

accounting principles—industry standards that govern current accounting practices, especially in complex transactions.

accounting procedure—the formalized accounting routines used by a business.

accounting records—all documents used to prepare financial statements.

accounting system—entire process that generates financial information, including all employees and equipment involved in the procedures.

accounts payable—current debts owed to vendors and suppliers; the "accounts payable ledger" is the exact listing of every service or product supplied to the business over an extended time and the amount the business owes.

accounts receivable—debts currently owed by customers to a business; the "accounts receivable ledger" is the exact listing of every service or product supplied to a customer over an extended time and the amount the customer owes.

accounts receivable financing—short-term borrowing secured by a firm's accounts receivable.

accounts receivable turnover—ratio that measures how often the receivables have been collected during the accounting period (divide total credit sales by accounts receivable).

accrual method—accounting for income and expenses as incurred, rather than as they are received or paid (the alternative is called the "cash method").

accrue—to increase by regular growth, such as interest; to include an item on the accounting records even though cash may not have changed hands.

accrued asset—assets from revenues earned but not yet received.

accrued benefit—benefit that becomes greater with length of service, such as vacation time earned.

accrued income—income that has been earned but hasn't been paid yet.

accrued liabilities—debts that have been incurred but haven't been paid yet.

accrued taxes—taxes owed but not yet paid.

accumulated dividend—dividend due but not yet paid.

ace—to win, do a perfect job, excel at a performance, such as a job interview or new business pitch (to "ace out" means winning at the expense of a competitor or co-worker); the best performer in an organization.

acetate—plastic overlay used for overhead displays as well as on posters.

acid rain—rain containing corrosive chemicals that destroy plants and wildlife, damage stone- and metalwork, and generally degrade the environment, typically a result of industrial and urban air pollution; potential business preventative and cleanup cost and/or public liability issue.

acid test—trial or analysis designed to show the true nature of the material or organization being tested; in accounting, formula used to measure liquid assets (divide cash, accounts receivable, and marketable securities by current liabilities), also called *quick ratio, acid test ratio,* or *quick acid ratio.*

acknowledgment—admission; faint praise; in law, the confirmation that a signature is voluntary and has been properly witnessed.

acquisition—process through which one company gains a controlling interest in another company.

acronym—word made up of the first letter or letters of a phrase or title (BOHICA, PAC, SEC, WYSIWYG)

across the board—including everyone or everything.

act of God—unavoidable catastrophic event caused by nature; informally, an explanation for any lucky or unlucky event no one has the time or willingness to analyze.

active—busy, displaying activity (e.g., an account, market, or relationship).

Active Corps of Executives (ACE)—association of volunteer executives established in 1969 to help small businesses.

active income—any income such as wages and commissions that comes in regularly and can be used immediately.

active manager—in quality, a manager who participates in the work of subordinates and actively seeks solutions to problems.

active market—characterized by a heavy volume of trading for one or many stock, bond, commodity, or other issues.

action—anything done, whether intentionally or unintentionally; in law, a legal proceeding.

action items—list of high-priority activities to be completed in a short amount of time; includes the activity, who is to take care of it, and the deadline for completion.

action plan—items to be completed to meet a specific objective, usually including a timetable for getting them done.

action programs—complex activities to be completed over a longer period of time to meet a specific objective or set of objectives.

actionable—subject to legal redress; an illegal act, especially in reference to corporate issues such as discrimination, liability, and slander.

activity report—recap of all contacts with a client, including decisions made and actions taken or pending, in a given period of time.

actuary—person who uses mathematics to figure the probabilities of insurance claims.

ad (advertising, advertisement)—space (usually paid for) in a newspaper or magazine, or time on radio or television, in which a sponsor presents information designed specifically to entice customers to buy a product or service.

ad agency—business that develops and contracts for ("places") advertising on behalf of a client.

ad appropriation—formula that allocates a specific proportion of a business's income for advertising over a set period of time.

ad response—change in sales or inquiries about a product in a timeframe directly after an ad has run.

ad infinitum—Latin for without end (literally: "to infinity").

ad litem—Latin for the purpose of a lawsuit or the duration of the suit.

ad valorem—Latin for something based on value; ad valorem taxes assess the value of the property, not the volume; property taxes are usually ad valorem.

adapt—typically used to mean adopt or use; actually means to adjust to new or changing conditions.

addendum—anything officially added to a document or agenda.

additional mark-on/mark-up—increase in the retail price of a product to take advantage of high demand.

adhesion contract—"take it or leave it" agreement in which standard items are offered by a business to its customers.

adjudication—judgment; determining the facts of a controversy and making a decision, usually in a legal setting.

adjusted gross income—income after deductions, the basis on which federal income tax is computed.

adjuster—insurance company employee responsible for examining damage and settling claims brought by the company's insureds.

administer—to take care of; can include planning, implementing, directing, budgeting, and accounting for activities on a project or overall program.

administered price—price set by a government entity or other nonmarket source.

administrative—any process that has to do with the overall running of the business or a portion of the business: planning, implementing, directing, and budgeting (the "paperwork and politics" of business).

administrative expense—cost incurred during the overall running of an operation that cannot be tied to the production of a specific product or service.

Administrative Management Society (AMS)—professional society that researches and promotes management methods designed to increase productivity, improve quality, lower costs, and improve employee/employer relationships.

administrative services only (ASO)—a technical term describing clerical services in benefits plans.

administrivia—trivial administrative items.

administrator—someone who administrates; in law, a person or entity appointed by a court to insure that the court's decisions are followed regarding property or an estate.

admiralty court—court concerned with maritime matters.

admitted carrier—insurance company authorized to do business in a state.

adopt—to take up or use; often refers the use of a technology for the first time by a consumer; *adapt* means to change.

adoption process—theory that different personality types will adopt (or adapt to) new technology at different points after the product's introduction: "innovators" buy the product soon after it's on the market; "early adopters" buy it once it's an established item, "late adopters" buy it once most of their friends and neighbors have the item, "laggards" buy it very late in the product's life cycle.

advance—to move ahead or make progress toward a goal; in finance, an amount paid before it is earned.

advanced biblical method—nonsystematic typing or research style explained by the phrase, "Seek ye and ye shall find."

advantage—superiority over a competitor.

adventure training—outdoor activities with varying degrees of controlled risk, from climbing ropes and towers to extended trips involving activities such as camping and white-water rafting, designed to build teamwork and camaraderie.

adversarial—relationship characterized by disagreement or divergent interest, such as labor relations in U.S. businesses, relationships between nonaligned managers and their subordinates, or relationships between poorly run businesses and their disgruntled customers.

adversary—opponent.

adverse effects—negative effects, usually associated with the use of a product.

adverse opinion—negative or contradictory opinion; in accounting, a CPA's finding that an organization's financial records do not reflect generally accepted accounting principles.

adverse possession—in law, a method of attaining property by occupying it, even if in opposition to the true owner; business slang for, "Possession is 90% of the law."

adverse selection—making a bad choice.

advertising—see *ad*

advocate—to support an idea or product; someone who supports an idea or product.

aerospace—literally, the earth's atmosphere and the space beyond; in business, typically applies to enterprises and products involving flight.

affect—to have an effect on, to cause change or put on a pretended behavior (when in doubt, use *impact*).

affective behavior—nonoriginal behavior used to elicit a specific response, such as rehearsed sales pitches or learned body language.

affidavit—a legally binding, written statement witnessed by a legally authorized person.

affiliated—connected to.

affiliated chain—group of geographically dispersed, noncompeting retail stores that act as a single entity when buying product or services.

affiliated company—two or more organizations that are subsidiaries of the same company; two or more organizations when one is a shareholder of the other but does not have a controlling interest; a company or other organization that is controlled by a bank through ownership or a majority interest of stock.

affiliated retailer—one of a group of noncompeting stores that buys products as a single entity.

affiliated wholesaler—a wholesaler that aligns with other, noncompeting wholesalers to purchase products in large volume to take advantage of volume discounts; a wholesaler that owns and usually is the primary supplier to affiliated distributors or retailers.

affirmative action—policies developed by organizations, often under government direction, to attempt to counteract past discriminatory situations, most often to encourage minorities to apply for jobs.

14

affluent—well off, rich; not the same as *effluent* (which means liquid waste).

aftermarket—market for items sold to customize, enhance, maintain, or restore a previously purchased product (for example, auto parts); a market where securities can be traded over-the-counter after their original issue in the primary market; the market that is used to buy and sell money market securities.

against the box—short sale by a stockholder who also holds a long position in the stock.

agency—organization that represents a person or business in dealing with a third party (for example, ad agencies design and place ads for their clients).

agency shop—organization in which all employees of a specific class that is represented by a union must pay union dues, even it they are not union members.

agent—person authorized to act for another person; in athletics and entertainment, the individual who negotiates contracts for services to be rendered.

agglomeration—many different entities combined into a single.

agglomeration diseconomies—expenses that occur because two or more organizations have combined, usually creating large, cumbersome bureaucracies that are less efficient than several smaller entities.

aggregate—total.

aggregate corporation—corporation having more than one stockholder.

aggregate demand—economic tool to predict the total of all goods and services that would be demanded in an economy at a given time at different income levels; the total demand for a given good or service during a specific time period.

aggregate economics—macroeconomics: the study of how major changes in society affect supply, demand, and price, and vice versa.

aggregate income—total income before adjusting for such things as taxes and inflation.

aggregate supply—economic tool to describe the total of all goods and services provided in an economy at different price levels; the total goods and services provided in an economy during a specific time period.

aggressive portfolio—securities portfolio designed to appreciate quickly.

agile manufacturing—term popularized by Tom Peters to describe a manufacturing business able to change rapidly to compete in global markets.

agribusiness—any business working in the field of agriculture: not only farmers ("production agriculture"), but producers of agricultural products and services and distributors and retailers of those products and services.

agricultural paper—financial instruments coming out of agribusiness ventures as opposed to industry.

airedale—a slick, high-pressure salesperson.

air bill—the papers sent with an express-delivery package so that it can be delivered and billed correctly.

aleatory—in insurance, a contract in which there is not equal distribution of risk and reward.

alert—to be on guard for a specific condition or occurrence (for example, a "blue shirt alert" tells workers that top executives are roaming the office; a "beefcake/bimbo alert" means that good-looking men/women are walking by).

algorithm—mechanical or repetitive sequence of computing instructions.

alien—from someplace else, whether another country (for example, an "illegal" alien) or another galaxy.

alien corporation—a corporation whose legal "residence" is in a foreign country because it is incorporated under the country's laws, even if it doesn't conduct its primary business in that country.

all-nighter—working past normal business hours, typically to finish a project due the following day.

allegation—assertion of fact that will attempt to be proved in court.

alligator hatchery—Joseph Juran's analogy of effective and ineffective ways to solve problems: Each live alligator is a potential quality improvement project, and each completed improvement project is a dead alligator. A "benign" hatchery produces new, useful quality plans; a "malignant" hatchery produces new alligators because nothing has changed. Juran contends that upper managers must supply the kind of leadership that shuts down rather than encourages the production of new alligators.

allowances—lower prices given by manufacturers, wholesalers, and distributors to retailers to offset expenses incurred for special projects such as marketing events.

allowed time—time it should take to complete a job at a reasonable level of performance.

alpha test—first official test in any series of tests, usually done on a very small scale.

alumni—graduates of a program, whether educational (as in a college or university) or business (as in former employees).

alumni relations—systematic way of maintaining and encouraging goodwill among past students or employees, often to make it easier to extract money from them at a future time.

amalgamation—the combination of two or more businesses or unions to form a single entity.

amass—to stockpile for use at a later time, whether physical items or intangibles such as support for an idea.

ambush interview—media tactic in which reporters and photographers arrive unannounced and begin an often hostile or adversarial interview before the subject has time to prepare (or hide).

amend—to change, but not destroy, by adding to something.

amenities—nonnecessary luxuries; social smalltalk.

American plan—hotel arrangement where meals, services, and room are paid with one fee.

American Stock Exchange (AMEX)—second largest U.S. securities organization specializing in the trading of stocks and bonds; in contrast to the New York Stock Exchange (NYSE), which specializes in very large companies, the AMEX handles primarily midsized and smaller companies.

Americans with Disabilities Act (ADA)—1992 legislation mandating full access to the workplace regardless of physical or other conditions.

amortization—the systematic liquidation or reduction of a financial obligation.

anal retentive—tight-assed.

analog—system in which numerical data or amplitudes are represented by "analogous" magnitudes or electrical signals; in analog recording, electrical signals are recorded to mimic sound waves; in "digital" recording, a coded pattern of ones and zeros reproduces the signal.

analysis paralysis—having so much information to study and weigh that no immediate or meaningful decision can be made.

analyst—professional who reviews information such as statistics or financial data in an attempt to predict future events.

analyst presentation—business presentation made specifically for financial analysts who make recommendations to buy, sell, or hold a company's stock.

anarchy—state in which no laws exist.

anatomy of processes—in quality, the breaking down of processes into their smallest parts to show how they interrelate.

anchor—to hold in place; something that enables an organization to ride out a business storm.

anchor product—product that accounts for the majority of sales in a product line or within an entire store.

anchor tenants—largest tenants in a shopping center or office complex, such as department stores or corporate headquarters.

ancillary—extra; of lesser importance.

anecdotal evidence—informal evidence, typically involving subjective observations and inferences, used in lieu of (or, not infrequently, in the absence of) conventional research and "hard data" to argue a point of view.

anecdote—a story told to illustrate a point (not the same as antidote).

annual—yearly, every year (*biannual* and *semiannual* mean twice a year, *biennial* every two years).

annual basis—statistical technique of taking a sampling of less than a year and extending it to cover a twelve-month period.

annual meeting—meeting held for stockholders of a publicly held company in which major decisions are announced or explained and the board of directors is elected.

annual percentage rate (APR)—amount of interest actually paid on an annual basis when interest is computed on a monthly basis.

annual report—official yearly report of a publicly held company's financial standing, including a statement by a certified public accountant as well as legally specified financial information; often includes additional information that represents the company in a favorable light.

annual wage—the set amount a person makes in a year, excluding overtime, bonuses, commissions, or other fluctuating income.

annuity—contract designed to disperse a sum of money in regular increments over a specific period of time.

antagonistic cooperation—human-resources theory that people suppress their dislike for one another when they see that working together offers mutual advantages.

antedate—to place a past date on a legal document.

antidote—substance or treatment that counteracts a poisonous or hazardous condition (not the same as *anecdote*).

antitrust—federal laws designed to encourage trade, thus discouraging monopolies and encouraging competition.

apparatchik—Russian for *bureaucrat.*

apple—something you shouldn't compare an orange to.

application—use or purpose; a form filled out to apply for something, such as a loan or a job.

applications programmer—someone who writes computer programs that solve specific problems.

applied economics—use of economic theories in real-life settings.

applied overhead—amount of overhead charged to a job or department when using a cost accounting system.

applied research—using pure research to develop practical applications.

appraisal—evaluation of a piece of property to determine its value.

appraiser—someone who estimates the value of property; most appraisers must be licensed and specialize in areas such as jewelry, land, antiques, etc.

appreciate—to gain in value; to understand (but not necessarily agree with) an opinion.

appreciation—amount a property gains in value from one time period to the next.

apprentice—historically, a trades- or craftsperson who is working toward mastery of a job or task by training under an expert or master; informally, anyone serving as an understudy (implies that the individual may eventually move up to the master's job).

appropriation—funds officially set aside to pay for something; not the same thing as *expropriation*, which is the act of taking another's property or rights.

approved list—securities or other investments that have been approved for investment by an organization or its customers.

aptitude—ability to learn something (used without a modifier, it implies a high aptitude).

aquaculture—fish farming.

arabesque—slang for a political move that takes you neatly out of the way when a difficult situation arises.

arbiter—court-appointed professional who specializes in settling conflicts (the court must confirm the decision's legal standing); often used interchangeably with *arbitrator*.

arbitrage—buying and selling to profit from price differences for the same or similar securities.

arbitrageur ("arb")—someone who engages in arbitrage; in the stock market, an individual or firm seeking to accumulate a block of stock of significant enough size to force the sale or restructuring of the company, or a buyback of the stock at a premium (see *greenmail*).

arbitration—process in which two parties submit a dispute to a disinterested third party; in "binding arbitration," they must abide by the arbitrator's decision; in "nonbinding arbitration" they don't have to.

arbitrator—someone appointed by a court or hired by independent parties in a dispute to help reach a compromise or resolution. In contrast to an "arbiter," an arbitrator's decision does not have to be approved by a court.

architect—someone who designs buildings; generally used to refer to anyone who designs or develops anything, such as a business plan.

archive—the area used to store old documents; to put something into storage.

arm's length policy—stated policy by a company to remain uninvolved in certain workings of employees or company divisions and, at the same time, not to allow those groups access to certain workings of the company.

array—series of related items arranged in a defined way; collection of data that is interrelated; range of options.

arrearage—amount of a loan past due.

art director—someone who sets the artistic direction of a print or video project, but not necessarily the person who produces the actual art.

articles of association—used by nonprofit organizations to show that the organization has met specific rules for existence; similar to articles of incorporation for a public business or entity.

articles of incorporation—official record that a company has met a state's laws for becoming a corporation.

artificial intelligence (AI)—the mimicking of human thinking by computers.

artisan—artist who produces work for a purpose other than pure art, such as a potter or weaver whose works have functional use.

as is—sold with no warranty as to condition or reliability (a clue that the material being purchased may be damaged or worn).

asbestos—mineral fibers frequently used in the past to make products fireproof; subsequently found to cause cancer; informally, refers to ideas or subjects that are difficult to understand, or describes a person who doesn't react to criticism.

ascertain—to find out.

ask—the requested sale price for a security.

aspiratory group—in marketing and sociology, a group to which a person or group "aspires" (wishes to belong), usually of a higher socioeconomic status than currently enjoyed.

assembly line—the production line (or any portion of it) that combines raw elements or components into a completed product; can connote mechanical, mindless, or unimaginative.

assembly plant—physical location of one or more assembly lines.

assembly tree—way of breaking down the processes in a company to show how all of the suppliers' inputs combine to create pieces of a whole product or process.

assess—to think about; to judge the value of.

assessment roll—official property-tax assessment record for a specific geographic area.

assessor—someone who determines property-tax assessments.

asset—item of value that could be exchanged for goods or services, or converted to cash.

asset management—practice of determining what items an individual or company will buy and sell at specific times to gain the greatest appreciation.

assign—to give a task to a subordinate; to allocate an individual to a group or department; to transfer ownership.

assignment—specific task to be completed; in insurance, the transfer of a policy owner direct to a third party.

assimilate—to learn.

associate—an employee who doesn't have a higher job title; a friend or colleague; to get together with someone for business purposes; a junior employee in a professional services firm, such as law or accounting, who has not been voted an ownership interest and partner status.

association—group of people who meet for a common purpose.

assume—to take over (as in a debt or obligation); to misjudge (as in "to assume always makes an 'ass'of 'u'and 'me.'")

assumed owner—in quality terminology, the manager of the most important portion of a major business process.

assure—to reassure or make sure; often used interchangeably with *ensure* and *insure*.

asynchronous—not synchronized; two people who do not work well together.

at sight—payment due on demand.

at will—whenever you want to; in many organizations, employees can be hired and fired "at will."

attach—to add to; in law, to take an asset or possession.

attachment—formal addition to a written document such as an insurance policy.

attitude—someone's emotions regarding a subject; used alone, implies a negative or cocky outlook.

attorney-at-law—professional who has been admitted to a state's legal bar; someone given official approval to represent others in legal processes.

attorney-in-fact—attorney who has written authorization to conduct business out of court for a client.

attractive nuisance—something innately dangerous yet interesting (such as a drainage pond in a residential neighborhood that is enticing to, and dangerous to, children); informally, a good-looking subordinate or co-worker.

attribute—to acknowledge the actual source of data, information, or a quote; a characteristic or quality.

attribute mapping—a way of measuring and analyzing quantifiable qualities of a group, such as income, education level, likes and dislikes.

auction—the sale of property to the highest bidder, whether verbally, by phone, or in writing. Public auctioneers must be licensed.

audience—any group that will somehow come in contact with a message.

audiovisual (AV)—pertaining to visual aids, typically low-end devices such as overhead or slide projectors (the high-end equivalent is "multimedia").

audit—review by either an outside or an inside entity to determine whether procedures (financial or otherwise) are being followed and whether controls are in place; may, but does not have to, include an opinion about the information.

audit trail—paperwork involved in an audit that shows correct audit procedures have been followed.

auditor—someone who performs an audit.

authoritarian management—style in which the manager's orders are never to be questioned.

automated teller machine (ATM)—electronic kiosk that dispenses cash, accepts deposits, and performs other standard banking transactions twenty-four hours a day.

automated warehouse—facility in which the items are stored and taken out of storage ("picked") by machinery.

automatic checkoff—voluntary amount deducted from a paycheck for items such as union dues, charitable contributions, investment funds, etc.

automatic deposit—paperless deposit of paychecks in the employee's bank account.

automatic merchandising—vending machines.

automatic number ID (ANI)—telephone technology that allows the person being called to know who is calling before answering (and hence allowing unwanted calls to be screened).

automation—use of machines to do work formerly done by people.

autonomous department—department that works separately from all others in the company; its work usually goes directly to a senior executive.

autopsy—detailed analysis to determine the cause of death; in business, determining what went wrong with a given product, service, or strategy.

average—arithmetic mean (divide the total amount by the number of inputs); informally, derogatory term for anyone who doesn't understand something as well as you do.

award—recognition for doing something well, often involving a gift of tangible or psychological value; the decision of an arbitrator.

ax—to fire; to completely eliminate anything, such as a department or a budget.

B

B-roll—generic video segments used to fill in when no germane footage is available

babel—corporate doublespeak, usually a lengthy speech or written document that, when deciphered, says very little.

Baby Bell—one of the seven regional telephone companies resulting from the breakup of AT&T.

baby boomer—someone born between the end of World War II (1946) and 1964.

baby bond—a bond worth less than $1,000 at maturity.

bachelor's degree—designation awarded for completing a defined course of study in a four-year college or university (common types are bachelor of arts, or B.A., and bachelor of science, or B.S., followed by the name of the subject).

back—to support; the part of the body you don't want to leave exposed to rivals.

back of the house—administrative support functions.

back office—administrative departments not directly involved in the major business of the company: payroll, personnel, records, communications, etc.

back pay—wages owed as a result of a pay change, for extra work, or in settlement of a dispute that was not paid at the time it was earned.

backdate—to put a past date on a document to take advantage of a legal or financial situation; usually illegal unless permitted as standard business practice (for example, life insurance policies often may be backdated up to six months to assess premiums on a younger age).

backdoor—to meet, decide, or gain access to something discreetly; in electronics, a computer access code, often created by a programmer or sophisticated user, that bypasses normal security procedures and allows entry into a system.

backdoor authority—unofficial authority to do something simply because the person is in the physical place to make the decision.

background—information given off the record and not for attribution or direct quotation; actions not happening for all to see; the interpretive history of something or someone.

backgrounder—written or video piece that explains the history or pertinent details of a product, event, or person.

backlog—unfilled orders or any work undone.

backstab—to betray someone to gain a business or personal advantage.

backtracking—displacing junior employees with senior workers when layoffs occur.

backup—duplicate copy of an electronic file, directory, or system.

backward compatible—new technology that will work with previous generations of the product or system.

backward integration—gaining ownership of the company's supply chain.

bail—money or property that releases a person from jail with the provision that the money is returned when the person appears in court; informally, to leave quickly, usually for fear that a situation will deteriorate; to help someone out of a bad situation.

bailout—loan or grant, often by the government, to help a business or industry remain solvent.

bait and switch—common, quasi-legal sales tactic in which advertising "baits" customers with a low price on a product, then salespeople attempt to "switch" them to a more expensive product; illegal if the company misleads consumers by not having the initially advertised product available.

balance—amount of money in an account; to account for deposits and withdrawals from an account; informally, to do more than one activity successfully at a time.

balance of payments—difference between trade payments made to foreign creditors and those paid by foreign debtors to a country.

balance of trade—monetary relationship between a nation's exports and imports; if exports exceed imports, the balance of trade is "favorable," if the reverse, "unfavorable."

balance sheet—financial statement showing property owned on the right side (credit) and any claims against that property on the left side (debit) as of a certain date; the total for each side must be equal (hence, balance).

balanced fund—investment fund balanced between stocks and bonds.

Baldrige Award (Malcolm Baldrige National Quality Award, a.k.a. "The Baldrige")—award process established in 1988 by the U.S. government to spur improved quality in products and services; up to two awards can be given in each of three categories: large business, small business, and service; no award is given if no candidates are deemed qualified. Named for the late Malcolm Baldrige, secretary of commerce in the Reagan administration.

balloon payment—large, lump-sum payment of the final balance owing on a loan or note.

ballooning—illegal practice in which prices of stocks are forced to levels far beyond their value.

ballot—any physical means of casting a vote; the method by which employees determine whether they'll be represented by a union.

band-aid approach—using superficial measures to cover up a minor problem without solving the underlying issues involved.

bank—business that offers one or more of the following services: savings accounts, checking accounts, loans, credit lines, negotiable securities; informally, to rely on something; to save.

banker's box—storage carton for business records that accommodates either standard- or legal-size file folders.

bankruptcy—legal actions taken to absolve a person or company of debts they are unable to pay.

banque—French for *bank*.

bantam store—new, small store that specializes in "quick hits" or onetime sales; often a trial store for a franchise or chain.

barcode—varying thin and wide stripes printed on an item in a unique arrangement so that information about it (such as price, expiration date, etc.) can be read by a computerized scanning device.

bare—operating without insurance.

bare bones—least amount with which something can be completed (for example, a budget or production team).

bargain basement—extremely low price on a product or service; derived from the retail practice of putting discounted merchandise in the basement of the store.

bargain hunter—price-sensitive consumer; investor who specializes in buying stocks that will gain in value appreciably and relatively quickly.

bargaining (collective)—process of negotiating work contracts and conditions between representatives of owners and workers.

bargaining agent—union or individual representing all the employees in a bargaining unit.

bargaining table—literally, the furniture around which union and management representatives meet; informally, active negotiations between a union and management.

bargaining unit—group of employees, usually at one company, who are eligible to be included in a union.

barometer—any selected group of statistics or other data that is used to predict larger trends.

barrister—British equivalent of a U.S. trial lawyer.

barter—to exchange goods or services for other goods or services rather than pay cash.

base pay—actual salary a person earns, excluding bonuses or fringe benefits.

base period—date from which economic data is measured and/or compared.

basic crops—in agriculture, the commodities that are eligible for price-support programs: corn, cotton, peanuts, rice, tobacco, and wheat.

basis—amount used to determine the value of something for taxing purposes; amount to which other amounts are compared, such as commodity prices at a large exchange; fundamental theory or principle.

basis point—0.01% of the yield of a mortgage, bond, or note; smallest measure used to determine yields.

batch—group of items completed or worked on together.

batch processing—in data processing, an entire job run as a whole (as opposed to an interactive process in which the computer user can enter new data and commands while the job is running); in time management, to save up minor individual tasks to be worked on all at once.

battle of the brands—fight between major brands for consumer marketshare, often consisting of widespread advertising designed to appeal to consumers' emotions because the products differ very little.

battery—two or more tests given to a large population; what the pink bunny is selling.

bayesian—decision-making method in which new information is constantly incorporated, causing assumptions to be continually refined to find the action with the highest expected payoff.

bazaar—store that offers a wide range of products; informally, marketplace where prices and conditions are constantly subject to renegotiation.

beamer—slang for BMW.

bean counter—accountant.

bear—someone who is pessimistic about the stock market.

bear clique—group of investors who work together to try to lower prices on securities or commodities by buying and selling the investment in a short amount of time.

bear hug—offer to buy a corporation for a much higher price than its market value.

bear market—period of declining stock and commodity prices.

bear position—"short position" in the market (a bear sells securities short in hopes that the market will continue declining so he can buy them back at an even lower price in the future).

bear raid—illegal practice of manipulating the price of a stock downward by buying a large number of shares, then selling them soon afterward.

bearer bond—unregistered security payable to the person possessing it; because payment is made on the basis of detachable coupons, it is also called a *coupon bond*.

bearish—pessimistic.

beauty contest—competitive review process in which several people, products, or agencies are looked at before a decision is made.

bedroom community—suburban community offering few jobs but close to a metropolitan area in which most of the residents work.

beef up—to build up, add more information, make more substantial.

beefcake—derogatory term for sexy, dumb men.

beeper—portable device that emits a beep when a phone number is called, alerting the holder to call in to work or another location.

behavior modification—trying to change a person's or group's actions by rewarding desirable behaviors and/or punishing undesirable ones.

behavioral model—model consisting of the behaviors rather than the duties involved in the position.

bellwether—indicator or leader (for example, a stock that often leads the market's movement); literally, the lead sheep in a herd, which often is belled to make it easier to identify and follow.

belly to belly selling—in-person sales tactics.

belt and suspender rule—having more than one alternative for a potential problem or backup systems in place in case a primary system breaks down.

belt line—rail line that surrounds or exists only within a city.

beltway—freeway or expressway that runs in or around a city; often refers to businesses located along the freeways that encircle Washington, D.C.

beltway bandit—derogatory term applied to consulting firms that specialize in federal government contracts.

bench strength—reserve talent, said of organizations that nurture backups for their top performers.

benchmark—to study another company's "best practices" in order to learn how it does something well, with the idea of applying the lessons to your own operations; a standard unit for the basis of comparison.

beneficiary—individual who benefits; in insurance, individual or group to whom a policy's proceeds are paid.

benefit—anything good or better than the competition; nonmonetary compensation in addition to wages or salary; event to raise money for a needy cause; payment received from life or disability insurance; to gain advantage from something.

benefit base—basic benefits the company provides to all employees (added benefits often can be purchased at less-than-market prices).

benefit cost analysis—cost of benefits provided to an employee as a percentage of the employee's entire cost to the company.

benefit, fringe—compensation provided to employees in the form of nonmonetary extras such as insurance, subsidized daycare, and pension plans.

benefit ratio—comparison of benefit costs to salary and wages for an individual or group of employees.

best case/worst case—advanced planning technique that involves developing scenarios that anticipate everything going perfectly and everything falling apart.

Best's rating—grade estimating financial stability given to insurance companies by A.M. Best's Rating Service. The highest is A+.

beta—Sony's proprietary video recording format.

beta test—second stage in many forms of new-product testing, usually larger and closer to a true sampling than an alpha test.

Bhopal—city in India that has become synonymous with chemical disasters as the result of a chemical plant explosion that killed thousands of local residents.

biannual—occurring twice a year ("biennial" occurs once every two years).

bias—prejudice.

bible—official sourcebook for a program.

Bible Belt—southeastern and south-central U.S., broadly consisting of the states within the box bounded by Florida, Texas, Kansas, and Virginia; the term stereotypes people of these states as displaying more conservative, religious-oriented beliefs.

bid—price offered for immediate acceptance on a stock or commodity; estimate of the cost of doing a job.

bid price—price at which the holder of an open-end share may redeem the shares.

biennial—occurring once every two years ("biannual" occurs twice a year).

Big Blue—IBM.

big business—large corporations, typically those with assets of several billion dollars.

Big Board—New York Stock Exchange.

Big Q—in quality, a company's attention to efforts that connect directly to the big picture.

Big Six—largest U.S. accounting firms. In 1993, they were: Arthur Andersen & Co., Coopers and Lybrand, Deloitte & Touche, Ernst & Young, KPMG Peat Marwick, and Price Waterhouse.

Big Three—three largest auto manufacturers in the U.S.: General Motors, Ford Motor Company, and Chrysler Corp.

bilateralism—commitments by both parties to do or not to do something.

bill—statement of charges for services rendered or products purchased; piece of paper currency; legislation under consideration; to send a statement of costs for payment.

bill of lading—document that itemizes goods shipped.

billable hours—in a professional service firm, hours worked for and billed to one of the firm's clients.

bimbo—attractive woman whose primary business asset is suspected to be her body, rather than her brain; ironically, prior to World War II the term applied to both men and women, and applied just to men in the early years of the 20th century (thought to derive from the Italian "bambino").

bimbo express—elevator used by secretaries and clerical workers for lunch and coffee breaks.

binder—in insurance and financial fields, temporary agreement that holds until the formal agreement is written, usually (but not necessarily) identical to the formal agreement; three-ring notebook; rubber band.

binding arbitration—when two parties (typically labor and management) submit a dispute to an impartial third party, whose decision must be followed by both.

bio—short biography, usually emphasizing work experience, but including personal items such as where the person grew up, family status, education, and other related personal background.

bioengineering—manipulation of biological elements to create new life forms, such as bacteria.

biological process—view of business processes formulated by Joseph Juran: Just as a cell divides into multiple cells, all coordinated by a "nervous system," an enterprise typically created by a single founder is "franchised" following the original model.

biotechnology—creation of new drugs or elements that use live items for their basis.

bird dog—someone who solicits business for a high-pressure salesperson; one paid to spread false or exaggerated information; to look for data or other information that will help in making a decision; to stay focused on a problem or project like a dog on a scent.

birth order—theory that people's behavior is predictable based on the order of their birth within a family.

black book—private address book; in some cities, annual listing of creative services, such as artists and photographers.

black box—flight recorder in the tail assembly of an airplane that records flight data (and hopefully survives a crash so the cause can be analyzed); central processing unit in a computer; any machine you don't understand that you nevertheless count on to operate reliably.

black hole—in astronomy, a star that has collapsed on itself, creating an entity with a tremendous gravitational pull from which nothing, not even light, can escape; in business, a project or operating entity that "eats" people, time, and money while showing little results; a workspace in which important items continually disappear.

black lung—disease resulting from breathing coal dust, one of the first widespread cases of proven industrial-related health problems in the U.S.

black market—illegal sale of merchandise that is in short supply or is illegal.

blackball—to work against someone; to convince an entire group of people that another person is undesirable for a position (derived from the practice of voting anonymously by using white and black balls).

blacklist—list of people considered unacceptable for a certain position; to place a person on such a list.

blackout—time during which certain activities cannot take place: in frequent-flyer programs, dates on which free-flight coupons cannot be used; in Social Security, the time during which a surviving spouse can't receive benefits.

blanket—all encompassing, covering everything.

blanket brand—brand of products offering something for

virtually every specific need (for example, separate grooming products for men, women, children, and infants).

bleed—to drain money or value from an organization through an activity that doesn't generate a good return; in management, using something to the utmost, often long after it should have been discarded; in printing, material such as pictures that run all the way to the edge of the page; informally, to extort or coerce regular sums of money from an organization (for example, through a succession of legal claims).

bleep—to block out certain socially unacceptable words with a masking sound.

blight—widespread, growing disintegration.

blind alley—path that does not work out.

blind man and the elephant—metaphor for not seeing the whole picture, and hence assuming the part you're in touch with is representative of the whole; from the story by Rudyard Kipling.

blind test—practice, common in medical and product preference testing, in which subjects do not know whether they are receiving the "real" product or a placebo or alternative; in a "double blind" test, the people dispensing the items also don't know which is which.

blinders—originally, tack for horses that restricts their vision to what is immediately in front of them so they won't be distracted or frightened by other horses, people, fires, and sudden movements; in business, working with blinders on means purposely ignoring the larger dimensions of a situation and focusing only on the task at hand.

blinding flash of the obvious—something so obvious that it should have been realized a long time before it was.

blip—short-lived phenomenon; derived from images on a radar screen that show up momentarily, then fade.

blister pack—clear, hard-shelled plastic shaped to hold a product to a cardboard backing so customers can see what they are buying before purchasing it.

blowout—sale of a product at a very low price, often below cost; fast-selling issue of a new stock, usually at higher prices than would normally be received because investors have a difficult time getting the number of shares they want and bid the price up.

blue chip—anything of exceptionally high quality; the generally high-priced, low-yielding stock in mature companies known for consistently paying dividends; derived from the most valuable poker chip.

blue collar—originally, skilled, semi-skilled, and unskilled workers who typically wore uniforms with blue shirts; blue collar workers must be paid overtime because they are not exempt from hour and wage laws.

blue laws—statute or ordinance that prohibits commercial activity on Sundays; refers to any strict statute or ordinance in a locality that seeks to define morality.

blue list—list of all current municipal bonds published every weekday.

blue sky laws—state laws that regulate the securities industry in the area of consumer protection.

blueprint—detailed patterns for a building; plan of action.

blues—in medicine, companies in the Blue Cross/Blue Shield system; in architecture, blueprints; in printing, photographic proof rendered in blue tones.

board of directors—people elected by stockholders to oversee the business.

board of managers—board of trustees for a mutual savings bank.

board of trustees—group of people that oversees the operations of a nonprofit organization.

board of trade—a produce exchange or chamber of commerce.

boardroom—room in a company's headquarters where the board of directors meets; a stockbroker's public office.

bobtail pool—group of speculators with a common goal but who do not act together.

body language—nonverbal communication consisting of facial expressions, tone of voice, and gestures that are clues to a person's emotional state.

BOHICA (Bend Over, Here It Comes Again)—used to describe the cynicism with which people greet new corporate pronouncements.

boiler room—usually fraudulent operation in which high-pressure telephone sales tactics are used to sell questionable securities.

boilerplate—design that can be used many times with only slight modifications; standard copy included in contracts, proposals, and other documents.

boink—euphemism for having sex, usually not for love but to gain an advantage in the business world; to take advantage of someone who is willing to have sex in hopes of gaining an advantage.

bona fide—genuine, not fraudulent.

bond—interest-bearing security issued by a corporation or public body; also, a financial guarantee that something will or will not happen (for example, fidelity bonds reimburse employers for dishonest acts by employees).

bonded—refers to a guarantee that an employee of a company has been checked for honesty and that a customer will receive a financial settlement if the employee performs a dishonest act.

bonus—anything extra that is of value; employees frequently receive financial bonuses for good work or when the company has a good year.

booby trap—situation that looks good in the beginning but is designed to make a person look bad or spend a great deal of money.

book—to officially record an item in a company's accounting books, as in booking a profit or loss; in hospitality, to reserve a room; activity record for a syndicate account; business's official accounting records; record of buy and sell orders in a security; trade journal.

book credit—ledger items that represent obligations not secured by notes to other collateral (also called *book accounts* or *open book accounts*).

book of final entry—book to which information is transferred.

book of original entry—book in which transactions are recorded chronologically.

book value—official value of an asset as carried on the financial records of an organization; value of an item as published in one of many books listing values, such as the Blue Book for used cars.

bookkeeper—person who records financial and other business entries for a business.

boom—period of rapid expansion or increase, often involving increased demand for goods and services, rising prices, inflation, high employment, and high demand for luxury items.

boondoggle—wasteful project that has the sole goal of creating work for a promoter or group of individuals and has little promise of economic payback.

boot—to fire someone or kick them out; in computers, to activate the software in the system.

bottom—lowest level in a market or cycle; lowest price a retail product can be sold for to break even.

bottom executives—top executives in a company using an inverted pyramid plan of organization.

bottom feeders—investors who buy stock in companies whose value is depressed due to adverse business conditions.

bottom line—final, succinct conclusion; in financial situations, net profit or loss.

bottom out—condition when something has reached its low point and is beginning to rise.

bottom up—opposite of top-down, participative management style emphasizing input from the frontlines.

bounceback card—response card included in a product or publication to allow someone to provide feedback or request additional information.

bounty—money given each time something happens; headhunters typically receive a bounty for each employee they place.

bourgeoisie—French word that describes the middle class.

bourse—European stock exchange.

boutique—store that carries a relatively small number of expensive or specialized items; a small shop within a larger store.

box store—low-service store that offers less expensive merchandise by buying in quantity; customers often literally buy items out of the box or by the box.

boycott—to purposely refrain from doing business with an organization in hopes of influencing its behavior.

brainstorming—free-associating ideas to solve a problem or formulate a policy, ideally with no criticism allowed.

brand—symbol or name that separates one company's product or line of products from another's.

brand awareness—extent to which consumers know about a particular brand of product.

brand extension—adding a product to an established line of products.

brand image—qualities that consumers associate with a brand of products.

brand loyalty—extent to which consumers prefer and will actually buy one brand over competing brands of the same basic product.

brand manager—person who directs the marketing activities for a brand of products; also called a product manager.

brand name—name of the brand line, not the individual product name, usually registered to prevent unauthorized copying or use and to protect its value in the marketplace.

brand share—percentage of sales on one product as compared to all competing products.

brandstanding—advertising and promoting an entire brand as opposed to a specific product.

brass—top management.

breadbasket—savings of an organization or its liquid financial assets; in marketing, the midwestern states that produce a high proportion of grains.

breach—not to do a legally required action.

break—good opportunity; quick, large downturn in an investment's prices; error in a brokerage firm's records of transactions; to provide different purchasing prices for different volumes.

break even—point at which income equals costs, which means the business is producing neither profits nor losses.

break up—to terminate activities; to officially disband a group.

breakout—smaller session at a meeting involving only part of those in attendance; written material (usually included in the body of the article) set in larger type within a story to highlight it.

breakthrough—major, often innovative action or idea that significantly changes a situation.

bridge loan—short-term loan made to "bridge" a period until money comes in or longer-term financing can be arranged.

brief—short written or verbal synopsis of a situation.

briefcase—small piece of luggage carried by business executives that stores the essentials needed for doing business for the duration of a trip.

briefing—short meeting that gives a synopsis of a situation.

broadcast quality—audio or video footage that is of high enough quality to be aired by a professional radio or television station.

brochure—small piece of literature that describes something.

broken lot—box containing multiple identical items in which some are missing; less than the usual amount of merchandise sold; fewer than 100 shares of stock.

broker—person who transacts business on behalf of someone but is not an employee of either party in the transaction.

brokerage house—business that specializes in transacting business (most often buying and selling stocks, bonds, commodities, and insurance policies) between two parties.

brotherhood—used to show unity among groups such as trade unions.

bubble pack—envelope containing air-filled plastic bubbles, used to protect items during mailing or shipping.

buck—to object; to go contrary to a person or a trend; to send to another person; to blame someone else.

bucket shop—illegal operation that takes orders from customers who want to buy securities, then waits to fill the orders when the price is lower than that quoted the customer.

budget—money or resources designated for a specific activity; estimate of the funds needed to conduct activities in a given period of time.

buffer—anything that stands between two other things, often for the purpose of diffusing communication between the two.

buffer inventory—inventory that serves as a reserve against higher than anticipated demand.

buffer stock—government-purchased excess agricultural

stock that is stored for sale in years of low production so that prices can be somewhat stabilized.

bull—in securities, someone who believes stock market prices will be rising; primary content of many official corporate pronouncements, especially alibis and excuses.

bull clique—investors who work informally as a group to push up stock prices through strategic buying and selling.

bull market—period of generally rising stock prices.

bull pool—illegal activity in which a group attempts to manipulate stock prices to higher levels.

bulletin—urgent, usually short announcement; written periodical that provides updates on a narrow subject.

bullish—optimistic.

bump—to take another person's job because you have seniority over that person and your position has been eliminated.

bump up—to raise a price or estimate to allow for unexpected costs or to generate extra revenue.

bundling—marketing several products and services together as a package rather than individually.

bureau—commonly, a government office, department, or agency.

Bureau of Labor Statistics—federal organization that compiles statistics having to do with the U.S. workforce.

bureaucracy—organizational system combining specialized functions and a fixed hierarchy of authority; government agency staffed by nonelected officials; favorite culprit for complicated, time-consuming processes in a large organization.

bureaucrat—someone who works in (and works for the preservation of) bureaucracy.

burnout—condition in which a person is so overworked that he or she cannot function normally in the workplace (and often at home); point at which a tax shelter is no longer advantageous because money is being withdrawn from it.

business—enterprise operated for the purpose of making a profit.

business agent—someone employed by an individual or a group to represent them and protect their interests.

business barometer—signal that business climate will be changing, such as unemployment figures.

business class—type of business being run as defined by the U.S. Department of Commerce; seats on an airplane between first class and the rest of coach, for which business travelers pay a premium price in order to get off the plane sooner; college-level course having to do with business or economics.

business climate—political and economic conditions that affect business.

business college—school specializing in areas such as business administration and secretarial training.

business cycle—regular, somewhat predictable cycles of economic strength and weakness in the nation as a whole or a specific market or industry segment; cycle of financial lows and highs experienced regularly by any business.

business day—hours that most businesses are open; days that financial organizations conduct business (excludes weekends and holidays).

business ethics—moral principles governing how a business is operated.

business office—physical location of the portion of a business that takes care of administrative and accounting duties.

business organization—structure of a business; how it functions.

business overhead coverage—disability coverage designed to cover the expenses of operating a business while the owner is disabled.

business plan—schematic for operating a business, usually over the next three to five years, that attempts to anticipate major decisions and create contingency plans for disasters; may also include individual plans for each department or division.

business reply card (BRC)—postcard preprinted with the business's address and sent or given to customers as a means to provide requested information, to request additional information, or to communicate complaints, suggestions, and (very infrequently) kudos.

business theater—use of entertainment activities such as dramatizations and celebrities in a business context.

business-to-business advertising—advertising that communicates directly with another business instead of consumers.

button down—neat and acceptable corporate style (derived from a collar style on dress shirts).

buy—to purchase; to believe another's theory or story.

buy in—to get others to go along with a proposed idea or course of action; in options trading, procedure used to terminate responsibility for delivering or accepting stock; transaction between brokers where the buying broker must obtain shares from other sources because securities are not delivered on time by the broker on the selling side.

buy on margin—to buy securities on credit.

buy the business—predatory tactic used in competitive bidding situations in which a firm (usually larger or better financed) underprices or promises to overserve in order to win the project, even though fulfilling under the proposed terms will not be profitable.

buy the farm—to die.

buy-sell—contract that allows a surviving business partner or partners to purchase the business from the deceased partner's estate.

buyback—contract in which the seller agrees to buy back the item under specific conditions.

buyer's market—situation in which supply exceeds demand, so buyer's can frequently negotiate good deals.

buyer's strike—situation in which even loyal buyers stop purchasing a product for any of a variety of reasons, including high prices.

buyout—contract provision that allows an organization to end a relationship before it is due to terminate by paying a pre-determined sum to the contractee; process in which one company buys a controlling share of another company's voting stock.

buzzword—frequently used (and often misused) term for a popular idea, practice, or technique; often doesn't have a clear meaning, but has become popular as a euphemism or synonym.

bylaws—rules adopted by an association or a corporation to govern its actions.

by-product—secondary product or substance, often marketable, occasionally hazardous, produced in the process of making something else.

by the book—according to strict guidelines.

C

cafeteria—lunch room, even if food can't be purchased there; describes any group from which choices must be made.

cafeteria plan—a system of fringe benefits where employees can allocate a total benefit amount among a number of options (health care, insurance, child care, etc.)

calculator—desktop or handheld device that performs mathematical functions; electronic substitute for learning how to add, subtract, multiply, and divide.

calendar—most dangerous tool in American business when it is used to drive or limit programs and actions instead of content value.

calendar-driven—sequence of business events, such as production, marketing plans, or financial statements, that is routinely performed at a specific date.

calendar year—January 1 to December 31.

call—demand from a lending institution that a loan be paid in full sooner than the original terms specified; in options trading, the right to buy a specific number of shares at a specified price by a certain date.

call protection—caveat typically negotiated in a private placement agreement protecting the buyer of the security from an early call.

call report—report from a salesperson or account executive describing a visit with a client.

call waiting—telephone service that allows a person to answer a second call while putting a current caller on hold.

cambist—expert or resource on foreign exchange rates.

camcorder—integrated video recording camera and deck, usually handheld.

campaign—organized series of actions designed to lead to a desired outcome; in marketing, a communications event or group of events (meetings, advertisements, and public relations activities) designed to influence someone.

canned presentation—largely predetermined presentation made the same way to different audiences.

canned program—any program that can be used as received, without being modified or customized. (e.g., a generic sales program or computer software package).

cannibalize—to take from one or more active sources for the benefit of another, as in a product that takes sales away from another of the company's products; to dismantle something and use or sell the parts.

canvass—to go door to door to present a message.

cap rate—short for *capitalization rate*.

capacity—amount that something will hold or produce in a given time period.

capital—money and property; city that serves as a government seat or primary center of an activity (a "capitol" is a building or complex of buildings where a government meets).

capital account—group of accounting records that revolve around the ownership of a business.

capital assets—physical property expected to last longer than ten years.

capital budget—money designated for widespread business activities such as research and development, advertising, or expansion.

capital formation—process of saving money that will be used as collateral or to purchase capital assets.

capital gains—profit resulting from the sale of securities or capital when they have been held for at least six months.

capital goods—items used in the production of other goods, such as buildings and machinery.

capital improvement—improvement to a building or equipment that increases its value, longevity, or usefulness.

capital intensive—requiring large investments of capital assets.

capital investment—money paid to acquire a capital good.

capital loss—loss from the sale of a capital asset.

capital movement—liquidation of a capital investment and reinvestment of the money in another area.

capital requirement—money needed for the normal operation of a business.

capital resource—item that is used in the production of goods.

capital stock—money or property contributed by stockholders to be used as the financial foundation for the corporation.

capital structure—corporation's financial framework, including long-term debt, preferred stock, and net worth.

capital turnover—annual sales divided by net worth.

capitalism—economic system in which capital goods are owned and managed privately rather than by a government, and where the profit motive of the individual is basic to the system of buying and selling goods.

capitalization—investment in capital goods, especially a major investment; a corporation's complete securities issuance.

capitalization rate—percentage of income compared to capital investment; baseline interest rate used to determine the present market value of a capital item that is not yet fully paid for.

capitalize—to invest in capital goods; to take advantage of a situation.

carbonless—paper with pressure-sensitive ink on the back that copies whatever is written on it to the sheet beneath it.

carcinogenic—cancer causing.

career—total work history of a person.

career limiting—activity that may prevent someone from advancing to a higher job as fast as he or she otherwise would (for example, having a child is often considered career limiting for a woman).

career path—jobs taken (or intended to be taken) over the course of a person's work history, typically leading to a management position.

career planning—deciding what jobs and coursework to take and what skills to acquire as well as which associations and clubs to join to reach desired jobs at specific points in a career.

career plateau—situation in which a person can't obtain higher-level jobs.

cargo—merchandise being hauled in bulk from one location to another via ship, truck, air, or train.

carpal tunnel syndrome—workplace injury sustained from limited repetitive motion.

carrier—vehicle, or company the vehicle belongs to, that carries goods for another company.

carrot and stick—negotiating or motivating strategy in which one offers something desirable and something threatening.

carrying charge—fee charged for buying something on credit; in commodities, charge for carrying the actual commodity; in real estate, cost of owning land before it is developed.

carryover—something old used on a new product; in finance, deductions and credits from one year used to reduce tax liability in the next year or years.

carryover effect—results of past experiences with a product or service on future transactions involving that good or service or others sold by the same organization.

cart—what you're not supposed to put in front of the horse; short for *cartridge*, as in toner cartridge or data cartridge.

cartage—charge for moving goods by vehicle.

cartel—two or more major suppliers who work together to increase the price and/or control the supply or distribution of their products through various means, but often by restricting trade.

cascade—dissemination of information level by level from the top down, similar to a fountain where water flows from the top to successively lower levels; arrangement of overlapping open windows on a computer screen.

case study—real or hypothetical example of a business situation, often used in business schools to study the circumstances and actions that led to a specific achievement or occurrence.

cash—money in savings, money orders, or currency; to convert a negotiable instrument into currency.

cash cow—mature, established product that is typically inexpensive to produce but brings in a great deal of money; line of business that generates a great deal of cash; stock that gives frequent large dividends.

cash basis—accounting method in which transactions are recorded as soon as money is received or paid (the opposite is the "accrual" method).

cash budget—amount of money expected to come into and go out of a specific account over a set period of time.

cash disbursement—money paid out.

cash discount—price reduction given for immediate payment; businesses often say "thirty days good as cash," meaning the cash discount can be received if the bill is paid within thirty days.

cash equivalent—amount of cash that could be received for an item if it were sold.

cash management—system by which an organization controls the use of its cash.

cash market—market that conducts business as soon as requested.

cash on delivery (C.O.D.)—transaction in which goods must be paid for in full by cash or the equivalent when delivered; also called collect on delivery.

cash on hand—amount of cash available at a given time.

cash order—transaction in which payment accompanies the order.

cash out—to sell off an interest with the intention of leaving a market or position; informally, to get what you can and get out; as identified by futurist Faith Popcorn, the social phenomenon in which people abandon a conventional career track to do what they really want to do, even though it typically doesn't pay as well.

cash position—total of cash and assets easily converted to cash available for use by a business at the present time.

cash ratio—accounting tool that measures the ratio of cash and marketable securities to current liabilities to give an idea of how quickly liabilities could be liquidated (also called "liquidity ratio").

cash reserve—cash that is not immediately needed but kept on hand against unexpected needs.

cash surrender value—amount of money a life insurance policyholder receives when canceling the policy.

cash flow—net income, depreciation, and other noncash charges as measured over a specific amount of time.

cashier—frontline employee who accepts payment for a product or service.

cast of characters—people participating in a major way at an event.

casual labor—part-time worker who makes a living by traveling from town to town to do seasonal or irregular work.

catastrophic coverage—insurance coverage for specific catastrophic events such as the death of a senior executive, a flood or a hurricane, a major fire, etc.; health insurance designed to protect against major, cash-intensive medical conditions and diseases.

Catch-22—no-win situation; situation with no solution (explored in Joseph Heller's novel of the same name).

catchall—program designed to reach a wide audience; purposely vague term intended to include a wide audience.

category killer—strip mall with one or more major tenants (typically a large merchandiser of clothing, toys, books, music and video recordings, sundries, or other soft goods), usually located near a major regional indoor shopping mall and offering more convenient access.

cats and dogs—speculative stocks that have short histories of sales, earnings, and dividend payments.

causality—literally, the relationship between a cause and an effect; typically, a big word used instead of *cause*.

cause—known or suspected reason for a problem or situation; issue or point of view; reason for firing or disciplining someone.

cause and effect diagram—diagram developed by Kaoru Ishikawa that identifies and links causes and effects (also called a "fishbone diagram").

cause marketing—public relations and advertising activities designed to persuade people to give money or think favorably of a nonprofit organization that uses the money to help people, animals, the environment, etc.

caveat—warning or mitigating condition.

caveat emptor—Latin for "let the buyer beware."

caveat venditor—Latin for "let the seller beware."

CD-ROM—compact disc, read-only memory (see Computer Appendix).

cease and desist—court order requiring that a person or business stop an activity.

cell—euphemism for a work cubicle with walls that don't reach the ceiling and (usually) no door; a data block on a computerized spreadsheet; in some types of quality and statistical testing, a group from which test subjects are randomly chosen.

cellular phone—portable telephone most commonly used as a car phone.

censure—formal act of disapproval; not allowing someone to participate in an organization or perform a job any longer because he or she broke one or more rules of the organization; not the same as "censor" (which means to delete or restrict information).

census—survey that physically counts something.

Central America—countries just south of Mexico and north of South America: Guatemala, Belize, El Salvador, Honduras, Nicaragua, Costa Rica, and Panama.

central planning—planning for an entire company, country, or other entity by a single organization, allowing little or no input from those outside the planning unit.

central tendency—expected average before data is analyzed; tendency of managers to give all their employees performance ratings that average out in the middle.

centralization—gathering everything into and administering out of one decision-making structure (a centralized business has a human resources department that oversees all divisions, as opposed to a human resources department in each division office).

central bank—country's formal bank, such as the U.S. Federal Reserve system, that issues currency, administers monetary policy, and holds deposits for other banks.

central business district (CBD)—downtown, in statistical parlance.

central buying—purchasing for a number of locations from the home office or another main location.

centre—British for *center*.

certification—process in which specific steps must be followed to obtain an official designation; documentation that something is authentic.

certified public accountant (CPA)—accountant who has completed at least four years of college, has passed specific exams, and has a minimum amount of experience as required by the state in which he or she works.

certify—in labor relations, determination by the National Labor Relations Board that a union has been properly selected by a majority of employees in a bargaining unit and is empowered to be the sole representative of those employees in negotiations with management.

ceteris paribus—Latin for "all other things being equal."

chachka—small promotional item (traditionally spelled *tchotchke*).

chain—group of stores carrying the same name, operating with nearly identical products and policies, and owned by a single organization.

chain of command—hierarchical system of authority and communications linkages in which each level of the organization works with those immediately above and below it.

chain feeding—continuously inserting something such as paper, envelopes, or labels into a machine such as a printer, either by hand or by loading items attached to each other.

chair—short for *chairperson*; used to avoid sexist language such as chair*man*; to run a meeting or function.

chairman of the board—member of a company's board of directors who presides over its meetings; company's highest-ranking executive, although not necessarily the one with the most actual authority.

chamber of commerce—nonprofit organization made up of business owners and executives, usually in a specific geographic area.

champion—supporter or sponsor of an event, cause, or product; to support a product or cause.

channel management—production setting where machines are laid out in order of their use.

channel of distribution—method of transferring merchandise from a manufacturer to a customer.

channel of sales—where and how a publication gets subscriptions.

Chapter 7—section of the 1978 Bankruptcy Act dealing with liquidation, under which a court-appointed temporary trustee runs the business.

Chapter 11—type of corporate bankruptcy that leaves the debtor in control of the business.

character generator (CG)—electronic device that allows letters and numbers to be superimposed on a video or still image.

charm school—euphemism for training course in which people attempt to improve their interpersonal skills in order to work better with others.

charter—government-issued document that establishes a corporation; to hire a vehicle or vessel, usually for exclusive use.

chartist—person who analyzes the patterns of securities and commodities.

chat—supposedly innocent, informal talk that isn't supposed to have career consequences, but often does.

chattel—tangible, transportable item.

cheap money—inflationary time when interest rates are low and prices are high, making it advantageous to borrow.

check—bank draft that is payable on demand; to look at something to determine if it is correct.

check sheet—form used to tally and informally analyze data, especially in quality control operations.

checklist—reminder of one or more things that must be done.

cheesecake—trite; often used to describe communications pieces that are old-fashioned, too cute, or too simplistic for the audience; common food item thought to most closely approximate the shelf life of management ideas that aren't seriously thought out or sustained.

chemistry—unexplainable closeness between two or more people that, in business, leads to a trust level beyond that found in most working relationships.

cheque—British for *check*.

Chernobyl—site of the 1986 Soviet nuclear power plant accident that has become synonymous with the potential for large nuclear disasters; thousands of people died and many more will die from the effects of the radiation, while the surrounding area may be uninhabitable for several hundred years.

chi square test—statistical analysis that measures whether variables are independent or dependent.

chicken coop—department in which a number of women work, especially when they are supervised by a man (it's the nature of a chicken coop to have but one rooster).

chief—informal term for leader.

chief executive officer (CEO)—highest-ranking executive in the corporation, responsible only to the board of directors.

chief financial officer (CFO)—highest-ranking corporate officer with authority to make major financial decisions for an organization.

chief information officer (CIO)—highest-ranking corporate officer dedicated to managing the organization's information systems and resources.

chief operating officer (COO)—person who ensures that the company runs smoothly day to day; usually the president, unless the CEO also fills that role.

child labor—historically, employment of children under age fifteen, a practice that, while legal, is governed by many guidelines; informally, dependence on teenagers for frontline workers.

Chinese menu—master plan that provides multiple options, allowing the client to assemble a program based on specific need, much like choosing items from a menu in a Chinese restaurant.

circular organization—organizational structure that, in contrast to conventional pyramid-style systems, is illustrated by concentric rings around an inner core.

chop shop—place where stolen cars are cut up and sold for spare parts; by extension, manufacturing organization in which poor-quality product is turned out quickly.

Christmas bonus—traditional check above and beyond salary and other wages that a company gives to employees at the end of the year.

Christmas turkey—token gift given to employees in November or December.

chronic fatigue syndrome (CFS)—disease characterized by unexplained and largely untreatable tiredness that often prevents an individual from staying awake and alert on the job; no cause has yet been found, but it is thought to be a set of viruses contracted as a result of extreme, prolonged stress.

chronic waste—Joseph Juran term for losses due to continuing, inherent quality deficiencies.

chronology—list of events in the order in which they happen.

churn—illegal but hard-to-prove practice of trading securities excessively to generate brokerage commissions rather than investment value; to use up an excessive amount of something, including energy and physical items such as paper; to worry excessively about something.

cipher—coded message; individual who is not particularly noteworthy and thus is interchangeable with others.

circular file—waste basket.

civil law—legal system concerned with activities not considered crimes, such as divorce and bankruptcy.

claim—formal request for payment from an insurance company because of a loss; assertion regarding a product's attributes or advantages.

Class A stock/Class B stock—shares of stock in a company that, based on its bylaws, have some difference, such as voting rights or dividend preference.

class action—lawsuit brought by one or several individuals that has been broadened at the court's direction to include in the final judgment all individuals who meet the criteria of the class.

class price—high price charged to unwary buyers.

Clayton Act—1914 amendment to the Sherman Antitrust Act that outlaws selling a product to different people for different prices (allowances, discounts, etc., are legal only if offered to everyone on an equal basis); also established that human labor is not to be considered a commodity.

clean—free of any defects or, in the case of a person, criminal history; in accounting, unqualified audit report; in finance, free of debt; in securities, trade that exactly matches an order.

clean hands—no previous record of misconduct; honest, ethical, and professional.

clean up—to finish a project; to solve the problems resulting from another person's mistake.

cleanup fund—amount of life insurance needed by a family to cover expenses when someone dies; environmental fund used to pay for the cleanup of a toxic waste site.

cleanroom—room used in research or manufacturing in which everything is sterile and people usually wear special clothing to prevent contamination.

clearinghouse—organization that buys outdated products from businesses going out of business and sells them inexpensively; organization that compiles or checks information (such as background checks on employees) for another organization; centralized location that sorts checks or other financial instruments and distributes them to the correct institutions; organization within a stock or commodities exchange that helps members settle debts made with each other.

clerical—having to do with the rote recordkeeping done by an organization.

clerical error—unintentional, usually minor error made while producing a document.

clerk—low-level administrative employee.

cliché—trite yet often accurate statement.

client—professional customer; the person whose happiness is more important than your child's school play.

clique—group of customers who informally agree to make purchases together; illegal agreement by a number of people to manipulate stock.

clock in/out—to begin and end work; refers to an actual timeclock, but is used by white collar workers to describe beginning and ending their workday.

clone—identical to another, although it may carry a different name (for example, many personal computers are clones of IBM or Apple computers because they contain identical internal components, even though their exterior cases are different).

close—price of a stock or bond at the end of a trading day; final half-hour of exchange trading; to stop doing business for the day or forever; to finalize a sale, loan, contract, or other agreement; to finalize accounting records for a specific time period.

closed-circuit television (CCTV)—distribution network for an internal television broadcast.

close corporation plan—arrangement for surviving stockholders to purchases a deceased stockholder's shares.

closed corporation—corporation in which all of the voting stock is held by a few shareholders.

closed option—illegal practice in which a customer is not given an option to opt out of a transaction.

closed shop—company that hires only union members.

closed stock—products that are sold in sets, such as cookware.

closed territory—salesperson's geographic area that cannot be intruded upon by another salesperson from the same company.

closely held corporation—public corporation that has only a few shareholders and whose stock is seldom traded publicly.

closeout—reduced-price sale of merchandise that the company doesn't intend to carry anymore.

closing bell—end of trading on the stock market for a day; end of the workday, especially in a plant or other area where a buzzer or bell signals quitting time.

cloud—item appearing in a legal document such as a property title that signals a possible problem with the document; past or current action that hinders a person's ability to work.

cluster analysis—statistical tool that analyzes data by dividing it into homogeneous groups.

co.—abbreviation for *company*, except in accounting, where it often signifies *co-partners*.

coach—least expensive fare for traveling by air, boat, or train; someone who works to improve another's performance.

coaching—trendy management technique in which managers work to motivate people to find solutions to problems instead of dictate the course of action, typically by trying to use team-oriented methods similar to athletic coaches.

coals to Newcastle—euphemism for trying to provide or sell something that people do not need (Newcastle is a seaport on the northeast coast of Great Britain, a coal-mining region).

coffee—magic elixir of American business (in some companies, if you don't drink it, you may be informally ostracized).

coffee break—short break from work taken in midmorning or midafternoon, often authorized or mandated by a labor contract or employee handbook.

cogeneration—use of waste heat from an industrial process to produce electricity or steam for heating.

cognitive—literally, having a sense of self or knowing you exist; in business, refers to a person who can reason logically.

cognitive dissonance—psychological theory that people will change their beliefs to justify their behaviors; in advertising, holds that consumers may become distressed about a purchase when they see advertising from a competitor, and consequently must be reassured that they have made the right choice so they don't return the item or switch to another brand when purchasing the next time.

cola—cost of living adjustment, usually tied to the rate of inflation.

cold call—calling on a potential customer you have never met before.

cold type—words and artwork printed directly on paper that then will be used to make a printing plate (printing originally involved "hot type" in the form of melted lead that was cast into lines of type).

collapse—to fall apart; to make smaller by combining.

collate—to put the pages of a document in order.

collateral—in finance, property offered as security when borrowing money; in advertising, the pieces of printed literature that are used in addition to major advertising.

colleague—business acquaintance, work associate, or fellow member of an association.

collection agency—organization that specializes in recovering overdue accounts for other companies, usually for a percentage of what they collect.

collective bargaining—meetings between company management and employee representatives to negotiate working conditions.

collectivism—system in which a central government makes most decisions about business and finance.

collusion—secret agreement among two or more parties to do something illegal.

collusive oligopoly—small group of producers (such as OPEC) that sets prices, production amounts, and distribution to customers.

color separation—set of negatives necessary to print a color image (usually blue, black, red, and yellow, but there may be as few as two or as many as eight, depending on the extent of color used).

coloration—intentional distortion of information.

colorize—to add color to an image that did not previously have it, such as a black-and-white movie.

commercial—advertising message inserted into broadcast programming; reason for the existence of free television programming (why else would it be called "commercial TV"?).

commercial paper—short-term loan obligations, often unsecured, issued by banks, corporations, and other organizations, usually maturing in several days to several months.

commingle—in finance, the often illegal practice of mixing a trustee's funds with those of client; to mix together.

commissary—store that sells food items at reduced prices because it is subsidized by a company or government; in food service, central facility that supplies ingredients and finished products to a network of outlying restaurants or other facilities.

commission—money paid to a salesperson or agent for making a sale, usually based on the volume of the transaction; government agency charged with writing and enforcing regulations.

committee—group of people who meet to discuss a specific topic on an ongoing basis; organization capable of designing a zebra, but seldom a racehorse.

commodity—tangible property that can be bought or sold; bulk goods (grains, metals, etc.) traded on a "commodities exchange."

common—pervasive; simple; derogatory term for people of lower-middle-class backgrounds.

common area—area in a corporate facility or office building that is open to all employees or tenants.

common carrier—regulated company or person in the business of transporting people, items, or information under a uniform pricing structure.

common courtesy—basic way of treating people nicely; with common sense, the primary component of intelligent personnel management.

common law—system of law derived from principles (often judicial decisions) rather than rules (as in legislation); the basis of English and most U.S. law.

Common Market—Western European countries that have low tariffs among themselves but maintain higher tariffs on imports into member nations.

common sense—inherent knowledge of right and wrong,

logic and balance, and ethical principles that many assume every person has but that, in fact, is often learned by experience.

common stock—document representing secured ownership in a corporation, usually involving voting rights for the board of directors; holders of bonds, debentures, and preferred stock take precedence in dividend distributions and in the event the corporation must be liquidated; common stockholders receive greater benefits if the stock performs well and take the primary risk if the company does poorly.

communication—exchange of information, whether verbally, in writing or through symbolic means.

communes—groups of people who live and work together, sharing all resources.

communism—economic system in which private property rights are subordinated to common ownership.

commute—to travel to and from work.

commuter—person who frequently travels between two places.

comp—short for *compensatory* or *complimentary*; in the former instance, usually refers to time that can be taken off from work in exchange for overtime, travel time, weekends, and other extra hours worked; in the latter, means giving someone something for free that they would ordinarily have to pay for, often as a goodwill gesture.

compact disc (CD)—optically read information storage technology in which data, images, and music are digitally encoded.

compact disc--read only memory (CD-ROM)—prerecorded CD that cannot be rerecorded or altered.

company—organization that produces and/or sells goods or services for a profit.

company car—vehicle given to employees free of charge for use primarily in business activities.

company rag—internal newsletter or newspaper put out by the company for its employees.

company song—literally, a song sung at corporate gatherings, more common in Japan than in the U.S.; by extension, any often-repeated message delivered by corporate executives.

company store—internal function that sells a company's products to its employees, usually for a small markup over cost.

comparable worth—theory that people should be paid according to their job's value to the organization, not according to age, sex, or other nonjob-related criteria.

compatible—two or more devices, or people, that can work together.

comparison shopper—customer who gathers and compares information about several competing products before making a purchase.

compensable factor—tasks that a company is willing to pay a person to perform.

compensation—wages, salary, and benefits, both tangible and intangible, that a person receives for doing a job; in law, money a person receives for having been wronged or injured.

compensation package—total collection of money, fringe benefits, incentives, and options a person receives for doing a job.

compensation system—system for determining which jobs are paid which amounts and what benefits are offered.

competence—ability to do a job in a satisfactory way.

competition—what happens when two or more businesses offer essentially the same product or service to the same potential customer; person or thing that could be a reasonable replacement for another; in marketing, product that may be purchased instead or yours, including "indirect" competition such as spending money on a new car instead of saving it to buy a new house.

competitive advantage—features of a product or service that make it more desirable than the competition's product.

competitive advertising—advertising designed to make a

competing product look bad or to make the company's product look good in comparison to the competition.

competitive analysis—analysis of the features, strengths, weaknesses, and performance of a company's products, services, and/or processes compared to those of competitors.

compilation—informal gathering of information or things; in accounting, does not have the accountant's assurances that it conforms to generally accepted accounting principles.

compile—to add up, collect, or systematically keep track of.

complaint—formal notice of a problem with a product, service, or employee's performance; in civil law, plaintiff's first discussion of facts; in criminal law, preliminary accusation made against a person.

complement—to fill out, complete, or supply something lacking (a "compliment" is something nice you say about someone or something).

complete meeting package (CMP)—arrangement that includes all lodging, food, and meeting-space costs in one package price.

compliance—meeting the terms of an agreement.

compliment—expression of admiration, respect, or affection.

complimentary—something given for free.

component—integral part of a system.

composition—how something is made up or looks; in finance, alternative to bankruptcy where creditors accept partial payment of the debt as full settlement.

compound—something made up of two or more substances; in finance, to continue to add to according to a fixed schedule (compounded daily, weekly, monthly, etc.), often increasing at a rate faster than arithmetic progression.

compound interest—interest paid on both the principal and the previously paid interest.

comptroller—company's head accountant, but not necessarily the manager of the accounting department (also called a "controller").

compulsory—mandatory.

computer—machine that can store, recall, and manipulate electronically coded instructions and information.

computer-based training (CBT)—training delivery system that uses computerized programs in lieu of or in support of live instructors to impart knowledge (also called *computer-assisted instruction [CAI]*).

computerese—jargon and slang used in the computer industry.

computerphobia—fear of using a computer.

concept—idea; in commercial design, a creative approach, usually well defined and including supporting documents (such as artwork, in the case of advertising) but not completed.

concept test—research conducted to gain feedback on an idea.

concept to customer—term coined by Ford Motor Co. to explain the steps from the initial idea for a new product until it reaches the market.

conceptualize—to think about.

concurrent—at the same time.

conference—meeting of two or more people to discuss specific topics.

Conference Board—business research organization based in New York City.

conference call—phone call in which at least three people are on the line at one time.

conference center—meeting facility designed specifically for business meetings; may or may not include overnight lodging facilities.

conference room—room set up for meetings, often containing presentation aids from whiteboards and flipcharts to sophisticated audiovisual equipment.

conference table—any table around which a meeting is held, although it implies a high-quality table with specific amenities such as space to spread out notes.

confidence game—scheme where a con artist wins the confidence of a person, then cheats the person out of money.

confidence interval—in statistics, a range that represents the probability within which something will occur in a given sample.

confidential—secret, not to be shown or told to anyone else; in government, lowest classification level (followed by secret, top secret).

confirmation—formal communication that reiterates an agreement; in government, approval by the legislative branch of appointments made by the executive branch.

conflict of interest—conflict between a person or firm's professional duties to a client and the personal interests of those involved, raising the prospect that they will serve themselves rather than the client.

conform—to fit your activities, ideas, or appearance to the norms of the group.

conformance—meeting any goal; within specifications.

confusion—state of being mixed up or perplexed; legally, mixing of goods from different owners into one group.

conglomerate—company that owns a number of businesses that operate in different markets.

congruence—fitting or working together.

congruent innovation—designing more than one product at a time to be used together (for example, developing a computer and a printer at the same time).

connotation—subtle implication or inference.

CONSCIOUS ERRORS

conscious errors—in quality, nonconformance to goals resulting from planned actions.

consensus—group agreement.

consent election—union election to determine the bargaining unit that will represent employees.

conservatism in accounting—understating assets and revenues while overstating liabilities and expenses.

consignment—selling articles for another person; majority of the sale goes to the owner of the goods while the seller takes a small commission.

consolidated metropolitan statistical area (CMSA)—largest census designation, including several primary metropolitan statistical areas (PMSA).

consortium—cooperative framework through which several independent organizations can work toward a common goal.

consul—government official who resides in and represents his or her nation in a foreign country.

consultant—someone external to an organization who is hired to advise a business on one or more areas of internal or external operations.

consumer—end-user customer of a product or service.

consumer confidence—relative faith (or lack thereof) in the current economy's prospects; when consumer confidence is high, people buy (and often borrow) more, fueling economic growth; when low, they are reluctant to spend as extensively, which can lead or contribute to falling sales and a period of economic decline.

consumer credit—loans used to buy consumer goods, primarily credit cards and loans for major purchases.

consumer goods—items bought for personal use.

consumer price index (CPI)—U.S. Bureau of Labor Statistics' monthly measure of changing consumer goods prices, based on key indicators; also called "cost of living index."

Consumer Product Safety Commission (CPSC)—federal agency charged with keeping defective products off the market.

consumer research—research to determine what consumers think of a product or service, what influences them to buy or not buy it, and what attributes can help a company better design and market its products.

consummate—very accomplished or professional; to finish or complete something.

consumption—how much of something is used in a given time period.

content—what something contains; satisfied.

contingency—something that may or may not happen, depending on other events.

contingency fee—in law, payment for services based on a percentage of a potential award or other basis other than the amount of work done on the case (in some cases, such as liability litigation, if there is no award, no fee is charged).

contingency fund—money set aside to be used in the event of a specific event, such as an emergency.

contingency plan—plan to be put in action if the original plan does not work or if a situation changes.

continuing education unit (CEU)—college or professional credit for courses geared to the continuing licensing or certification needs of practicing professionals such as realtors, nurses, etc.

continuous audit—examination of accounting records during the year, prior to the year-end report, to find and correct mistakes.

continuous improvement—theory (called "kaizen" in Japan) that seeks to continually eliminate defects to improve quality.

continuous process—manufacturing or service operation that never stops or closes.

contract—legally binding agreement that sets the terms for a

71

relationship between two or more entities under which each is expected to perform or refrain from performing one or a series of actions; agreement for the supply of certain goods or services at a set price; to hire someone to do something for you.

contract farming—raising crops or animals to be sold to a predetermined entity.

contract manufacturing—producing a product under contract from, and to the specifications of, another firm that will sell or incorporate the product into its own offerings.

contraction—reduction in business activity or the gross national product (euphemism for a mild recession).

contractor—professional who arranges for others to do work for a third party; business or worker performing work for a second or third party.

contraindicator—observation, fact, or feeling that makes a course of action inadvisable.

contrarian—someone who routinely takes an opposite stance to the prevailing viewpoint, sometimes just for the fun of arguing; in investing, someone who acts against the current market trend, investing when most people expect a decline, selling when most people expect further increases.

contributory—something that is a factor in, but not the entire cause of, something else.

control—norm against which research is compared; essential ingredient in functional empowerment; to have the final say in how something will be done; to regulate a machine so that the final product is manufactured within specified parameters.

control chart—measurement device that continuously tracks significant variation in product or process over a specified period of time.

control station—in quality, an area that carries out a specific quality-oriented activity.

control subject—in quality, any feature of a product or

process that must be regulated to ensure that the end result is within specified parameters.

controllable costs—all costs, including labor and materials, that can be controlled by the area to which they are charged.

controlled company—company in which at least 51% of the voting shares are held by another company.

controller—company's head accountant, but not necessarily manager of the accounting department; also called "comptroller."

controlling interest—literally, ownership of the majority of a company's voting shares, but may also refer to the largest shareholder when ownership of the majority of the company's stock is widely dispersed.

convenience sampling—testing based at least in part on choosing items that are easiest to measure rather than a true random sample.

convention—large gathering of people with similar interests, often including trade show exhibit areas where vendors can display products and give informational programs on topics of interest to the attendees.

convention bureau—local organization that markets a city or region as a convention destination and assists convention organizers with the details of holding their gathering in that area.

conversion—changing something from one form to another of equal value or utility, such as bonds to shares of common stock or shares in one mutual fund to others in the same family; process of changing existing military-industrial manufacturing and development facilities and organizations to nonmilitary uses.

convertible—investment or asset that can be converted from one form to another, such as a stock to cash.

convertibles—preferred stocks and bonds that can be exchanged at a set price for other forms of securities issued by the company.

cook the books—euphemism for making the financial statements and other documents look as good as possible through legal as well as illegal practices.

cooling-off period—in securities, the time (usually twenty days) between the filing of a preliminary prospectus with the Securities and Exchange Commission and the public offering of those securities; in labor negotiations, period during which a union cannot strike and/or an employer cannot lock out employees.

co-op (short for *cooperative*)—organization (common in agriculture) for the production or marketing of the members' goods; corporate ownership of real estate in which stockholding tenants can use space within the building and deduct interest and property taxes paid by the corporation; an arrangement in which two real estate agents split the commission.

co-op advertising—arrangement under which a manufacturer reimburses all or part of a retailer's cost of advertising placement (and generally also creates the advertising materials) to help get its products advertised in local markets.

copier—machine that makes low-cost, on-the-spot, black-and-white or four-color duplicates of printed material, although not of the quality of a printing press.

copreneur—person or business that acts as a formal or informal partner with an entrepreneur.

copy—reproduction of an original; in media, the words.

copy-protected—computer disk that cannot be duplicated (for example, to protect software) or to which new material cannot be added (to preserve the integrity of the data already on it).

copy stand—a piece of metal or plastic that keeps papers upright and in line with a computer screen or typewriter keyboard to make it easier to input the material.

copyright—legal protection that allows writers, artists, and publishers to determine when and where their work will be published and to prevent unauthorized use or duplication of their creations.

core—central memory of a computer.

core business—major area of business in which a company operates.

core competencies—key technologies, skills, or other competitive features that form the basis of a company's business activities.

corn-hog ratio—difference between the price that could be obtained by selling an input and by selling the completed product, deriving from the farming practice of deciding whether to feed the corn to the hogs and then sell the hogs, or just sell the corn.

corner the market—illegal attempt to control the price or disposition of a security or commodity by purchasing it in large volumes.

corp and gown—cooperative efforts between corporations and universities.

corporate—having to do with or sponsored by a corporation.

corporate campaign—organized program of advertising and public relations designed to make a company look good as opposed to selling its products or services.

corporate collateral—printed (and increasingly multimedia) material used to inform interested audiences of an organization's activities; typically includes brochures, catalogs, price sheets, annual reports, white papers, and other prepared material.

corporate credit card—credit card issued to the company or to an employee to be used for company expenses.

corporate counsel—lawyers who work directly for the corporation.

corporate culture—informal and formal rules of behavior for people who work for a company.

corporate dress code—informal or formal rules for what type of clothing can be worn to work by people of different rank within the organization.

corporate identity—view that customers and the general public have of a corporation; includes logos, brand names, and other identifiers.

corporate insider—person who has such intimate knowledge of the financial situation of a company that he or she is legally barred from using that knowledge to make gains in the stock market.

corporate raider—someone who specializes in buying companies against the will of their managements.

corporate university—organized curriculum specific to the job skills and management-development needs of an organization, usually run under the aegis of the corporate training department.

corporate video—informational videotape produced for internal or external audiences, usually designed to introduce employees or customers and prospects to a concept, not to solicit sales directly.

corporation—organization chartered under the laws of incorporation of a state or country; it is legally separate from the owners and is treated as an artificial person.

corporeal—tangible.

correlate—to determine the relationship between two or more things.

correx—in media, short for corrections to be made to a script or printed piece before production.

corridor—narrow area providing access from one place to another; one of the two major landscape features in an office building (the other being cubicles or offices).

correspondent—businesses such as banks or securities brokers that conduct transactions for third parties in markets unavailable to the third parties; in media, reporter who covers a specific region or subject.

corroborate—to confirm or support another's position.

cosign—to sign a contract in addition to the signature of the principal, thus taking responsibility for the debt if the principal signer does not meet the obligation.

cosine—something you studied in high school trigonometry and promptly forgot.

cost—total money, time, resources, and/or discomfort that must be put out to get something.

cost accounting—accounting concerned with detailing the cost of producing a product or service.

cost application—allocating costs to the department or other entity that incurred them.

cost basis—using the purchase price of an asset to derive other numbers, such as tax or depreciation rates.

cost-benefit analysis—deciding whether the benefits of doing (or not doing) something outweigh the costs involved.

cost center—nonrevenue-producing department within an organization.

cost containment—financial restraint designed to keep budgets from growing; sometimes a euphemism for cost cutting.

cost-effective—providing more benefits (although not necessarily profits) than it costs to produce.

cost method—means of accounting for a controlling company's investments in its subsidiary companies.

cost objective—budgeted ceiling for a project.

cost of goods manufactured—total costs of all goods produced during an accounting period.

cost of goods sold—combined costs of buying raw materials, producing finished goods, and marketing the goods.

cost of living adjustment (COLA)—periodic adjustment to a group's salary or wage that reflects the inflation rate but is not necessarily equal to the inflation rate.

cost of living index—U.S. Bureau of Labor Statistics'

monthly measure of changing consumer goods prices; also called "consumer price index" (CPI).

cost of poor quality (COPQ)—costs that would disappear if products and processes were perfect.

cost overrun—amount a project costs above that budgeted.

cost per thousand (CPM)—in advertising, cost of reaching 1,000 prospects or households (divide the cost of the advertising by the circulation of the medium in thousands); in manufacturing, cost of producing 1,000 units of the product.

cost-plus—contract to produce a product for its cost plus a set percentage above cost.

cost-push inflation—rising prices resulting from rising costs.

cottage industry—production of items by people working in their homes.

council—advisory or legislative group ("counsel" means advice or a lawyer).

council of economic advisers—economists designated by the president to advise the federal government on economic matters.

counsel—attorney; advice; to give professional advice to a person or business.

counselor—attorney; may also refer to any professional consultant.

countdown—list of tasks to be performed in a specific order.

counter—surface in a retail establishment across which business is conducted; action taken in reaction to an opponent's actions; in negotiations, offer whose terms are different from those proposed by the other party; to make such an offer.

counter check—check provided by a bank to a depositor that can be cashed only by the person to whom it is issued.

counter program—marketing program designed to thwart negative advertising about a company's product or service by the competition; in television, to schedule a strong show against a strong show on another network in hopes of weakening its audience and hence its appeal to advertisers.

   counterfeit—imitation that can be passed off as the real thing.

   countermand—to change an order prior to its being executed.

   countermarket—often small market that has a narrow use for a product.

   countersign—to add your signature to a document to confirm it is genuine.

   country club—often expensive private club that provides facilities for tennis, golf, and other activities only to members and their guests.

   country store—large store outside of an urban area that offers a wide variety of products at relatively low prices for customers in a surrounding rural region.

   coup—sudden, successful move to gain control over a situation.

   coupon—attachments to a bond that can be turned in after specific dates for interest due; marketing device designed to build consumer traffic in a product by offering a financial inducement for purchase.

   covenant—formal, legally binding agreement to do or refrain from doing something; clause in a lease or contract.

   cover—in finance, to meet an obligation; in the workplace, to do someone else's job while he or she is gone; to make an excuse for a mistake; to attend a function and report on it to others.

   cover letter—letter accompanying a résumé, proposal, goods, or other material that explains what has been sent.

   cover memo—short note accompanying a report or other document, often containing routing instructions and other action items.

   cover sheet—protective title sheet on a document.

cover story—detailed account designed to explain why someone is doing or has done something in such a way as to deflect close scrutiny or cover up wrongdoing; in media, story featured on the cover of a magazine, which means it is usually (but not always) the most important story in the publication.

cover your ass (CYA)—defensive tactic designed to make sure no colleague or superior can blame you if something goes wrong.

coverage—amount and type of insurance a person or business carries.

craft union—union made up of people who perform similar, specific jobs (bricklayer, plumber, etc.); the opposite of an industry-wide union where anyone working in one industry is a member.

craftsman/craftsperson—worker with a specific skill, usually involving work done by hand.

craftsmanship—quality; literally, the work done by a skilled laborer, such as an electrician or carpenter.

crank—someone who makes repeated demands or complaints of little merit or value; to produce something quickly and generically.

crash—in investing, large, quick drop in securities prices; in electronics, computer failure that makes the computer temporarily or permanently unusable; in work style, to sleep after working long, intense hours.

cream—to take the best of something.

creative accounting—recording items under accounts for which they don't apply or in ways designed to make the financial picture look better than it is.

creative director—person at an ad agency or production studio who oversees art development and writing on a project.

credenza—sideboard that accompanies an executive desk.

credit—system through which a customer is given immediate use of a product or service, with payment to come later; acknowledgment of success or approval; to post funds to or remove an obligation from a customer's account.

credit analyst—someone who analyzes the credit-worthiness of a person or business to determine if a loan or credit can be issued, or who sets credit ratings for bonds.

credit bureau—organization that maintains credit files on consumers.

credit card—card accepted by businesses in lieu of cash and in promise of payment upon billing (in effect, a short-term loan); plastic money.

credit report—official report of a person's or company's credit standing based on information sent by creditors.

credit union—state or federally chartered financial cooperative formed by members of a specific group (such as employees, churches, or unions) to offer its members selected financial services.

credited service date—date on which your employment began, used to determine benefits such as retirement; may be different from the actual date you were hired due to various policies (for example, the first of the month, quarter, or year following your hiring date).

creditor—someone to whom you owe money.

crescendo—slow, steady increase to a dramatic peak.

crisis—important problem.

crisis management—common but largely ineffective management style in which a crisis is provoked to enable a manager to make a decision.

criteria—standards (always plural) used to judge something.

criterion—singular of *criteria* (means just one standard).

criterion predictor—standard measure, such as a test, that predicts how a person or group will perform in a situation.

critical—extremely important; near a danger point.

critical incident—event that results in a major change.

critical path method (CPM)—method of determining the most cost-effective steps to take to achieve a desired outcome.

critical process—extremely dangerous process that could result in large monetary, social, or physical costs.

criticality analysis—process used to identify product features that are extremely important (for example, safety, meeting government regulations, etc.).

cronyism—favoritism to an old friend.

crop—in agribusiness, a year's or season's production of a commodity, usually limited to grains but colloquially used for animals that will be marketed at the same time; in media, to mark a photo or piece of art to show a printer the area that is to be included in the finished piece; to cut something out of a process or document.

crop mark—marks that show the printer what area of a photo or piece of art to include in the finished piece.

crop year—period of agricultural production from the harvest of one crop until the harvest of the next.

cross—situation in which one broker handles both the buying and selling in a securities transaction.

cross-functional—involving employees, products, or processes from more than one department or functional area.

cross-merchandising—putting related items on display together (e.g.; strawberries, whipped cream, and shortcakes displayed in one area at a grocery store).

cross-training—training employees to work at more than one job in the company; fitness equipment used for more than one form of athletic activity.

crosstabs—short for *cross tabulations*; breakouts of major findings in a research study by subcategories for detailed comparison and analysis.

crown jewels—company's most desirable properties, especially at a time when the company is being examined for a takeover or merger.

cube—short for *cubicle*; what you get when you multiply something by itself twice.

cubicle—corporate equivalent of a fishbowl; small, modular work area, generally without a door, the height of whose walls often signifies relative stature in the organization.

cue—signal to begin doing something.

cue card—card that has written directions for people performing for television or live theater.

culpable—guilty, especially when a person has acted immorally without regard to others.

cult—small, secretive group of people who meet to discuss or act on specific items.

cult of personality—corporate culture in which people blindly follow a charismatic leader, for better or worse.

cultural needs—needs that consumers have as a direct result of the culture in which they have been nurtured or currently live, such as degree of self-respect and continuity of habit patterns.

cultural resistance—resistance to change due to the possible social consequences of the change.

culture—behaviors and values held by a group.

cumulative—made up of things added together.

cure-all—widely used remedy that solves (or is purported to solve) many problems.

curmudgeon—continuously crabby, ill-tempered, or sarcastic person, generally older than the rest of the group.

currency—physical form of money used by an economy; in banking, refers exclusively to paper money.

current—happening now; account on which payments have been kept up to date; what flows through an electric wire.

current assets—cash or other assets that likely will be depleted within the next twelve months.

current liabilities—debts that must be paid within the next twelve months.

current ratio—in accounting, company's ability to pay its debts (divide current assets by current liabilities); also called a "quick ratio."

curriculum—in education or training, systematic progression of courses followed in an area of study.

curriculum vitae—detailed résumé of a person's career (literally, the course of your life).

custom—habit or tradition that often becomes an unwritten rule; way of behaving or activity that occurs primarily because it has occurred regularly in the past.

customer—where your work goes, who it's important to; the person or entity that buys what you make or deliver.

customer-driven—process or product that is continually modified based on customer input.

customer expectations—peripheral list of tangible and intangible features in addition to the basic need that customers have from a product or service.

customer needs—specific customer desires that can be met in part or in whole by products or services.

customer perceptions—customers' conclusions based on their experience and observations, subject to modification by your marketing and management activities.

customer satisfaction index (CSI)—statistical measure of the degree to which products and services are currently meeting customer needs and expectations.

customer service—in traditional companies, internal department responsible for solving customer complaints and problems; in progressive companies, what everybody is paid to provide, whether internally or externally.

customer service representative (CSR)—someone whose primary job involves dealing directly with customers, either face to face or by phone.

customs—charges levied on imported goods; checkpoint you must pass through for registration and declaration purposes in traveling from one country to another.

cut—to eliminate or stop something.

cut off—to bar a person from something, especially an informal process such as the flow of information through a gossip chain.

cutoff—point at which an activity will stop or change.

cybernetics—field of technology that compares the human nervous system to computers.

cycle—periodic repetitions that are similar or identical.

cycle of service—predictable, repeatable steps involved in providing a service to a customer.

cycle time—amount of time elapsed from the beginning of a process to its completion.

cyclical—happening on a regular basis.

D

D&B—report on the credit-worthiness of a business, prepared by Dun & Bradstreet, a diversified information firm.

daisy chain—organized manipulation of trading in a security by promoters who use the appearance of high interest and activity levels to lure unwary investors, then unload their own purchases.

dark ride—in the amusement industry, a roller coaster–style thrill ride literally in the dark, such as Disney's Space Mountain; applies to situations marked by rapid and unexpected change with no way to maintain orientation or to estimate how long the ride will continue

Darwinism—Charles Darwin's theory of survival of the fittest, which can also be applied to products in the marketplace and people in the workplace.

data—factual information used to develop theories, justify opinions, or guide actions (literally the plural form of "datum," which vernacular vigilantes use to justify their insistence on the awkward "data are" instead of the more colloquial "data is"; either is correct according to *Webster's*).

data bank—compilation of data that is organized for easy retrieval.

data processing (DP)—using a computer or other system to help generate, organize, and analyze data.

database—intermingled set of data derived from previous activities that can be accessed, sorted, and used in a number of ways; computer program that allows entry, classification, manipulation, and updating of data entries.

dated—something with a date on it, such as a check or report; old, often in the sense of too old to be of use, or outdated.

dawn patrol—tour through the workplace shortly after arrival to greet co-workers, check on projects in progress, and see who's in and available for brief consultation or longer meetings later in the day; sometimes recommended as a time management tool to get socializing out of the way before settling down to work.

daycare—the care of preschool and grade-school children during work hours.

Daytimer—popular brand of small notebook used to record personal business information, keep schedules current, and track activities.

daytripper—someone who travels to field locations but does not stay overnight.

dBase I-II-III—popular business management software that combines graphics, spreadsheet capabilities, and other data management abilities.

de facto—Latin for *in fact*, used to describe a situation in which a nonlegal entity is acting as though it were official, or in which an unwritten law or custom has become a functional standard.

de jure—Latin for *by right* or *by law*; official.

de novo—Latin for *anew*; starting over again, disregarding any previous incidents or encounters.

dead letter—mail that cannot be delivered by the U.S. Postal Service; often said of projects or proposals that have no chance of being launched or accepted.

dead presidents—paper money.

dead stock—items that no longer interest consumers at other than extremely low prices; items that can't be sold because they no longer meet consumer safety requirements.

dead time—time a worker is unproductive because of a machinery breakdown, a meeting, the absence of a key participant or component, or other reason beyond the individual's control; time spent commuting or traveling.

deadbeat—employee who doesn't perform up to standards; client who doesn't pay bills.

deadend—something, such as a job or project, that has no future.

deadline—date or time when something is supposedly due; most projects have many deadlines (small d) prior to a final or drop-dead Deadline (big D).

deadwood—employee who is no longer contributing significantly to the company.

deal breaker—negotiating point considered so important by one party that failure to accept it will terminate further negotiations.

dealer—retailer that maintains merchandise in stock; in securities, broker who takes legal title of the item being sold before transferring it to the customer.

debenture—debt backed only by a company's general credit line and good faith; debenture holders are compensated before stockholders when a firm is dissolved.

debit—costs chargeable to a person or project; to enter on the debit side of a ledger.

debit card—card that can be used much like a credit card, but with funds immediately subtracted from the bearer's checking account.

debt—money owed to a person or organization for product or services provided.

debt/equity ratio—measure of business solvency (generally, divide total liabilities by total shareholder's equity; alternatively, total long-term debt divided by total shareholders' equity or long-term debt and preferred stock divided by common stock equity).

debt retirement—repayment of a loan.

debt service—money needed to pay the interest and an agreed-upon portion of principal on a loan during a specific time period.

decaf—decaffeinated coffee.

decentralization—systematic breaking up of formerly centralized or consolidated decision-making processes to provide local, line, or operating-unit autonomy or control.

deceptive packaging—packaging that gives the illusion the product is larger or nicer than it is in reality.

decertification—in labor relations, formal finding by the National Labor Relations Board that a union no longer represents a majority of the workers in a bargaining unit.

decision—committing yourself or those under your control to a course of action.

decision model—formal representation of the way decisions are made in an organization.

decision package—choices and documentation of each potential decision given to upper management by middle managers doing planning in a zero-based budgeting system.

decision support system—segment of a management information system that provides data to decision makers and integrates their decisions into the broader MIS flow.

decision tree—graphic representation of the various consequences of various decision options available in a process.

decisive—capable of making up his or her mind.

declare—to formally announce or record something; in finance, to authorize payment of a dividend; in tax matters, to acknowledge income or assets for tax purposes.

decommission—to retire or discontinue use of a piece of equipment, including all actions and costs necessary to clean up, dispose of, store, or secure the equipment and its site.

deductible—in insurance, amount of loss or cost you must pay before the policy kicks in.

deduction—something subtracted from your paycheck before you get it; amount the IRS allows you to subtract from gross income when figuring income taxes.

deductive reasoning—starting with things you know or assume to be true, then using logic to reach a conclusion; going from the general to the specific.

deed—legal document that conveys title interest, usually in real estate, from one person or entity to another.

deep discount—substantial discount, well in excess of what is normal for the business (and which probably can't be sustained for long without harming the business), used to attract new customers or reward good customers.

deep six—to bury or throw away (derived from the naval custom of burial at sea).

defalcation—embezzlement.

default—in finance, failure to make timely payments on a debt or to fulfill the provisions of a contract; in computers, menu or setting that a software program will use until other choices are selected.

defendant—someone charged in a legal action.

defective—said of something that doesn't work properly, often because of a design flaw or faulty production.

defer—to hold over so action can be taken at another time.

deferred compensation—salary to be paid later.

deficiency—something lacking.

deficit—in finance, excess of spending over revenue; loss or lack that must be made up; in government, amount of money borrowed to cover spending beyond that collected in taxes and other forms of income, payment of interest on which erodes the government's ability to fund other programs.

deficit financing—method used to finance operations for which there is no direct revenue support, such as borrowing, the sale of bonds, etc.

deflation—falling prices combined with stagnant business activity.

defunct—no longer working or no longer in business.

degress—progressive, consistent decline.

dehire—euphemism for laying off or firing.

delay—to make late.

delayer—removal of middle management from an organization so that there are fewer layers between frontline and top executives.

delegate—authorize a subordinate or peer to handle something.

delete—to remove.

deliberate—refers to an action taken without rushing and after some thought; to think about prior to reaching a decision.

delimit—to set boundaries.

delinquent—overdue payment.

delist—to remove a stock's listing on an exchange, usually because it failed to meet the requirements of the exchange.

delivery—in law, the transfer of ownership rights.

Delphi method—consensus decision-making tool used when a group's members are dispersed or when you want people to provide individual input without being influenced by group discussion; coordinator collects written comments from all members of the panel, circulates each one's comments to the others for review, then compiles feedback and continues the process until a decision is made or consensus reached.

demand—amount of a product or service that consumers are actually willing to pay for.

demand curve—chart that shows the demand for a product or service at different prices.

demand deposit—money on account with a financial institution that must be available to the depositor within thirty days on demand and without further advance notice.

demand loan—loan that doesn't have a predetermined maturity date but must be paid when the lender demands it.

demand-pull inflation—price increases fueled by a shortage of goods or services compared to demand.

demarketing—intentional effort by a company to reduce demand for a product or service.

demassification—breaking of a large business into autonomous, small groups.

Deming Prize—award given in Japan to organizations that have completed rigid quality criteria; named for W. Edwards

Deming, who was instrumental in the adoption of quality techniques in Japanese industry after World War II.

demographics—statistics such as income, age, and education level, used in defining target markets for a product or service.

demonstrate—to show how a product works or how a manufacturing or service operation is performed.

demotivate—to remove or reduce someone's motivation through thoughtless, stupid, or punitive actions and inactions.

denationalize—to convert nationalized businesses and industries to private ownership.

department—work group that deals with one product or process, usually consisting of one supervisor and several non-supervisory workers.

department store—retail store that carries a wide range of items arranged in small areas according to use.

deplete—to use up.

depletion allowance—credit on taxes paid on the development of natural resources.

deploy—to send something out to the field or to put in place; to spread out.

deposit—in finance, funds credited to a customer's account; prepayment held as a security on a purchase or customer relationship.

deposition—in law, written testimony taken under oath.

depositor—individual or entity that maintains funds with a financial institution.

depot—storage facility; transit facility for trains, buses, or freight.

depreciation—allowance for tax purposes that reflects the progressive decline in estimated value of equipment or property to reflect its obsolescence or physical wearing out.

depression—in economics, large decrease in business activity combined with falling prices and rising unemployment; in medicine, mental disorder involving deep sadness, inability to concentrate or work effectively, feelings of despair, and other debilitating symptoms.

deregulate—to loosen or remove government regulations, often in hopes of encouraging free enterprise or stimulating competitive activity.

design—preliminary drawings of how something will look; schematic outline of a process or program; to determine how something will look when completed; to create, as in a program or process.

design review—process for gaining input from a number of employees on how well a design meets customer needs and how cost-effective it will be to produce and market.

design shop—company specializing in the design of advertising materials, graphics, logos, and/or magazines.

desk—in finance, place where a specific function takes place (as in a trading desk); in the workplace, flat, horizontal surface on which someone works (having your own is the first sign that your work is important, after which you can concentrate on aspects such as size, style, and placement).

desktop publishing—production of type and graphics from a personal computer.

desktop video—video program edited on a personal computer.

detail person—manufacturer's representative who serves as a liaison with the customer to solve problems and enhance loyalty and satisfaction; retail salesperson whose job is to increase business by providing personal attention to customers.

detect—to find defects before the product is in the customer's hands.

deterministic—refers to a philosophy that says actions are largely predetermined by a combination of genetics and the environment.

deutsche mark—German currency.

devalue—to purposely lower something's value; in monetary policy, to lower the value of the country's currency in relation to others (or a gold standard, where still in effect).

developer—person who takes land without buildings and finances the building of structures; in photography, chemicals that bring out the image on a piece of film.

deviate—someone who looks or acts differently than the group norm and is shunned or feared accordingly; to take a path different from that expected or assigned to.

deviation—in statistics, degree of departure from a fixed value or norm.

diagonal expansion—development of new products that can be made with existing equipment.

diagnosis—sequence of events used to determine the cause of a problem or defect.

diagnostic journey—term used by Joseph Juran to define quality-improvement activities that start with discovering the signs that a problem might exist and end with determining the problem's causes.

dicker—to bargain.

Dictaphone—recording device with an attachment that allows the playback to be started and stopped with a foot pedal so it can be transcribed easily.

dictation—recording of words (either with a machine or having another person write them down) that will later be transcribed into a formal document such as a letter or report.

difference—in arithmetic, what you get when you subtract something from something else.

differently abled—politically correct term for what used to be referred to as physically or mentally handicapped.

differentiation—process of making a product or service noticeably different in the eyes of a customer.

diffuse—to spread something out, often weakening or softening it in the process; to use more words than are needed.

digest—summary of a larger body of information; to assimilate.

digital—in computers, refers to the basic form of encoding data as a combination of the numbers 1 and 0; something that can be manipulated by hand.

digitize—to convert an image or signal into digital information.

digress—to leave the main subject to make a point that may be tangential or irrelevant to the central theme.

dilution—something made less strong by adding something to it (such as adding water to a concentrated solution); in finance, a lowering of value caused by addition (such as issuing more stock, which reduces the percentage of ownership of current stockholders).

diminishing returns—rate of return that fails to increase in proportion to the cost of adding additional labor or capital to an investment or asset.

dingbat—small icon placed at the end of a story; slang for a very dumb person.

dinosaur—extinct animal characterized by a large body and a small brain (provoking Darwinian analogies with the state of the corporate art as practiced in larger U.S. businesses).

direct deposit—funds deposited directly to a financial account rather than dispensed by check to the recipient.

direct mail—advertising or other sales and promotional materials sent to consumers through the mail system.

direct marketing—marketing delivered directly to a person, usually via mail, telephone, or in-person contacts at the customer's home.

direct selling—selling from the manufacturer to the customer with no intermediary.

director—member of a company's board of directors; person who makes final decisions for a project or process; title usually (but not always) above that of manager; in film and theater, person responsible for staging and the performance of the actors (the "producer" handles the financing of the production).

directorate—board of directors; executive staff.

disability—persistent handicap or condition that prevents an individual from doing a job or limits his or her ability to meet all the requirements of a position (discriminatory if the requirements are arbitrary, artificial, or not truly reflective of the needs of the job).

disability insurance—policy that compensates individuals disabled or injured on the job in ways not covered under worker's compensation.

disburse—to pay out.

disc—optically recorded or read data storage medium (a "disk" is magnetically recorded, although the two are often used interchangeably).

discharge—waste stream released into the air or water around a plant; to fire; to pay off a debt or be released from having to pay it through some means, such as filing bankruptcy.

disclaimer—notice that a person or company is not responsible for something, most commonly the misuse of a product; CPA's decision not to give an opinion on a company's financial statements, usually because incomplete information was provided.

disclosure—required release of all information relevant to making an informed purchase or investment decision.

discount—in securities, difference between the value stated on a bond and amount it would receive if sold at this time; to lower a price; not to believe information because it came from an unreliable source.

discount broker—securities firm that charges clients a lower transaction fee or commission on sales.

discount rate—interest rate banks must pay when borrowing money from the federal reserve.

discount store—retail store that offers a wide variety of merchandise at low prices.

discovery—pretrial period when both parties seek information from their adversary.

discovery sampling—research to determine if something, such as a product defect, is within established parameters.

discrepancy—deviation from what is expected, such as the amount the cash register memory says has been rung up and the actual amount of cash in the drawer.

discretionary—not mandatory; up to the responsible choice of the individual.

discretionary income—money that is not needed to provide basic necessities such as food, clothing, and housing.

discrimination—treating a group or class of people, or a member of that class, different from everybody else because of age, sex, race, religion, physical appearance or abilities, or other characteristics.

disinflation—slower inflation; reduction or turnaround in inflationary pressures ("deflation" means prices are actually falling).

disk—magnetically recorded or read data storage medium (a "disc" is optically recorded, although the two are often used interchangeably).

diskette—small computer disk, typically 5-$1/4''$ or 3-$1/2''$ in diameter.

dismember—to tear apart quickly or violently, such as breaking up an acquired company and selling off the pieces.

dismiss—to fire; not to take into account.

displaced—out of place or not having a place anymore as a result of factors such as layoffs, business closures, obsolescence, or other outside forces.

disposable income—money left after taxes have been paid.

disruption—unwanted break in a process.

dissociate—to separate; to take a new job.

dissolution—ending the existence of a corporation or other entity; to dissolve a contractual relationship.

dissonance—lack of agreement or unity; in advertising, consumer confusion caused by conflicting claims.

distress sale—forced liquidation.

distribution—movement from the point of production or storage to the point of purchase; funds received from an investment or estate; in statistics, spread of data in a sample.

distribution allowance—reduction in price a distributor receives from a manufacturer to defray the costs of distribution.

distributor—company that acts as an intermediary, usually purchasing products from many manufacturers and reselling them to retailers.

diversify—spread risk by having a variety of operations or investments; to increase variety.

diversified company—organization with a wide variety of products and services that reach many markets.

diversity—variety; in the workplace, applies to issues involved in combining employees from numerous ethnic, cultural, and other backgrounds.

divest—to sell; to remove.

divestiture—getting rid of assets as a result of a court order, often to enforce antitrust laws.

divide et empera—Latin for *divide and conquer*.

dividend—corporate profits distributed to shareholders, usually on a quarterly basis.

division—major corporate entity that contains all of the departments and resources needed to operate independently within the parent company.

division of labor—dividing up the tasks to be performed among different groups of employees; putting workers with similar skills into categories for purposes such as statistical analysis or collective bargaining.

document—written paper that provides information or gives evidence of something; in computers, a file; to record events or other information for future use; to explain how something works.

documentary evidence—legal evidence based on written sources.

documentation—instructions for a product or process.

dog—product that costs more to produce than it brings in in profits.

dog and pony—extensive, prepared presentation of a firm's capabilities, designed to impress a client or prospective client, often involving a number of people, including top executives.

doing business as (DBA)—formal notice that an individual is conducting business under an assumed name.

dollar cost averaging—investment technique in which you use the same amount of money each month (or other period) to purchase securities, regardless of what the individual units cost.

dominant variable—most important variable in an equation or process.

done deal—finalized contract or agreement.

door—increasingly rare fixture in all but the most senior managers' offices.

dot pitch—sharpness of the image on a computer screen, literally the distance (in millimeters, such as 0.29) between the dots that form an image; the lower the number, the sharper the screen image.

dot structure—in printing, combination and distribution of ink dots that make up an image.

double budget—accounting system that keeps capital expenditures separate from ongoing expenses.

double dip—legal but sometimes negatively perceived status in which someone receives or qualifies for two pensions from different organizations, typically involving military and government service.

double indemnity—in insurance, payment of twice the face amount of a policy under specific conditions, such as death by accident.

double jeopardy—legal principle that an individual cannot be tried twice on the same charge if the previous trial resulted in acquittal; portion in the television game show *Jeopardy* during which the dollar value of answers is doubled ("and scores can really change").

double time—twice the normal wage for working holidays or overtime; in the military, twice the standard marching pace, or running in cadence.

doublespeak—intentionally vague and confusing wording designed to sound positive or impressive, but in fact giving very little information.

Dow Jones Industrial Average (DJI)—indicator of stock market performance based on the average performance of thirty large industrial (and, increasingly, service) companies.

down—said of a system that is not working; depressed.

down payment—amount paid at the time of purchase or delivery, with the balance to be paid at a later date.

down tick—when a stock or bond price falls.

downgrade—to reduce a recommendation or rating; to criticize.

downlink—in satellite communications, equipment that allows a ground site to receive a transmission; act of receiving the information.

download—to transfer a file from a central computer to a terminal or PC, or from a remote recording device to a central computer.

downplay—to treat something as unimportant.

downscale—to move to a smaller or more modest scale of operations; to reduce a production level.

downside risk—what an investor could lose due to adverse conditions or performance.

downsize—to make the organization smaller through means such as layoffs, early retirement options, and selling off operations.

downshifting—deciding to put less emphasis on work, often by taking a less demanding or time-consuming job or declining promotions.

downtime—time during which machinery is not working.

draft—preliminary form of a legal document, presentation, or proposal; written order authorizing a second party to pay a specific amount of money to a payee; to produce a preliminary version of something, such as a speech or presentation script; to produce a legal document; to conscript citizens for military service.

draw—money obtained in advance to pay for reimbursable expenses, such as travel, that you expect to incur in the near future, or as an advance against sales commissions; to take cash out of an account; to write and format a legal document.

drayage—fee paid to have someone move something (a "dray" is a cart used to haul goods).

dress for success—popular theory (and 1970s book) showing office workers how (and attempting to explain why) to dress appropriately for the style of the companies in which they work.

drive—campaign or sustained effort toward a goal; quality of people who work hard to succeed; in securities, illegal effort by a group of investors to try to drive down stock, bond, or commodity prices through strategic buying and selling.

drive time—time it takes to commute to work via car; in

101

radio, hours during which most of the audience is listening in their cars on the way to and from work.

driven—compulsive quality, positive if the results are generally desirable (for example, "service- or customer-driven"), negative if it comes at the expense of personal or professional health or balance.

drop ship—to send goods directly to the purchaser from a producer or distributor.

dry goods—product made of fabric, such as clothing.

dry hole—dead end; product that doesn't produce a profit; derived from the drilling-industry term for a well where nothing is found.

dry run—preliminary run of a production process to find any problems; dress rehearsal for a presentation.

dual career track—two options, both advancing the individual's career (and compensation), but with one typically allowing the individual to stay in a chosen job or specialty area instead of moving into a management position along the traditional career path.

dub—to put additional sound or special effects on a video or audio program; to copy.

due date—date on which payment is due or a project or product is to be delivered.

due diligence—in finance, disclosure of negative and other information, such as pending litigation or relative solvency, that might affect a purchase decision.

due process—following the correct legal procedures.

due professional care—in law, finding that someone performed a job to the prevailing standards of the profession.

dumb down—to make complex or technical information or processes more easily understood or more palatable; connotes oversimplification

dumb up—to make technical information understandable to

those who lack technical knowledge but must make use of the information.

dummy—corporation set up to shield participants from public view or liability; something that holds something else's place, such as a stand-in; in media, mockup of a magazine or newspaper; in bridge, partner's hand when played face-up.

dump—in foreign trade, to sell merchandise in a foreign country at a price lower than that in the producer's domestic market to weaken competitors; to sell goods abroad that cannot be sold in the domestic market due to inferior quality or regulatory prohibitions; to sell large amounts of stock with no concern for the effect it has on the market; to print or transfer a computer file.

dun—to ask repeatedly that a past-due account be paid, sometimes to the point of harassment or intimidation.

dupe—duplicate or copy; duplicate slide or transparency used in presentations or publishing in order to safeguard the original; to fool someone (or, someone who is easily fooled).

durable goods—items made to last, such as those made of metal or wood.

duress—illegal pressure brought to bear to produce an action (a contract signed "under duress" is not binding because it was not entered into voluntarily).

dutch auction—type of sale where the item is offered at a high price and the auctioneer continues to lower the price until someone buys it.

duty—obligation; tax on imported or exported goods.

duty free—goods that may enter or leave a country without being taxed.

dysfunctional—system, product, or person that is not functioning as intended.

E

E-mail—electronic mail sent through a company's computer system.

early adopter—someone who buys new products or technologies, or assumes new lifestyle habits and practices, as soon as they become available, providing initial word-of-mouth information to everybody else.

early involvement—business-to-business practice of working closely with major customers early in their product and service design stages so that the vendor's offerings most closely match the customer's needs.

early retirement—method of reducing the company's employment rolls in general, and the rolls of those earning generally larger salaries and fringe benefits in particular, by offering retirement benefits before the previously established target for age or length of service has been reached.

earned benefit—benefit contingent on length of service, such as sick leave, vacation, service bonuses, etc.

earned income—income from work, pensions, or annuities, but not from stock dividends or similar sources.

earnest money—deposit put down as evidence of intent to buy.

earnings—company's net income over an extended period; individual's income.

earnings per share (EPS)—amount of profit allocated to each share of common stock for a given time period, such as a quarter or year (divide the dividend allocation by the number of shares outstanding).

easy money—period when loans are relatively easier to obtain because of the amount of funds available in the banking system.

echelon—level of power in an organization.

ecology—study of how living things interact; often used as a synonym for plants and animals.

economic factors—trends and phenomena that have an influence over the amount of money people and corporations have.

economics—study of the economy, including individual monetary habits and large trends.

economies of scale—savings that result when products are mass produced.

economist—professional who studies information related to the economy.

economize—to make do with less; to reduce expenditures or use of corporate resources while attempting to maintain existing levels of service.

ecotopia—marketing term for the northwestern United States, so called because much of the population has a deep attachment to the land.

ECU—European Currency Unit, the common currency that is supposed to be created as part of the economic integration of Europe in the 1990s.

edge city—demographer's term for suburbs of major cities that have become relatively autonomous and self-sustaining centers of business and civic activities; typically a middle-class area, not defined by conventional suburban borders, surrounding a central city (or "urban core") where people live, work, and shop.

edict—official announcement that often states a policy or rule.

edifice complex—propensity of business executives to feel that the company with the bigger building is the better company.

edit—in video, the process of assembling a finished program from separate pieces of video footage and voiceover narration; to correct, revise, enhance, or otherwise change another's piece of written, audio, or video work, often shortening it in the process.

edit suite—studio and equipment used to edit audio or video works.

effect—result of something ("affect" is used as a verb only); to produce, accomplish, or make something happen ("affect" means to have an effect on or to influence); when in doubt, use "impact."

effective—something that works.

effective date—date when something actually happens, such as a law being enforced or a contract being considered binding.

efficiency expert—specialist in the management of work whose supposed skill is arranging people and processes for maximum time- and cost-effectiveness; typically disrespected (because sometimes their efforts have made matters worse instead of better) or feared (because people don't like to change, and some people might lose their jobs as a result of change).

Efficient Customer Response (ECR)—grocery industry program that envisions a nationwide network of computers and scanners that will improve the efficiency of relationships between wholesalers and retailers.

efficient markets—in investing, controversial theory that says you can't beat the market by finding undervalued stocks or forecasting movements because stock prices accurately reflect the true value investors put on the company and its actions.

effluent—liquid wastes, sometimes toxic, discharged from a process ("affluent" means you have a lot of money).

effort—work made visible.

effortless—characteristic of skilled work that makes it appear easy to do and hence can be dangerous to the doer, because people don't think you're doing anything that's all that hard or valuable.

egress—means of exiting.

eight-hour chair—ergonomically designed chair that meets comfort standards for use over extended periods of time.

80/20 principle—marketing axiom that says that about 20% of a company's customers will account for about 80% of its sales; often applied to other situations with multiple causes and multiple effects; also called "the Pareto principle."

86—slang for killing a program or idea.

elastic—relative measurement of how fast and how extensively a market or situation changes when prices change.

elasticity—amount of responsiveness shown by buyers (demand) or producers (supply) when prices change; the less something reacts to price changes, the more elastic it is said to be.

electronic—systems that operate through the controlled conduction of electrons or other carriers of an electrical charge.

electronic data interchange (EDI)—computer-to-computer interface that allows businesses to share forms, access technical and account information, and transact paperless business activities in computer real-time.

electronic funds transfer system (EFTS)—paperless computer-managed system that credits and debits funds far faster than the old manual systems.

element—piece of something else; in marketing, refers to the various individual pieces and activities that will be developed and employed in a campaign.

elephant-sized project—extremely large project.

elevator—means used to communicate in person between levels of an organization's hierarchy; place where entry-level employees can attract the notice of senior management, for good or ill.

elevator music—generic, ideally inoffensive music played in elevators, over the telephone while on hold, in waiting areas and other public places to mask background noises and create a pleasant environment; like fingernails on a chalkboard to people whose tastes run to forms of music with more style and character.

Elks—nonprofit fraternal organization.

embargo—formal, often government-mandated restriction against sending or selling specific items to another country, business, or person; in business communications, forbidding the general release of information before a specified date.

embezzlement—sophisticated form of stealing that usually involves falsifying financial records to allow an individual to improperly take money or property without being noticed.

emboss—to create a raised design on a surface, often used in expensive or image-creating printed pieces such as letterheads, annual reports, and corporate brochures.

emergency—sudden crisis that demands action; something you have to resolve under pressure as the result of someone else's poor planning or inept actions.

emerging market—demographic group newly identified by marketers as having a number of factors in common.

eminence grise—French for an older person whose authority and experience is respected.

eminent domain—government's right to take a person's private property for public use without that person's permission, subject to compensation for the market value of the property.

empathy—ability to understand what another person must be feeling without sharing the same feelings ("sympathy" involves the sharing of feelings).

employee—person hired by a company for an indefinite period.

employee assistance program (EAP)—program provided by an employer to help its employees cope with problems resulting from conditions in or out of the workplace, such as alcohol and drug abuse, stress management, health improvement, and balancing the competing needs of job and family.

employee development—activity that makes a person a better employee, most commonly training, but including apprenticeships, continuing education courses and advanced degree work at educational institutions, and rotating through a succession of jobs to gain experience and understanding of the various facets of the company's business.

employee manual—handbook that officially explains the policies, procedures, and benefits of the organization.

employee of the month—common recognition tactic in which one employee's performance is chosen as being exceptional for a given time period, usually with a token award such as a plaque, a photo on a bulletin board, and an article about the person in the company newsletter; may demotivate more people than it motivates by virtue of passing over others whose performance also merited recognition.

employee retirement stock ownership plan (ERSOP)—employee-owned stock fund whose assets and dividends are put into a tax-deferred retirement account.

employer—person or corporation that pays another person to do work for them.

employment—your paid job.

employment agency—company that specializes in finding candidates for a company's job positions or jobs for people who are unemployed or want to change jobs and are willing to pay a fee for placement in a new position.

employment contract—contract stating the details of an employment relationship.

employment test—test given to applicants for a job to help determine which is the best choice.

employment parity—attempting to hire members of minority groups at the same percentage as that in which they are represented in the community.

empowerment—practice of making it clear that employees have both the responsibility and the authority to make decisions within the scope of their jobs.

empty nesters—demographic term for couples whose children are grown and not living at home.

encode—to translate a message into coded form; to put a coded message onto an item or in a document, such as a computer file.

encumbrances—in real estate, preexisting legal rights or interests (such as mortgages, leases, or easements) that diminish the value of a property but do not prevent its title from being passed to a new owner; informally, things that weigh down or complicate an activity or relationship, such as conditions, caveats, or limitations.

end cap—shelving or display space on either end of an aisle containing retail merchandise, often considered a prime position to display product.

end product—final result of a process.

endorse—to sign a check; to publicly approve of the merits of an individual or product.

engage—to hire; to enter into competition with; to put a machine or process into operation.

engine—a machine that converts energy into motion.

engineer—person whose education and training are in one of several technical areas of the science of engineering; to design or bring about a result.

enhance—to make something better by adding incremental improvements that are not necessary to the main purpose; a person enhances his or her education with courses such as music appreciation; an enhanced product has added features (which may or may not be considered valuable or desirable by the customer).

ensure—to insure (used interchangeably); to make certain.

enterprise—activity with a specific goal in mind; often a synonym for a new or entrepreneurial business.

enterprise zone—area, often depressed or in need of revitalization, in which favorable conditions are created by government actions (such as tax reductions or tax credits, or relaxed employment or planning rules) to attract businesses.

entertain—to offer hospitality or diversion; to think about an idea; to keep people interested in a subject without providing a great deal of specific information about it.

entity—legal form in which a business exists and holds property.

entree—access; main course of a meal.

entrepreneur—person who starts a business, especially if the venture is considered risky or unique.

entry-level job—job for which someone with little experience is qualified, typically low-paying and offering few opportunities for significant advancement without additional experience and/or education.

envelope—what you push when you're trying to expand the way people look at an idea or activity; container for printed and other materials; to surround or enclose.

environment—physical or intellectual area that surrounds a business or activity.

environmental impact report (EIR)—planning document that attempts to forecast the environmental effects of a proposed activity; also called an *environmental impact statement (EIS)*.

Environmental Protection Agency (EPA)—federal agency concerned with how the actions of people and corporations affect their surroundings.

environmentalist—person concerned enough about the environment to put its interests ahead of strictly commercial considerations.

environmentally correct—actions taken to protect water, air, wildlife, and the natural setting in which business is conducted; connotes actions taken to allay the fears and suspicions of environmentally sensitive constituencies.

environmentally sound—products and actions that do not harm nature.

equal employment opportunity (EEO)—right of every person to compete for a job and to be promoted on the basis of ability, without artificial barriers based on race, sex, age, disability, or other nonjob-related conditions; often refers to procedures and rules used to ensure adherence to this right.

Equal Employment Opportunity Commission (EEOC)— federal agency created by the Civil Rights Act of 1964 to ensure equal employment opportunity.

equilibrium—balance; point in a market when nothing is forcing a change in price or demand.

equity—in corporate finance, ownership interest held by shareholders in the form of stock; in real estate, amount actually owned in property that isn't fully paid for yet; in the workplace, fairness, but not necessarily equality.

ergonomics—study of designing workspaces, furniture, vehicles, and other areas in which people function for lengthy periods of time so that they are most comfortable and easy to use.

error-proofing—reduction of the probability of inadvertent human errors through better procedures and better workspace design.

escalator clause—contractual clause through which increases in costs are passed on to another party; in a labor contract, clause that increases wages in conjunction with increases in the cost of living index.

escrow—in law, giving a document, such as a title or deed, to a third party until the terms of an agreement are met, at which point it is delivered to the acquiring party; in real estate, money deposited or deducted from mortgage payments in advance for payment of taxes, insurance, and other charges.

esquire (esq.)—honorary title used by attorneys.

et al—Latin for *and others*.

ethical—fair treatment that meets the professional standards of a group; in medicine, drugs that can be sold only by physicians or veterinarians.

ethics—moral and professional principles.

ethnic—anything to do with a culture; in the U.S., typically describes cultural characteristics other than those of white European ancestry.

ethnic market—group of people whom marketers have identified as having certain specific needs and wants as a result of their ethnic backgrounds.

Euro—having to do with Europe.

Eurobank—bank that accepts deposits from corporations and governments outside their home country; the bank itself does not have to be based in Europe.

Eurodollar—U.S. dollar on deposit in a European bank, often used as a reserve currency by European nations.

European Economic Community (EEC)—alliance formed by Western European countries in 1957 to promote and coordinate trade and production activities; the twelve full members include Belgium, Denmark, France, Germany, Great Britain, Greece, Ireland, Italy, Luxembourg, the Netherlands, Portugal, and Spain.

European Monetary System (EMS)—European Economic Community concord stipulating consistent monetary exchange rates.

European Plan (EP)—hotel rate that includes the room only.

everyday low pricing (EDLP)—strategy of setting and maintaining one price on a product or service rather than muddying the marketing waters with a succession of discounts, sale prices, promotions, rebates, and other changes (often increasing costs for the seller and confusion for the customer).

ex gratia payment—settlement by an insurance company for a claim it doesn't feel it should pay, made to avoid the expense of going to court.

ex officio—in law, by right of position or office; often incorrectly used in an instance when an officer of a company makes a decision without being present at the meeting.

Exacto knife—small, scalpel-like knife used by artists and designers to make delicate or intricate cuts.

excel—to do exceptionally well compared to others.

excellence—what everybody in business is supposed to be in search of; hard to find because, by definition, there's not very much of it to go around.

exchange—place or system in which or through which securities are traded, such as the New York Stock Exchange; to trade goods or services for goods or services of equal value (if money changes hands as part of the transaction, it's a "sale").

exchange rate—price for which one country's currency can be changed into another country's currency.

exchequer—formally, the account of the chancellor of the Exchequer of the United Kingdom; informally, a national treasury or any large amount of funds.

excise—to cut something away or remove it from a larger piece.

excise tax—tax imposed on something specific, such as consumption of an item, practice of an occupation, or anything else not taxed as income or property.

execute—to do; in law, to complete or sign.

executive—employee of at least managerial level, although the term usually applies to vice presidents and above and is rarely used for those directly supervising manufacturing operations.

executive secretary—secretary who works directly for a top executive and whose duties frequently include general administrative activities as well as clerical work.

executive session—meeting of a board, committee, or other group from which the general public is barred.

executive summary—short summary (usually no more than a page or two) of detailed material, designed to give the reader the gist without the time-consuming details.

exempt—position not covered by hour and wage laws and hence not eligible for overtime pay; excluded from anything that would normally apply to the broad situation.

exemption—deduction from taxable income allowed to a taxpayer due to specific circumstances, such as having children, or business or medical expenses.

exercise—designed activity or hypothetical situation discussed or worked through for learning purposes; activity intended to improve personal health and fitness; to do something you have the right to do under the provisions of a contract; to work out.

exhibit—illustration in a document; in law, an item introduced into evidence in court; to show or display.

exhibit hall—large area at a convention or trade show devoted to displays of products and literature.

exhortation—very strong recommendation or appeal.

exit interview—meeting with a supervisor or human resources person to discuss why you are leaving the company.

exit polling—questioning people as they leave a polling place to determine how a vote is going before returns are counted.

exonerate—to clear someone from blame or suspicion.

expand—to grow or spread out.

expansion—growth, whether through investment in new facilities or purchase of existing facilities and capabilities of another organization.

expectations—what customers feel they should receive from a product or service in addition to the core need that it satisfies; customer expectations are a basic component of market research and new product development.

expected return—amount of net profit projected from a venture.

expendable—something that can be used, deleted, or discarded without hurting the end product or the organization's viability; frequently refers to budget items or employees about to be laid off.

expenditures—amounts spent on specific projects.

expense—amount spent for any reason; in accounting, deductible cost.

expense account—allotment for travel and expenses incurred in the course of doing business; in accounting, account in which expenses are recorded.

expense report—detailed report, including receipts, of when and why money was spent in the course of traveling for business.

expensed—paid for out of a specific budget, sometimes over a period of time.

experience—the best teacher; previous work (and the knowledge gained from it); past history or norm for an activity or situation; to undergo.

experienced amateurs—employees who have a great deal of experience in doing something but no formal training in the area.

experiential education/learning—learning by doing something rather than being taught about it by another.

expire—to end, as in a contract or option.

exploit—to take advantage of or use; often refers to an extreme or unethical use of a person or situation for personal or business benefit.

exponential—in mathematics, relative relationships involving multiplying something by itself (doubling, tripling, etc.); informally, describes a rapid rate of increase.

export—to ship a product outside of a country or from one region or zone to another.

Export-Import Bank (Eximbank)—U.S. bank whose lending power is used to stimulate international trade.

exposition—large event usually open to the public; detailed explanation of something.

exposure—in marketing, measure of how many people see or hear advertising or public relations messages; in finance, probability and degree of risk in a venture; in career development, value of an individual's contacts with upper management.

Express Mail—overnight delivery service provided by the U.S. Postal Service.

extant—living.

extension—time added after a deadline for payment or submission of a project; addition to a product line; individual's internal phone number.

extent—scope; how far something extends.

extenuating circumstances—unpredictable events or mitigating conditions that at least partially explain why rules weren't followed or an objective wasn't accomplished as expected.

external audit—audit performed by people who do not work for the organization.

external customer—individuals and groups that purchase what an organization makes or does.

external equity—pay received for a job in an organization as compared to that received for similar jobs in other organizations.

extinct—no longer in existence.

extinction pricing—pricing a product extremely low to sell off remaining inventory.

extortion—obtaining money or advantage through intimidation.

extraordinary income—unexpected income derived from nonusual sources.

extraordinary loss—large, unplanned loss.

extrapolate—to add new values beyond those now known (as opposed to "interpolate," which involves determining intermediate values in a series).

extrinsic reward—nonessential gift given as a reward for doing something well.

executive washroom—private bathroom, often locked to control access by the less mighty, where top executives sometimes take advantage of informal meetings to make decisions (may be one of the key reasons why the glass ceiling continues to exist).

eyeball—to inspect visually for general appearance; to read.

F

fabricated materials—items or components in a finished product that have been processed to some extent before use or assembly.

fabrication—lie.

facade—outside wall or "face" of a building; actions designed to make persons or products appear better or more substantial than they are.

face value—amount noted on a check or security; amount of insurance a policy provides at death or maturity.

facility—building or other physical place set aside for a specific function.

facilitator—person who guides a meeting or activity in which participants are expected to generate their own ideas or find their own solutions rather than be given those of the discussion leader or an outside authority.

facsimile—originally, a copy of an original; now refers primarily to a telecommunications device ("fax") that transmits scanned documents over telephone lines to another machine or a computer.

faction—relatively small group of people who have a different opinion from a larger group.

factoid—number, statistic, quote, axiom, or other small, unrelated piece of information that provides the illusion of knowledge (the Dow Jones Industrial Average and the barometric pressure are factoids in the sense that most people can repeat the numbers but have no real knowledge or understanding of what they mean).

factor—cause that contributes to an effect; individual who acts as an agent.

factor analysis—analysis of complex situations done by consolidating data into groupings of related items.

factory—manufacturing facility.

fail-safe—measure or device designed to keep a disaster from happening, such as a pressure-relief valve that keeps a furnace from blowing up; contingency actions developed in advance to be implemented if a proposed plan of action backfires.

fair rate of return—financial return permitted to a utility or other controlled organization by the regulatory body involved.

fair representation—union's duty to represent all members of a bargaining unit equally.

fait accompli—French for something done before anyone finds out about it.

fam tour—in hospitality, an all- or most-expenses-paid visit to one or several potential meeting and convention sites provided to meeting planners so they can "familiarize" themselves with the capabilities of the facilities to handle their meeting needs.

family—group of products bearing the same brand name or group of products with similar uses, such as a company's family of soap products; also used (usually by management) to describe a company's workforce when trying to create goodwill.

family business—private business all or substantially owned and managed by members of the same small or extended family.

Fannie Mae—nickname for the Federal National Mortgage Association, a publicly owned government corporation that buys and packages home mortgages, primarily from the Federal Home Administration, for sale to investors; shares are traded on the New York Stock Exchange.

fast track—path to quicker promotion than your peers, often because you have been selected and are being groomed by management for bigger and better things; to accelerate a process.

faux pas—French for *mistake*, usually in a social setting.

fax—message sent or received by facsimile machine, or the machine itself.

feasible—possible or likely.

featherbedding—getting paid for work you don't do; in labor relations, refers to contract provisions designed to preserve jobs by requiring that workers are paid even if they no longer do what they used to.

feature—aspect of a product; to highlight or emphasize.

features, advantages, and benefits (FABs)—in marketing communications, showcasing a product or service's value by explaining its significant features, showing its advantages compared to competitors' offerings, and pointing out how it will benefit the purchaser.

fed—federal reserve system; employee of the federal government, often representing a regulatory agency.

federal—refers to the national government of a country.

Federal Aviation Administration (FAA)—agency of the U.S. Department of Transportation that oversees airlines, airports, and air traffic control.

Federal Communications Commission (FCC)—agency of the U.S. Government that regulates the broadcasting industry by issuing licenses to radio and television stations.

Federal Deposit Insurance Corporation (FDIC)—federal agency that insures bank deposits.

Federal Housing Administration (FHA)—agency of the U.S. Department of Housing and Urban Development (HUD) that administers loan programs designed to make housing more affordable.

federal ID number (FIN)—number assigned to an incorporated business for tax purposes, equivalent to an individual's Social Security number.

Federal Reserve—system of twelve regional banks (located in Atlanta, Boston, Chicago, Cleveland, Dallas, Kansas City, Minneapolis, New York, Philadelphia, Richmond, St. Louis, and San Francisco) and their twenty-five branches that take actions to regulate the national money supply.

Federal Reserve Board (FRB)—federal reserve system's seven-member governing board.

Federal Savings & Loan Insurance Corporation (FSLIC)—government agency that insures savings and loan deposits.

Federal Trade Commission (FTC)—government entity responsible for protecting the free enterprise system by ensuring competition; among other things, it regulates advertising practices.

Fedex—short for Federal Express, the overnight-delivery company; to send something overnight.

fee—amount paid for professional services.

feedback—return flow of information regarding an individual or group's performance, or consumers' likes and dislikes, communicated after an event has been completed or a product has been used; informally, applies to information used to guide another's performance based on past actions.

feedback loop—data returned from the field to the people or processes that need to be adjusted to correct problems and improve performance.

feeder line—transportation that takes traffic or people from several areas and routes it to a major line.

feeding frenzy—derived from the actions of predators in the wild, such as sharks or piranha, which swarm a victim; applies to investors who aggressively buy stock in a company whose resistance to a takeover is weakening or reporters who jump en masse on a breaking story in search of all the sordid details.

fiber optics—technology involving the transmission of information in the form of light carried by a cable made up of spunglass fibers or other materials.

fiche—short for *microfiche*, the transfer of documents to extremely small photos that must be read on magnifying machines; before computers, a common way for companies to store old documents as well as accounts payable and accounts receivable information.

fiduciary—person or business that holds something in trust for someone else and, as such, must act responsibly with that trust.

field intelligence—data gained from talking to external customers about how a product or service meets their needs or affects their lives.

field staff—salespeople who work out of remote offices.

field work—work done directly with customers, at their place of business or in a neutral setting.

fifth color—in printing, addition of a special color or coated effect, such as clear varnish or a gold tone, to a conventional four-color (black, red, yellow, blue) piece; used on materials designed to convey an image of success and class.

file—folder or computer document holding information on something; to put away, store, or stop working on something.

file cabinet—place where a pile of paper can be stored vertically instead of horizontally .

file folder—document file in an Apple system.

file 13—euphemism for *waste basket*.

fill or kill (FOK)—order to buy or sell a particular security immediately if it is available, otherwise the order is canceled.

film—covering or coating; in printing and photography, negatives used to make printing plates; to photograph on motion picture film or videotape.

finance—science of money; to pay for a purchase over time.

financial relations—special area of public relations dealing with the communication of financial information directly to interested audiences, including shareholders, brokers, and analysts.

financial statement—report on a business's financial condition.

financial supermarket—financial services company that offers many different products and services.

financier—expert in large-scale financial affairs, often one who arranges financing for a venture and may consequently have some control over the project.

finder's fee—bonus paid for landing a large account; fee paid to a person or company that locates a new business opportunity for a community or large organization.

finished goods—products ready to sell to customers.

fire—to terminate someone's employment for reasons other than lack of work available.

firefighting—solving problems, usually ones that have been allowed to become serious because they were neglected.

firm—unincorporated business, although often used as a synonym for any kind of business; strong or steadfast, such as a firm agreement to do something; to make more detailed and definite ("to firm up an offer").

first class—anything measurably better than the norm; the way you get to fly if you're a company officer.

first in, first out (FIFO)—inventory valuation system in which the first goods manufactured are considered the first ones sold; in inflationary times, tends to inflate profits because the first materials purchased, which were the least expensive, are charged against current sales.

first law of organizational physics—dynamic that explains the relative lot of people in a hierarchy: "shit flows downhill," as explained by drill sergeants in basic training; "the trickle-

123

down theory," as popularized during the presidency of Ronald Reagan.

first law of program probability—theory that any program with more pieces, parts, steps, or elements than the statistically normal human being has fingers on one hand is unlikely to succeed.

first mortgage—original mortgage on a property, which is considered senior to additional mortgages arranged.

fiscal—having to do with money, although literally it refers only to the public treasury or finances.

fiscal responsibility—company's legal responsibility to its shareholders to make wise financial decisions.

fiscal year—business's twelve-month accounting period, sometimes beginning on January 1, but often instead commencing on the day the company became incorporated or started business, or set to reflect the seasonal swings of the business.

fishbone analysis—analysis technique that charts the linkages between causes and effects (the result often looks like the skeleton of a fish, hence the name) by asking why until root causes are found; also called an "Ishikawa diagram" after its Japanese originator.

fission—breaking items into their basic components; splitting an atom ("fusion" means putting things together).

fit—suitable; in good health; to adapt easily to the corporate culture or needs of the situation.

fitness for use—pragmatic definition of the quality of a product, including both its features and its ability to meet customer needs.

five-percenter—company that earmarks five percent of its pretax profits for community and philanthropic causes, the maximum allowable deduction on federal taxes.

fixed—nonvarying; constant.

fixed asset—physical resource or facility used to make a product or provide a service.

fixed fee—predetermined price for doing something, no matter how long it takes; the vendor assumes the risk for cost overruns and unforeseeable expenses, but benefits if the job is finished sooner or at less expense than anticipated.

fixture—something or someone that has been around for a long time; in real estate, something that can't be removed without affecting the value of the property.

fizzle—to fail in a disappointing way.

flack—public relations specialist who works to get a company's name in the press; abuse or criticism (although the real word for that is *flak*, meaning "antiaircraft fire"); to push a specific point of view based on selfish or commercial interest, not necessarily because it meets the needs of a given situation.

flag—marker or cautionary note in a file designed to call attention to a specific condition or circumstance; in publishing, the logo, including the name of the publication, on the cover or front page; to highlight or call attention to; to tire or lose enthusiasm.

flagship—product or service for which a company is best known, whether or not it brings in the most profits; largest or most extensive property in a chain's holdings.

flak—abuse or criticism.

flameout—to lose momentum and die; derived from what happens when a jet engine stops working in midair.

flank attack—unanticipated opposition to a proposal or program on the basis of a side issue, rather than through objection to the main premise or thrust; in advertising, a campaign that seeks to steer customers away from a competing product by highlighting minor features and advantages rather than directly confronting or criticizing the competition.

flanker product—in marketing, extension to a line that is only slightly different from existing products, such as a new flavor or size.

flat—showing neither growth nor decline.

flat scale—pay that doesn't fluctuate with productivity.

flat tax—tax assessed at the same rate to everyone, regardless of income or other circumstances.

flexible budget—multiple contingency plan that provides for different amounts of income and expenses as a result of different levels of production or sales.

flextime—system that allows employees to vary their work hours rather than adhere to a strict schedule in order to balance personal and professional commitments.

flight—in advertising, a series of ads that runs or is mailed in one time period.

flipchart—a stand with a large pad of paper that can be written on so that everyone in a small meeting can see it.

float—funds in transit that are credited to the depositor even though they haven't yet cleared the originator's bank, or are treated as still in the originator's account because they haven't yet been deposited by the recipient, in either case allowing very short-term use of money that really isn't there; checks that haven't been paid yet; to offer new securities; to take out a loan.

floating holiday—paid day off that can be taken at the employee's discretion, usually requiring a supervisor's approval.

flood the market—predatory marketing tactic in which so much product is put on the market that consumers have a difficult time finding competing products, or prices fall significantly, hurting smaller competitors.

floor loan—smallest loan available from a lender.

floor plan—schematic of a building showing the arrangement of offices and equipment.

flowchart—graphic representation of the succession of steps
126

and decision points in a process; to develop a flowchart on a process.

fluctuate—to change, usually within a given range.

flush—financially well off; to discard something; to stop making a product or providing a service.

fly-by-night—shady or unreliable; not likely to be around for very long.

flyer—one-page printed announcement; calculated risk.

flyspeck—to examine carefully and in minute detail.

focus group—research technique in which people representative of customer demographics or target audiences discuss their opinions on an issue or a company's products or services to provide insight for design, development, or marketing specialists.

folio—page number.

followership—theory that says businesses need people who know how to follow their leaders.

Food and Drug Administration (FDA)—federal agency that writes and enforces regulations ensuring the safety of food, drugs, cosmetics, and medical devices.

food chain—in ecology, successive levels of plants and animals that feed on each other; refers to where people are in a company's hierarchy.

foolproof—device, program, or system that can be run even by a person of limited intelligence who isn't paying attention (usually the fools prove able to screw things up anyway).

footer—information printed at the bottom of a document; unlike a footnote, the same information appears on each page; foundation support.

force field analysis—identification and analysis of the strength of driving forces and restraining forces in a process.

force majeure—action or event that has major consequences.

forecast—estimate of future trends based on past experiences and data.

foreclosure—forfeiture of property to a lender because a debt on the property wasn't paid in a timely manner.

foreign—located in a country other than your native country; strange or unfamiliar.

foreign corporation—corporation doing business in a country or state other than the one in which it is incorporated.

foreign exchange—methods that two or more countries use to pay or make loans to one another.

foreign trade zone (FTZ)—enclosed area near a port where goods from one country en route to a third country can be stored, inspected, or processed with no duty being assessed as long as they are shipped out; also called "free trade zone."

foreman—person who supervises laborers.

form—document template with blank spaces for specific information.

format—standardized written or verbal presentation; to make a computer disk ready to receive information.

Fortune 500—*Fortune* magazine's annual listing of the largest industrial companies in the United States.

forward integration—diversification of a business into areas that are closer to the end user of its product, most commonly a manufacturer or wholesaler opening retail stores.

four Cs—the four items that make up 80% of vending machine sales: candy, cigarettes, coffee, and cold drinks.

four Ps—in product marketing, the four basic considerations: product, price, place, and promotion.

four-color—in printing, black, red, blue, and yellow, the four colors used in varying percentages.

401(K)—company-run investment fund into which employees can put pretax earnings, with taxes deferred until the funds are withdrawn; also called a salary reduction plan.

fragment—small part that has been broken away from something larger; to break a small piece or group away from something larger.

fragmented industry—industry in which companies face many opportunities for differentiation, but each is of small importance (restaurants, for example).

franc—French monetary standard.

franchise—license to use a company's name, products, and marketing support in exchange for meeting certain conditions; government-granted permission to use public property.

fraternal—organized group of people who meet for social purposes; in the past, referred strictly to all-male organizations, but now applies to any such group.

fraternize—to make friends with people who work for your competitors, either out of naïveté or in an attempt to gain insight into their actions and plans.

fraud—misrepresentation of a situation or product to harm someone or gain money from them; impostor.

Freddie Mae—nickname for the Federal Home Loan Mortgage Corporation, a government agency that buys and packages home mortgages, primarily from the Federal Home Administration, for sale to investors; shares are owned by savings institutions.

free enterprise—system in which (ideally) business is conducted based on the rules of a marketplace rather than government regulation.

free lunch—what there's no such thing as; reflects the sense that in business, everything has a cost.

free market—market in which prices are determined by supply and demand.

free on board (FOB)—in transportation, means that the invoice price includes delivery to a specified point and no further, with the buyer paying for any additional shipping needed.

free trade agreement—agreements between two or more countries to have no tariffs or restrictions on trade.

free trade zone (FTZ)—same as *foreign trade zone*.

freebie—sample product or small item given away at a trade show, convention, or retail store to familiarize people with a product, company, or brand name.

Freedom of Information Act (FOIA)—law that outlines what federal documents are open and available to the public and how they can be obtained.

freelance—people who provide their services to businesses on a per-job basis; freelancers are not considered employees, but may be held to employee standards of conduct while working on a project.

frequency—amount that something happens over a specified period of time.

frequency distribution—relationship between the value of a variable and the frequency with which it occurs; graphic representation of that relationship.

frequent customer program—marketing program that provides special benefits or incentives to repeat customers to build loyalty and repeat sales.

frequent flyer program—first frequent customer program, developed in the airline industry to reward passengers who fly large numbers of miles with free seat upgrades or tickets.

Freudian motivation theory—Sigmund Freud's late-nineteenth-century theory that all actions are motivated by sexual needs.

friendly acquisition—corporate takeover or merger in which the company being acquired is (or professes to be) happy about it, seeing it as a business advantage.

fringe benefits—nonmonetary compensation provided to employees, such as health insurance, company cars, and retirement plans.

frivolous—anything not worthy of attention because it is unimportant to the matter; in law, small claim or piece of information that a judge deems to be not worth pursuing.

front—innocent-seeming image or facade that may be used to hide an illegal business or activity; to serve as the visible agent for a project that may involve unidentified participants.

front money—money needed to begin a project.

front office—offices of the major executives of a company.

frontage—part of a business's property that is located along a street or other traffic corridor accessible to customers.

front-end load—in investing, charge for buying an investment assessed at the time of purchase; in the workplace, to give employees a large amount of information so they can understand a more difficult concept; to give managers information before their subordinates so they buy into a new program first.

frontline—employees who work directly with customers; the point at which customers and employees interact.

frozen—not able to be used, such as frozen assets or accounts.

FUD (fear, uncertainty, and dread or doubt)—basic components that lead people to consider changing what they are doing.

fudge—extra time built into a schedule to account for delays; extra money put into a budget as a contingency against likely cost overruns or as added profit; to make up information.

fudge factor—when budgeting or scheduling, a number by which base figures are increased to reflect contingencies.

fulfillment—process of filling orders placed by direct mail or direct marketing.

full disclosure—legal requirement to tell someone all specific and relevant information before a sale is completed.

full employment—level of unemployment (usually between 3% and 7%) determined by economists to be a natural result of people switching jobs, not caused by an adverse economy or a lack of jobs.

full faith—government's promise to use all its income-generating power to repay a bond; used colloquially to mean you have done something in complete honesty.

full service—in brokerage, investment company that provides research and other services in addition to executing trades; business that provides a range of after-sale or continuing services to its customers.

fully vested—in pension funds, refers to ownership of all of the money contributed by the employer, usually after a number of years with the company.

functional—operating; convenient or practical.

functional illiterate—someone who is unable to learn how to read and write, or has so far avoided learning to do so well enough to be employable (often despite having been graduated from high school).

functionality—how well something suits the purpose for which it is intended.

fund—amount of money or an account to which money is contributed that is to be used for a specific purpose; to finance or underwrite.

fund accounting—accounting system used by nonprofit organizations, including government, to account for the dispersal of funds.

fundamentals—basics of a business; something you know that a newly hired employee doesn't know.

furniture disease—occupational hazard of office workers whose inactivity causes steadily increasing waist measurements.

fusion—combining two items to create a third completely different item ("fission" means splitting things apart).

futures—in investing, agreement to buy or sell a specific amount of a commodity or financial instrument at a particular price on a specific date.

futurist—someone who focuses on current trends and their likely future outcomes.

fuzzify—to make something less clear, usually with the purpose of trying to hide the true message or bury a potentially embarrassing or damaging fact.

fuzzy logic—computer term for calculations that involve multiple variables and contingencies rather than strictly either/or decisions; used to provide fast approximations from databases and to explore "what if" scenarios.

FYI (for your information)—notation on a document you should read for the information in it, but need not take action on; in investing, price quoted for general information, but not as a firm offer to buy or sell.

G

gaffe—social mistake, such as wearing casual clothes to a formal party.

gain—increase in value; volume produced from an electronic signal.

gain sharing—management practice of paying employees a bonus or incentive based on the percentage of improvement they help generate in sales or other standards.

gambit—initial action or statement, sometimes intended to confuse a competitor about the actual strategy to be employed; in chess, refers to the sacrifice of one or more usually minor pieces early in the game to obtain an advantage as the game develops.

game—ready and willing, but not necessarily happy about trying something; metaphor for business competition.

game plan—strategy and tactics for solving a problem or attacking an issue in a specific time frame.

Gantt chart—graphic representation showing the succession of tasks that must be accomplished in the production of a product or completion of a process (developed by Henry Laurence Gantt).

garnish—little piece of fruit or lettuce that adds color to a plate of food (you "garnish" a salad; you "garnishee" someone's paycheck).

garnishee—to get a court order to withhold money from a person's paycheck to pay a debt.

garnishment—court order telling an employer to withhold money from an employee's paycheck and send it to another source for repayment of a debt.

gatekeeper—someone who controls access to another individual, usually an executive or top-notch specialist; anyone who tries to keep you from seeing or talking to his or her superior or associates.

GBC binding—type of binding that uses a plastic comblike tube, popular for small documents that will not have materials added or taken out.

gender analysis—ascertaining which names on a list are male and which are female, usually for the purpose of tailoring marketing promotions.

general—applying to all or most, usually without including a great deal of detail; opposite of *specific*.

General Accounting Office (GAO)—agency set up by Congress to ensure that the federal government's financial transactions are legal.

General Agreement on Tariffs and Trade (GATT)—continuing negotiations on trade matters among the seven largest industrial nations, including the United States, Canada, Japan, Great Britain, France, Germany, and Italy.

general contractor—person who organizes and supervises

the construction of a building, often employing "subcontractors" for specific parts of the project.

general ledger—formal accounts of a business.

general partner—in a limited partnership, the partner who typically provides administration and management of activities and funds, and whose liability and exposure are not limited to the amount of funds invested.

general session—at a conference, meetings intended for all attendees.

generalist—someone who knows a little bit about a lot of different things but has no specialized knowledge or skills, ideally making him or her capable of growing into a variety of positions and changing with changing conditions and needs.

generally accepted accounting principles (GAAP)—recommended procedures established by the Financial Accounting Standards Board for formally recording and reporting financial information.

generation—people born, educated, trained, or experienced during a specific time period; run of a product that has changed from the preceding run.

generic—pertaining to an entire class or large group; product or service that meets basic needs, but typically does not have elaborate features or packaging; common name or substance that cannot be trademarked.

genetic—having to do with a physical aspect that can be inherited.

genetic engineering—science of studying and perhaps ultimately controlling the characteristics of a life form through changes in the genetic code that determines its makeup.

gentleman's agreement—unofficial contract based on the parties' trust that each will honor the promises made.

GIGO (garbage/gospel in, garbage/gospel out)—term popularized by computer programmers to explain that your conclusions are only as good as the data on which they're based.

gilt-edged—literally "edged with gold," usually refers to something of high class or status; in investing, stock or bond with a continuing record of dependability; in bonds specifically, equivalent to a blue-chip stock.

Ginnie Mae—mortgaged-based securities issued by the Government National Mortgage Association; the Association itself.

giveback—in labor negotiations, return of something previously negotiated, such as raises or more favorable work rules, generally due to threats to the organization's viability or survival.

glamor stock—stock with a widely held reputation for paying increasingly larger dividends.

glass ceiling—invisible barrier on the ladder of success that is said to keep women from rising to high-ranking positions; implies that although no recognizable barriers to advancement exist for women, something unseen must be stopping them, since they are not represented in top jobs in numbers anywhere proportional to their representation in the workforce in general.

glitch—usually minor problem that delays or prevents a project from being completed as quickly or smoothly as expected.

global—having to do with the entire world.

global project—project that touches most of the departments in a company and is expected to produce significant results for the company.

globalization—when a product or company is taken international.

glocalization—maintaining a focus on local needs and conditions in a global context.

gloss—superficial luster or shine.

gloss over—to minimize the impact of something or to talk about it superficially.

glossary—short list of words and their definitions, usually pertaining to a technical or specialized subject or piece of work.

glut—oversupply of something.

go—what you get $200 for passing in Monopoly; Japanese game of strategy; official permission to commence a course of action.

go ballistic—when a project suddenly "blows up"; to lose your temper; to get unreasonably upset about something.

go long—in investing, to buy stocks, bonds, or futures contracts because you think they will increase in value over time.

go/no go—final decision point at which you must commit to do something or give it up.

go private—to repurchase all outstanding shares of stock, either by the company or a private investor, in the process ending public ownership of interest in the company.

go public—to offer shares of stock to the public for the first time.

go short—in investing, to sell a security the investor does not own in hopes that it can be bought back at a cheaper price to cover the position, thus generating a profit.

goals—agreed-upon objectives for something or someone.

gold—precious metal that many countries base their currency on.

goldbrick—lazy; to waste time or otherwise shirk responsibility.

golden handcuffs—situation in which an employee makes too much money and has too many benefits with an organization to be able to take an otherwise appealing job with another firm whose compensation package is lower.

golden handshake—financial and benefits programs offered to long-term employees to encourage them to retire before they are sixty-two years old.

golden parachute—clause in a hiring contract that gives the employee, usually a high-level executive or specialist, a large settlement if he or she is fired for any reason other than illegal actions; popularized in the 1980s by managements seeking to ensure their own financial status in the event of discharge after a hostile takeover.

golf—framework within which to conduct informal business meetings, build and maintain networks, and escape the button-down realities of the conventional workplace; the perfect metaphor for business: you set goals, strive to achieve them, record your proficiency in doing so, then move on to new goals; may also be an apt metaphor for American management from the standpoint that the person who does the least wins.

good faith—acting honestly with no intention to cheat someone.

goods—items, other than real estate, produced and/or sold by a company or person; negative information about someone.

goodwill—intangible asset of a business derived from the favorable attitudes of its customers and other stakeholders.

grace period—time between when a payment is due and the assessment of penalties or declaration of default or cancellation; time before a law, rule, or other important judgment takes effect.

grade—level or measure of quality or achievement.

graduated wage—paying people in the same job differently based on their experience, number of years with the company, and other factors.

graft—money or another advantage that a person obtains by dishonestly using his or her position; money paid to corrupt a public official; to add something to an existing organization or program.

grain exchange—trading market for agricultural commodities.

grandfather—to allow preexisting situations to continue under new guidelines, even though they would not be accepted under the new rules.

grant—funding for a nonprofit project; to concede as true; to transfer property by deed.

grapevine—informal communications network in a company, community, industry, or other group of people that often knows what's going on before the official line is released and has a fair degree of influence over career prospects at the lower levels of an organization.

graph—chart that displays data relationships.

graphics—artwork and type styling in a printed or video piece.

graphology—handwriting analysis to assess an individual's character.

gratis—free.

graveyard—late evening/early morning shift, usually from 11:00 P.M. to 7:00 A.M. or midnight to 8:00 A.M.

gravitas—weight; significance; staying power.

gravity filing system—euphemism for stacking and piling files instead of putting them into file cabinets or another, more organized storage system.

gray collar—manual laborers working in the public sector, such as sanitation-truck drivers.

gray market—legal market for selling scarce goods at higher than normal prices.

gray scale—degree of contrast in a graphic display.

Great Depression—period of high unemployment and stagnant economic growth beginning (in the United States) at the end of 1929 and lasting until World War II.

green—new and inexperienced in an area; ecologically safe or sensitive.

green card—card issued by the U.S. Immigration and Naturalization Service allowing noncitizens to work in the United States.

green eyeshade—refers to accounting activities.

green field—new field of operations.

greenback—U.S. paper currency.

greenmail—purchasing your stock back from a company or speculator that wants to acquire you at a price above market value in hopes of preventing a hostile takeover.

grid—simple graphic device in which the axes and value limits form squares; size is measured by the numbers of squares vertically and horizontally (2-by-2, 3-by-3, etc.).

grid training—teamwork training.

grievance—complaint, usually by a union employee, against a company or nonunion supervisor.

grievance procedure—successive stages of review to be followed in handling an employee's complaint.

gross—total before anything has been deducted; crude or distasteful; significantly overweight; in mathematics, twelve dozen.

gross billing—total amount billed for goods or services before deduction of commissions and other allowances.

gross domestic product (GDP)—more popular measure of the nation's economy, obtained by subtracting payments of foreign investments from gross national product.

gross impressions—in marketing, estimate of the number of times an advertisement has been viewed by a given target audience.

gross national product (GNP)—total value of goods and services produced by a nation in a given time period, usually a year (gross domestic product is becoming the more popular measure of a nation's economic strength).

gross sales—total value of sales before deducting customer discounts, allowances, and returns.

gross weight—combined weight of contents and shipping materials.

ground floor—first stages of a new business or market.

ground up—starting with the most basic activities or entities and moving to the more complex.

ground zero—refers literally to the point above which an atomic bomb is detonated; in business, refers to going back to or being at the absolute beginning.

groundbreaking—ceremony that marks the beginning of construction for a new building; pioneering effort that "breaks new ground."

group—collection of people or things that share common characteristics, however tenuous or arbitrary; to combine individual elements into larger collections for easier management or analysis.

group dynamics—how members of a group interact with one another.

group incentives—incentives provided to a group rather than to individuals, such as price breaks given by travel agents and hotels to organizations to encourage them to send more people to an event; financial or other incentives offered to a group of employees to try to improve their performance as a whole.

grow—in investing, to become larger; in employee development, to develop people's talents in a way that makes them more valuable to the organization; in a personal sense, to become more mature and well-rounded with time.

growth fund—mutual fund invested primarily in companies expected to grow over the long term and provide capital appreciation (relatively riskier than conservative funds, such as money markets, designed for principal protection).

growth industry—business category that is expected to see greater demand for its products or services in the years ahead.

growth share/stock—security that is expected to offer bigger dividends or split over the long term.

GS (government service) rating—public employee's personnel ranking, used to determine pay scale, perks, and qualification for new positions.

guarantee—legally binding pledge to do something; manufacturer's promise to pay for repairs or replace an imperfect product within a certain time period; to promise to take over payment of a loan if another person doesn't make payments in a timely manner.

guarantor—someone who makes a guarantee.

guerrilla action—marketing technique in which a company attacks competitors in a nonsystematic way so that no one knows who will be attacked next or what the attack will consist of.

guild—association that represents the interests of a professional or business group, usually more loosely organized and less influential than a union; medieval system of craft management.

gundeck—to falsify a report to provide the appearance of compliance with a schedule, production quota, training regimen, or other requirement.

H

hack—someone whose skills are good enough to get by, but not good enough to produce outstanding work, for example in writing; taxicab; to cut vigorously (as in words from a document or people from a department).

haggle—to argue with the hope of reaching a compromise; although it usually refers to sales situations, it can be applied in any compromise.

halo effect—ability of a reputation, good or bad, to stick to a person, product, or company.

hammering the market—effect when many investors sell large amounts of stock they believe to be too expensive.

hand off—to delegate; to turn a project, and responsibility for it, over to someone else.

handicap—physical or mental deficiency that prevents or hampers normal performance; socially less acceptable term for disability.

handicapped access—generally refers to providing wheelchair accessibility to a physical structure, but in a broader sense can be applied to making anything fully accessible to anyone with a disability.

handling charge—fee added to the price of a product to cover transportation, packaging, or other services involved in getting it to the customer.

hands-on—actually performing an activity (hands-on learning means learning how to do something by doing it).

happy hour—promotional period in a bar or restaurant (typically sometime between 4:00 and 7:00 P.M.) when drinks are cheaper, to attract people on their way home from work.

hard copy—paper copy of something created on a computer.

hard-core—highly resistant to change; offensive.

hard currency—originally, coins made of precious metals, such as gold and silver; now, any currency with a reputation for stability that is accepted in international transactions; also called "hard money."

hard goods—durable merchandise that can be expected to hold up for a significant length of time, such as appliances and furniture.

hard hat—helmet worn by construction workers to protect them from falling objects; typically refers to a blue collar worker or someone who sympathizes with labor as opposed to management.

hard sell—situation in which a salesperson will not take no for an answer and frequently uses coercive statements to try to make a person buy something.

hardware—machinery and other equipment used in industrial processes; in computers, the actual equipment absent the operating software.

hardy—strong; durable; capable of surviving adversity.

harvest—in agriculture, bringing in the crop; allowing market share to decline by maximizing short-term cash flow at the expense of long-term sales.

hatchet man—subordinate whose duties include firing employees, closing operations, and negotiating in unpleasant situations, often at the behest of a superior who doesn't want to do the dirty work personally.

Hawthorne effect—phenomenon that productivity will improve in any group being studied as a result of the added attention given to it (whether positive or negative), first observed in the Hawthorne plant of Western Electric in the 1920s and '30s; when interest wanes, improvement ceases.

hazard—danger or obstacle; to offer or venture.

hazardous waste—by-products of production that are considered dangerous to the health of people, animals, or the environment.

head—to lead.

head's up display—virtual-reality image that appears before the viewer's eyes.

header—repeated message at the top of every page in a document; headfirst dive.

headhunter—someone who finds candidates for high-level jobs; as a business, called "executive search firm."

health maintenance organization (HMO)—healthcare system that provides prepaid services to members for a fixed premium, emphasizing preventive care and somewhat restricted access in discretionary areas to keep costs lower.

heartland—primary market area for a product; in U.S. geography, the crop- and livestock-oriented midwestern states.

heavy industry—businesses in fields such as steel, automobile manufacturing, refining, and others that produce large volumes of hard goods using large facilities and large numbers of employees.

hedge—to take counterbalancing actions to mitigate risk; to evade the truth.

heel—jerk.

heir—someone entitled to inherit.

heir apparent—individual considered most likely to succeed a current manager or executive, even though no formal designation has been made.

hemline theory—whimsical theory that stock market prices mirror the lowering or raising of hemlines on women's dresses.

hertz—measurement of frequency equal to one cycle per second.

heterogeneous—consisting of different or varied things.

heuristic—finding an answer by trying different solutions, a form of trial-and-error learning.

hidden agenda—real objectives a person or group has for an activity, in contrast to the formal agenda, which lists activities but not motives or goals.

hidden assets—properties that a company has undervalued on its financial statements to hide their true worth.

hidden inflation—charging the same price for poor quality or a reduced quantity of a product.

hidden plant—quality term for the amount (often estimated as a third or more) of a production facility or business in general that is primarily occupied with correcting mistakes made by other parts of the business.

hierarchy—method of organizing a bureaucracy in layers of importance, with the most important at the top and the least at the bottom.

hierarchy of needs—Abraham Maslow's theory that humans have five needs that, until satisfied, motivate them in ascending order of importance: physical, safety, companionship, respect, and self-actualization.

high flyer—speculative stock whose price moves up and down quickly and dramatically.

high rise—building with six or more floors.

high tech(nology)—technology that uses electronics to allow the performance of increasingly sophisticated functions.

high touch—futurist John Naisbitt's observation that as the level of technology increases, displacing people from processes, we place a higher premium on the quality of personal interactions.

highball—alcoholic drink served in a tall glass; to give a cost estimate on the high end of what you really think it will come in at.

highs—stocks that on a given day have hit their highest price of the year.

hire—to employ a person.

hiring hall—union office where workers come to see if work is available.

histogram—graphic representation of a frequency distribution or data using rectangular bars whose widths are in proportion to the range of values within the class and whose heights are in proportion to the frequencies reported.

historical—refers to figures and norms derived from past performance.

hit and run—in sales, process of making a quick, hard sell, then not following up with the prospect; in marketing, short, intense advertising campaign; in management, technique of criticizing subordinates, then leaving them to stew about it.

146

hit list—names of top prospects to be contacted; key competitors to be eliminated or surpassed.

hit the bricks—go on strike.

hold—what you put people on while you're trying to locate someone who can take care of them; in investing, qualified recommendation that current stockholders keep their shares but new acquisitions may not be in order at this time; to reserve.

hold-harmless—legal clause in a contract establishing which party is responsible for claims arising from the issue involved.

holding—property to which you have legal title and of which you have possession.

holding company—company that manages other companies in which it owns stock.

holistic—using nonintrusive methods to solve a problem or cure a disease; also spelled "wholistic."

holy joe—interoffice envelope.

home office—corporate headquarters; for people who work out of their homes, an area set aside for their business, the costs of which can be deducted for tax purposes.

homestead—home and its adjacent property, in many states exempted from all or some property taxes and protected from seizure in the event of personal bankruptcy.

homework—finding out background information on a person or company you are about to deal with; doing work in your home.

homogeneous—same or very similar in composition.

homogenization—act of making things the same.

hon—short for *honey*; what you call someone of lower status and younger than you, especially if you're a man talking to a woman; what an oldtime waitress calls you, regardless of your age or sex.

hon.—short for *honorable*; title often used for elected officials.

honeymoon—time immediately following a hire or promotion when faults go unnoticed or are deliberately overlooked.

honor—to pay something on time; to accept a third party's payment, such as a check or credit card; to give a nonmonetary reward to someone.

honor bar—assortment of drinks and snacks for which you pay as you take them by putting money into a box.

honorarium—modest fee given to a professional for his or her services in lieu of a full calculation of their worth.

horizontal—sideways (like the horizon; vertical is up and down).

horizontal integration—company that seeks to own much of its competition, a practice that may put it in conflict with antitrust laws.

horizontal marketing—agreement between two companies producing different products that are used together to jointly market their products, or for one of the companies to use its expertise to market the other's product; also called "symbiotic marketing."

horizontal publication—magazine that reaches a wide audience with varying interests.

horizontal union—union that represents people of similar status but in different occupations.

hospitality industry—hotels and restaurants.

hospitality suite—small room (often a hotel room) set up with snacks and alcoholic drinks for visitors at a convention or trade show, usually sponsored by suppliers to entertain current and potential customers.

host—person or company sponsoring an event; computer that controls other computers and electronic devices.

hostile takeover—merger or acquisition in which the company being purchased does not want to be, but can't stop it from happening.

hot property—something for which there is a great deal of short-term demand.

hot spots—parts of the country or a region that represent significant problems or opportunities for a business.

hot under the collar—about to lose your temper.

hot stove rule—disciplinary action that starts with a warning, then provides consistent, immediate follow-up.

hourly employees—those who are paid on the basis of hours worked, including overtime since normally they are not exempt from wage rules.

house—can refer to any business, but usually refers to a small business that specializes in one area; in gambling, casino you're playing against.

house account—client whose corporate contact is a company executive or a salesperson working out of the home office instead of allocated by sales territory; usually but not always an extremely important client.

house agency—advertising function of a company that is set up as a profit center so that it may receive commissions on advertising that normally do not go to companies that place their own advertising.

house bank—company department that offers many banking functions to employees, such as loans and savings accounts.

house brand—brand of merchandise specifically produced for the company, usually by a third-party manufacturer, and often priced below its name-brand competition.

house mark—trademark affixed to items produced by a company.

house organ—company publication that goes to employees and/or customers and interested third parties.

households—for marketing purposes, any dwelling in which one or more people live as a unit (advertisers measure households reached as opposed to people reached).

149

housing starts—key indicator of economic growth derived from the number of houses, including attached housing units, for which construction is started in a given time period, usually a quarter.

huckster—someone who tries to sell by making false or extravagant promises.

HUHA (head up his/her ass)—discreet notation put on a memo to alert others that the information is flawed.

human relations—behavioral science concerned with interpersonal issues in the workplace and motivating employees.

human resources—employees of an organization; company department concerned with hiring, coordinating benefits, and motivating employees.

human resources development (HRD)—training and other activities designed to improve the skills of a company's workers.

hybrid technology—technology that uses two or more components from different manufacturers or different technological areas.

hype—large-scale, orchestrated advertising, especially in television and radio, that is designed to generate a great deal of attention over a short period of time.

hyper—prefix signifying very high levels or scales.

hyperbole—exaggeration used as a figure of speech ("he's got an ego wider than the central time zone").

hyperinflation—period of rapid inflation that renders a nation's currency essentially worthless.

hypermarket (hypermarche)—extremely large department store that generates high per capita purchases because it offers lower prices than smaller operations.

hypothesis—statement made early in the study of something that directs further research designed to discover if it is true.

I

iceberg principle—theory that any problem reveals only a small portion of its true size, the most important aspects being hidden from immediate view.

icebreaker—generic, inoffensive remark or story used to open a conversation or presentation.

icon—small, usually simplistic graphic representation of a message, topic, or computer command.

ideal—perfect or nearly perfect.

ideation—big (probably unnecessary) word for the process of having an idea or of relating one idea to another.

identity—image that other people have of a person or thing.

idle—not working; lazy; to shut down a production line and lay off its workers.

illegal alien—someone from another country prohibited by law from being in, or holding a job in, this country.

illegible—unreadable; too messy to be read.

illegitimate—unlawful or unauthorized.

illiquid—not liquid, as in not having sufficient cash flow to meet obligations, or an investment that cannot be readily converted into cash.

illiterate—unable to read or write.

image advertising—advertising used to create a good image

151

or impression of a product or company, not directly to sell the product.

image selling—selling a product by convincing customers that others will think better of them for owning such a splendiferous item.

imagineering—Disney concept of engineering everything guests can imagine: what they see, what they hear, what they feel, what they experience, even how long they wait, to provide a carefully controlled, multidimensional experience.

imitation—not real, but looking like the real thing on the surface; the sincerest form of flattery.

immune system—Joseph Juran's observation that organizations, like biological immune systems, tend to reject the introduction of new concepts.

impact—effect an action has; the word to use when you're not sure whether to use "affect" or "effect"; to hit something.

impasse—roadblock or dead end; problem that cannot be easily solved; labor negotiations where no progress is being made.

implicate—to imply or incriminate.

implication—meaning implied by a statement or action.

implied consent—legally dubious contention that by not saying no, someone has said yes.

implied warranty—unwritten warranty that exists because of a law.

implode—to collapse violently inward, often used to describe a project that falls apart before it reaches the marketing stage; the opposite of *explode*.

import—product that is produced in one location (usually another country), then moved to another for consumption; foreign-made car; to bring products produced abroad into the country; to bring workers in from another location.

import quota—limit, usually government-mandated, on the

maximum amount of a product or commodity that may be imported in a given period of time.

impose—to create a hardship; to place a tax or fine on an item.

imposition—hardship; in printing, the precise laying of pages on a printed form so that more than one can be printed at a time.

impound—fee or premium collected prior to its coming due; to legally seize something.

impregnate—to make pregnant; to saturate.

impression—feelings people have toward a product after viewing advertising for it; in advertising, one exposure to an advertisement.

imprimatur—official permission or license to do something, especially to print something.

imprint—mark or impression; notation in a book giving facts of its publication; to make a mark or impression on a surface; to learn tasks and behaviors from a senior or more experienced worker, much like a baby duck learning how to walk, swim, and fly from its mother.

improve—to make something better, in the process increasing its valuation for taxes or sale.

improvise—to make up on the spot.

impulse item—product bought on the spur of the moment, often placed near the cash register.

in absentia—Latin for *in the absence* of someone.

in camera—Latin for *in private*; secret session of a governing body; in law, meeting held in the judge's chambers or in the presence of the judge alone rather than in open court.

in flagrante delicto—Latin for getting caught in the act (literally, "while it's on fire").

in-house—something done within a company that could be done by an outside source.

in kind—paying for something with a similar item or service, such as a legal firm swapping legal advice for accounting advice from a CPA, or paying for a new photocopier by giving the seller a computer.

in medias res—Latin for *in the middle of the thing*, such as when you begin a narrative partway in rather than at the beginning.

in perpetuity—forever.

in play—said of a company whose stock is being acquired for a possible takeover; able to be used or pursued according to either formal or informal rules.

in-service—short training or informational activity on a specific topic presented to employees.

in stock—in inventory and ready for immediate or quick shipment.

in the tank—failure; defeated proposal or project that has been killed.

inadvertent errors—unintentional human errors.

inbound—materials designated for a specific location such as a company plant.

incentive—predetermined reward for doing something, provided above and beyond the normal pay of the job itself, offered to enhance motivation and performance.

income—money or value that an individual, family, or business earns in a specified period of time.

income averaging—calculating federal taxes by averaging current-year income plus income for the preceding three years.

income distribution—how people in a defined geographic area differ in their amount of income, especially in terms of disposable income; how people of different incomes spend their money.

income fund—investment fund, usually heavily invested in bonds, whose primary objective is to produce current income for investors.

income statement—profits and losses incurred over a given period of time.

income stream—flow of money from a business or investment.

income tax—personal or business tax based on income received.

incoming—items arriving at a specific location; warning of the imminent arrival of a manager or bad news (deriving from the Vietnam era warning to take cover from artillery bombardment).

incompetent—unable to do what needs to be done; legally unable to enter into a binding contract.

incorporate—to meet the legal requirements for becoming a corporation; to include something, especially interspersed throughout the entity.

incremental—increasing or decreasing by steady steps or amounts.

incubator—project or committee designed to come up with and nurture new ideas.

indemnify—to insure; to pay for a loss.

indemnity—amount given as compensation or security for a loss.

independent—autonomous; capable of making its own decisions; self-employed or not allied with a larger company or group; in retail, small chain of privately owned stores.

independent agent—someone who sells products from several different providers and is not affiliated exclusively with any one company.

independent contractor—someone engaged to perform a task for another, but who is not subject to the customer's direction, only the results of the commission.

index—a single indicator created by combining data from a number of different sources used as a baseline comparison for future compilations of data from the same sources; list of key topics, ideas, and individuals and the page numbers where they are discussed in a book; to link wages, taxes, or other rates to an index.

indicators—values, norms, and other benchmarks used to evaluate progress or quality.

indirect cost—cost that cannot be directly attributed, such as the electricity used to run manufacturing machinery.

individual retirement account (IRA)—account in which pretax money is saved for retirement and taxed upon withdrawal (primarily used by people who don't have company-sponsored retirement plans).

inducement—incentive to do something.

inductive reasoning—going from the specific to the general, using a limited amount of information to extrapolate major conclusions.

industrial—anything having to do with businesses that manufacture products; in investing, stocks of companies that produce or distribute products and services, excluding utilities, finance, and transportation.

industrial advertising—advertising aimed at businesses rather than individual consumers.

industrial democracy—idealistic theory of participative management in which workers have a voice in the operation of the business.

industrial engineer—engineer who specializes in designing systems to efficiently build a product.

industrial espionage—spying on competitors to determine how they make a product or how they are planning to market a product.

industrial park—planned unit development zoned and developed for businesses.

industrial psychologist—psychologist who specializes in workplace problems.

industrial relations—study of employees and their relationships with employers.

industrial revenue bond—business development incentive provided by state and local governments through which the government finances the construction of a facility that is then leased to a business.

industrial revolution—period beginning around 1850 in which the introduction of new production, transportation, and communication technology brought about a transition from an agrarian society to city living where people worked in factories that greatly increased productivity.

industrial union—union that represents employees who work in manufacturing or heavy industry, regardless of their skills.

industry—designation for businesses that produce a common product or service.

industry standard—generally accepted specifications for an industrial product.

inelastic—inflexible; market condition where price increases quickly bring falling sales.

inept—incompetent; stupid; incapable of doing something.

inert—inactive; having no effect, good or bad.

infer—to deduce; to conclude on the basis of evidence.

inflation—continuous increase in the price of goods and services brought about by too much demand chasing too little supply.

informal leader—leader whose influence with a group comes from the group's acceptance as opposed to the person's position.

information advertising—advertising designed to tell consumers about a concern, but not directly to sell a product or service.

information systems—technology or system of technology and people used to produce data and convey information to others.

informational picketing—picketing by a union to encourage a vote that would install it as the bargaining agent for the company being picketed; picketing by an interest group to win public support.

informational violence—futurist Alvin Toffler's term for using information strategically and tactically to achieve competitive goals.

infrastructure—basic physical systems that support a business or nation, such as highways, power generation, communications, and water and sewage.

infringement—violation of another's right, such as a trademark or copyright.

ingress—means of entrance.

inherent—intrinsic; a natural part of.

initial—first; to acknowledge that you have seen and understood information in a document by writing your initials on it.

initial public offering (IPO)—company's first offering of public stock.

initiative—effort; venture; ability to start something and/or follow it through to its conclusion.

injunction—legal method of stopping an activity for an indefinite period.

innovation—process of developing something new.

input—all information or physical means used to produce a product; data entered into a computer.

insegrevious—wild-card word that has no root in any language and consequently can mean anything you want it to mean (legend has it that it was invented by a linguistics class in the late 1950s).

insertion order—order to place print advertising in a publication.

inside information—information about a company not yet available to the public that could be used to your advantage when buying securities (use of inside information for personal benefit is illegal).

inside track—advantageous competitive position (in racing, the inside track around an oval is the shortest distance to the finish line).

insider trading—illegal buying and selling of securities based on inside information, especially when more than one person is involved in the scheme.

insolvent—having more debts than the business or individual can pay even if all assets were liquidated.

institute—educational or research center, often affiliated with an organization with a cause to promote; to start.

institutional investor—organization, such as a mutual fund, pension fund, or nonprofit organization, that invests large amounts of money in securities.

institutional sales—sales made to businesses or large nonprofit organizations such as hospitals.

instrument—tool; measurement device; legal record of an event or action; means used to obtain an end.

insurance—financial protection against a disaster by paying premiums to an insurer that pledges to reimburse you for losses from specific hazards or circumstances.

insurance company—organization that collects premiums and underwrites policies; a stock company is owned by stockholders, a mutual company is owned by policyholders.

intangible—something valuable that cannot be physically touched or sensed, such as a person's talent, a copyright or patent, customers' goodwill, or the way in which a service is provided.

integrate—to combine two or more different things to make a whole.

intellectual property—intangible property that consists of a person's ideas and creativeness, such as the design of a magazine.

interactive—multimedia system in which a user can interact with a program through a computer keyboard, touch screen, or other electronic device.

intercom—electronic device for talking from one office or area directly to another.

interest—ownership right in property; money you pay a business or person to borrow their money, usually a percentage of the remaining balance; desire to further pursue an activity.

interest rate—rate of return on the principal borrowed.

interface—device that converts signals from one system into signals another can understand; to make two different things work together; to discuss something with someone.

interim—time between two major actions or events.

intermediary—person who comes between two others, usually to settle an argument.

intern—in business, college student or recent graduate who is working at the company temporarily to gain experience, usually unpaid or paid very low wages; in medicine, recent or near graduate working in a supervised setting to obtain practical experience.

internal—inside.

internal audit—audit of any procedure or process performed by employees of the organization.

internal control—accounting procedure that assures financial records are kept according to policy.

internal customer—employees of a company who are affected by the activities of any given project.

internal failures—product and process failures that occur before product is delivered to end customers.

internal rate of return (IRR)—annual rate of return on an investment, including cash flow and interest aspects.

Internal Revenue Service (IRS)—agency of the Department of the Treasury charged with administering the U.S. tax code and collecting income taxes.

international—having to do with more than one country.

International Monetary Fund (IMF)—Washington, D.C.-based organization that works to encourage international trade.

International Organization for Standardization (ISO)—Geneva, Switzerland-based association of independent national standardization organizations in most of the world's industrial and industrializing countries (the common nickname "ISO" is a Greek prefix meaning "uniform," not an acronym).

interoffice mail—system used within a company to send physical items from one location to another.

interpolate—to insert additions between existing parts; in mathematics, to determine intermediate values in a series (as opposed to "extrapolate," which involves projecting new values beyond those now known).

interstate—from one state to another in the United States.

interstate banking—banking operations between two or more states.

Interstate Commerce Commission (ICC)—federal entity that regulates transportation services crossing state boundaries.

intervene—to get involved in hopes of helping solve a problem or resolving a dispute.

interview—asking someone questions to obtain information; important screening stage in obtaining a new job.

intestate—dying without leaving a will.

intrapreneur—entrepreneur based within a company, using company resources to develop new products and services.

intrastate—within the state.

intrinsic—involving the essential nature of the thing.

inventory—detailed listing of items, including raw materials and finished goods, in a specified location and their value.

inventory control—system that keeps track of what is in inventory, what is scheduled to be moved out of inventory, and what is ordered to come in.

inventory turnover—ratio of annual sales to inventory; how often a company's inventory is completely sold, usually in a one-year period.

inverse relationship—reversed order (as one increases, the other decreases).

inverted pyramid—method of writing where the most important information is presented first; upside-down organizational chart showing customers on top, then frontline people, narrowing down to senior executives, shown at the bottom.

invest—to exchange capital for a secured interest in a property or security in expectation of income and/or profit over the long term.

investment banking—underwriting or acting as an agent in the issuance of securities to the public.

investment club—group of investors who pool their funds and decide together in which securities to invest.

investment grade—system of designating the stability of top-ranked bonds for conservative investors.

investment portfolio—listing of all investments a person or organization holds.

investor—someone who buys investments.

investor relations—corporate communications function designed to keep investors informed of the state of the company.

invoice—bill outlining exactly what services or products were provided and how much each cost.

ironclad—rigid or inflexible, such as an ironclad pledge not to join a union.

irrevocable—incapable of being revoked or changed.

island—small retail display (usually no larger than 6 feet by 6 feet) set anywhere in a store; small division of a company separated by a great distance.

ISO 9000—series of five quality-documentation standards promoted as a worldwide basis for quality assurance.

issue—large offering of stocks or bonds by a corporation or government; any subject over which two or more people disagree; to release securities for purchase.

issues analysis—to determine what the major issues are in a given situation and to offer solutions for compromises between groups.

issues management—public relations tactic of helping groups define what issues are involved in a given situation and providing information that attempts to sway one or more groups to a particular view.

italics—"tilted" typeface used to add emphasis.

iteration—repetition of an action; subsequent version of a document or product.

itinerant worker—someone who moves from one low-paying job to another, often traveling throughout a region or from state to state.

J

jack-of-all-trades—someone with a wide range of skills and experience (although he or she may have mastered none).

janitor—someone who cleans up after everybody else at work; maintenance engineer without a beeper.

jargon generator—paper grid or computer program that

combines large words in new combinations to aid in creating prolix corporate prose.

jawboning—in labor relations, political intervention in a dispute in an attempt to avoid prolonged strikes and keep settlements from aggravating financial conditions, such as inflation; by extension, using your status or power to try to talk someone into doing something.

jet lag—tiredness that accompanies travel when several time zones are crossed.

jingle—short, catchy song or musical theme used repeatedly to enhance recall of an advertising message.

job—defined duties a person performs for pay; defined project; to subcontract; to cheat someone.

Job—Old Testament character made to suffer in endlessly creative ways.

job action—movement by a labor organization to shut down a job site due to a grievance or dispute.

job bank—computer listing of jobs available by category, often maintained by organizations such as a public unemployment service or a private employment agency.

job bidding—internally, applying for an open position on the basis of seniority; externally, submitting a bid for a job being subcontracted, often in competition with others, with the expectation that the job will go to the lowest bidder whose proposal meets the needs of the task.

job classification—category a job fits into in determining compensation and comparisons with other jobs.

job description—formal, written description of the duties to be performed in a job.

job enrichment—adding more, ideally more interesting, duties to a person's job; also called "job enhancement" and "job enlargement."

job evaluation—determining the value a given job has to the organization to make sure compensation is appropriate.

job hopping—moving to a new job less than a year after taking the previous position; pattern of continually changing jobs, spending only a year or two in each (depending on the desirability of the skills you obtain from this process, it can either work against you, making you look undependable, or for you, making you look highly versatile and capable).

job lot—contract for producing a specific amount of product.

job placement—attempt to fit workers into vacant jobs for which they are qualified.

job posting—internal notice of a job opening, often "posted" on a bulletin board to allow the company's current employees to apply before outsiders are considered.

job preview—screening and hiring technique in which qualified candidates are given the opportunity to actually see and perhaps perform a job they are applying for to determine whether they really want to do it and demonstrate their aptitude for it.

job ranking—ordering of jobs in terms of difficulty.

job rotation—moving people between several different jobs on a regular schedule, either because no one has the jobs permanently or as a way to keep people fresh and interested (and get them cross-trained) by offering variety in their work.

job satisfaction—how much you like your job (when someone tells you, "We know you're not satisfied with your job," chances are they're hinting that you may be fired or laid off if you don't move on on your own).

job scope—extent of the duties involved in a job.

job security—relative likelihood that your job will be eliminated or you will be fired; measure of the extent to which the job itself, or the employee in it, is important to the company.

job sharing—splitting a full-time job's hours and benefits between two people who cover it at different hours or on different days, often setting their own schedule for doing so.

job shop—company that performs specific duties for larger companies, such as making products to order.

job surfing—changing jobs within an organization, often as a result of coping with reorganizations that eliminate or change the nature of the previous job.

job ticket—order documentation that accompanies a job.

jobber—person who buys goods from a wholesaler or manufacturer and resells them to retailers, often providing such additional services as maintaining store displays.

jog—to nudge something slightly, like your memory; to run slowly as a form of exercise.

joint account—account that can be accessed by several individuals, such as a family's checking account.

joint planning—quality strategy in which planning is done by a team of employees, customers, and suppliers.

joint venture—when two or more entities combine resources for a onetime or ongoing project, but do not merge all their business activities.

journal—in accounting, first place financial transactions are recorded; in media, professional publication.

the Journal—short for *The Wall Street Journal*, the Monday through Friday newspaper that covers major and publicly held businesses based in the U.S. and abroad.

journalize—to enter something in a journal.

journeyman—in labor and craft unions, someone who has successfully completed an apprenticeship in a trade and is considered skilled enough to work independently; in general usage, someone with adequate but not outstanding skills, a role-player rather than a star.

judgment—decision of a court; amount of money awarded on the basis of legal action; discretion and reasoning ability (the British spell it "judgement").

juice—connections, as in your ability to get someone else to do something for you; electrical power.

junior—put-down term for one of the boss's or owner's children working in the business.

junior executives—entry- and midlevel managers being groomed for advancement.

junior partner—lower-ranking partner in a professional services firm who generally receives a smaller share of the profits and has less power and authority than senior partners; in a two-person partnership, the one with less invested in the business.

junk bond—bond issued by a company with poor or questionable financial performance, often secured only by the prospect of future earnings rather than physical collateral; popular if dubious form of financing during the merger mania of the 1980s.

junket—free trip provided to members of a legislative or regulatory body, the press, or other interest group in an attempt to build greater understanding of and goodwill toward the sponsor of the trip.

jury—group chosen to sit in judgment in a court trial; in professional journals, board of reviewers that evaluates articles submitted for publication to assure that they contain valid and noteworthy content.

jury-rigged—in sailing, something rigged for temporary use; implies makeshift or haphazard plans, programs, and processes rather than careful design.

JUSE (Union of Japanese Scientists and Engineers)—standards-setting and technical education organization in Japan known for its promotion of total quality management.

just in time (JIT)—manufacturing inventory system in which raw materials and components are delivered from suppliers shortly before they are needed, reducing inventory costs; requires close coordination and a high level of confidence between the company and its suppliers.

justified—allowed; in document composition, lines that are even on both right and left margins.

K

kaizen—Japanese discipline of continuous improvement to reduce defects and variation and enhance the quality of the end product.

kanban—Japanese term for a just-in-time inventory system in which materials are scheduled to arrive when needed rather than stockpiled in a warehouse (the word means "reminder").

kanban square—hybrid form of inventory management in which physical space is allocated for each item to be stocked and only that much is kept in inventory; when the square is empty, or almost empty, the item in it is reordered.

karoshi—Japanese phenomenon of people working themselves to death.

Keogh plan—retirement income plan in which self-employed workers or those employed by unincorporated organizations can place pretax dollars, the money taxed when withdrawn.

kerning—in typesetting, manipulating the space between two letters.

key—what you use to open a lock; what you strike on a keyboard to type a given character; answers to a test; most important or one of the most important; to arm or disarm a security system; to concentrate on; to type.

key account—account that brings in a large portion of business, usually more than 20%.

keyboard—keys on a typewriter or computer; to type or

enter numerical data, especially when putting information into a computer.

Keynesian—economic theory developed by Great Britain's John Maynard Keynes in which government intervention in the form of taxation and policy is used to balance the economy between unemployment, resulting from insufficient demand, and inflation, resulting from too much demand.

keynote—most important speech at an event.

keypad—numerical keys on an electronic device, such as a calculator, telephone, or security control panel.

keypunch—early form of entering data into a computer in which holes were punched into a card that could be read by the machine; today refers to menial data-entry work.

keys to the boardroom—means one or more members of the board of directors think the person can do nothing wrong and will consider any idea offered seriously.

keys to the executive washroom—legendary symbol of success embodied in being given access to the bathroom used only by top executives rather than having to take care of this particular kind of business in the company's common facilities.

keystone—most essential element; in early architecture, the center stone in an arch that holds the span together.

keystone markup—100% markup on retail merchandise.

kickback—money (usually a percentage of the value involved) given to the source of a job, contract, or other financial advantage; most kickbacks are illegal, or at least unethical.

kill—to stop, end, or discontinue; to shut down a machine or process; to end a test or experiment by deciding not to go forward with the actual project.

kill the messenger—to take action against the bearer of bad news, even though the individual isn't responsible for it.

killing—having done very well in a business venture or investment program.

kilo—Greek prefix meaning 1,000; a kilowatt is 1,000 watts, a kilobyte is 1,000 bytes.

kinetic—involving energy from motion.

KISS—short for "keep it short and simple" or "keep it simple, stupid," good advice in making sure presentations lead to desired outcomes.

kite—use of illegal or unethical trading methods to increase stock prices; sophisticated practice of depositing money in two or more banks, then writing criss-crossing checks off the accounts to take advantage of the float; to write a check when you don't have the money to cover it; to alter the amount on a check.

Kiwanis—nonprofit fraternal organization.

klingon—intimidating, often unethical or ruthless, competitor, but one you think you can eventually outsmart.

kludge—bug; temporary fix within a computer program or piece of computer hardware; computerese for junk; also spelled "kluge."

knowledge—third and soon to be most important form of power in business and society, surpassing violence and wealth, according to futurist Alvin Toffler.

knowledge-driven—business or activity where what you know and what you do with what you know is more important than traditional driving forces such as production capability, company size, market share, and other variables.

Kondratieff cycle—theory of 1920s Soviet economist Nikolai Kondratieff that, over the longer term, capitalist economies go through predictable "supercycles" that last fifty to sixty years.

kryptonite—what Superman can't handle; surprise tactic or action that provides an advantage competitors aren't prepared to counter; conversely, a competitor's advantage the company can't counter.

kudos—recognition in any form, but usually insubstantial such as a thank-you note or verbal recognition.

L

label—piece of paper affixed to something so that it can be filed or put into a category; display area on a product that provides information on the producer and the contents; to put someone or something into a broad category; to put a label on a file or other document.

labor—short for unionized workers ("organized labor") in relations with management; employees, usually blue collar workers or white collar nonexempt employees; to work.

labor force—number of people over sixteen years old who are employed.

labor-intensive—requiring a large amount of human work to produce.

labor pool—group of qualified workers from which employees are hired.

labor relations—how management relates to employees, often used in the context of unions and contract negotiations.

labor union—organization formed or selected by all or part of a firm's employees to represent them in negotiating wages and working conditions.

laboratory (lab)—literal or figurative place where new products and services are developed and tested.

lackey—someone who will do anything to please his or her boss.

Laffer curve—theory developed by economist Arthur Laffer that tax rates and revenue received can be plotted on a curve;

171

suggests that for every revenue level other than the optimum there are two possible tax rates, one too high, one too low; if the tax rate is too high, decreasing it will actually result in increased tax revenues.

lagging indicator—statistical category in which changes typically occur after a major event, used to verify theories.

laissez-faire—French for *allowing to do;* as an economic philosophy, holds that an economy is best served by letting it do what it wants to do, with as little government regulation of the marketplace as possible.

lame duck—someone who will be leaving a job in the near future but is still doing that job, implying that any decision made or actions taken may be reversed or ignored by the successor; in politics, defeated politician or one not running for reelection who is serving out the end of the term.

landlord—person or company that owns residential or business property and rents it to someone else.

landmark—event that will change the way something is done for a long time to come; object that marks a geographic area.

language barrier—business obstacle presented by not being able to speak the customer's native language.

lapel pin—company, fraternity, sorority, or club pin worn on the lapel of a jacket to identify the wearer as belonging to the organization.

lapse—mistake due to inattention; in insurance, to allow coverage to cease by not renewing a policy.

laptop computer—portable computer that can operate either on batteries or electric current (notebook computers operate on batteries only).

laser—coherent beam of single-wavelength light (the word is an acronym for "light amplification by stimulated emission of radiation"); applies to any device or philosophy that is notable for its sharp and unwavering focus and power.

laser disc—computer disc that is read by a beam of light, resulting in no wear and tear on the disc; sometimes called a "platter."

laser pointer—presentations aid that projects a fine beam of light for pointing out details of material projected on a screen or wall in a meeting.

last in, first out (LIFO)—inventory accounting method in which the most recently manufactured products are considered the first sold, resulting in a tendency to show lower profits during inflationary times than the FIFO method.

latent demand—demand for a product or service that has been temporarily suppressed by adverse conditions, such as a recession or lack of supply, but will still be there when conditions improve.

lateral—sideways.

lateral file—horizontal file cabinet.

lateral move—moving to a new job, often with the same employer, that offers the same pay and status as the old one.

Latin America—countries of the western hemisphere where Spanish or Portuguese is spoken.

latitude—discretion or freedom to act; in geography, degrees north or south of the equator (the horizontal lines on a globe or map; "longitude" is degrees east or west of the prime meridian that passes through Greenwich, England, or the lines that run vertically).

launch—in advertising and marketing, the beginning of a new campaign or the introduction of a new product; to introduce.

launder—to run illegally obtained funds through a legitimate business.

lavalier—small microphone that can be clipped to clothing or hung around the neck, allowing the speaker some degree of movement.

lay audience—people, no matter what their educational level, who have no special knowledge of the product or field being discussed.

layoff—elimination of jobs, and the people in them, due to a lack of work or other circumstance (if conditions may improve enough to hire back at least some of the people, it's a "temporary layoff"; if that's unlikely to happen, it's a "permanent layoff").

layover—time spent in an airport while making a connection; one or several nights in a city between flights.

LCD (lighted crystal display)—technology that uses polarized crystal material to form and project electronic images.

LCD panel—electronic device that is laid on an overhead projector to display information from a computer on a large screen.

lead time—time to prepare before a major activity begins; time needed to accomplish a preliminary stage in a process before the next stage can begin; time between placing an order and taking delivery.

leaded—coffee with the caffeine still in it.

leadership—ability to persuade or inspire others to follow a course of action (not the same thing as managing).

leading (LEDD-ing)—in printing, space between lines of type.

leading indicators—economic statistics, such as interest rates and housing starts, used by the U.S. Department of Commerce to forecast the direction of the economy.

learner—someone in a training course (the corporate equivalent of "student").

learning curve—phenomenon by which productivity increases as people become more familiar with and experienced in their jobs.

lease—contract that spells out the conditions for renting something; to rent something for a specific period of time by signing a contract.

leaseback—practice by which an owner sells property, such as a building or equipment, then leases it back from the buyer.

least best—ego-salving way to highlight needed performance improvement by working with groups of people rather than singling out any one worker for attention.

leave of absence—extended (usually two weeks or more) unpaid time away from work with the provision that the employee will return to the same (or similar) job with no loss of seniority or other perks.

leapfrog—to skip one or more steps in a process; often used when technology makes major advances or when an employee is promoted to a position at least two steps ahead of his or her past job.

LED (light-emitting diode or lighted electronic display)—technology used in display readouts.

ledger—official book of financial transaction entries for a business.

leg up—making progress or gaining a foothold, derived from the act of mounting a horse (to "give someone a leg up" is to help them).

legal—meeting the requirements of law or permitted by law.

legal entity—something other than a person, such as a corporation, that can be legally treated as a person and has the same legal rights, such as entering into contracts, suing and being sued, and owning property.

legal tender—money and other items, such as federal reserve notes, that by law must be accepted as payment.

legion—organization with many loyal and dedicated members; multitude or impressively large number (originally the major unit in the Roman army).

legs—staying power or ability to move beyond the initial prospects ("the program's got legs").

leisure—time, and activities to fill it, for the hours during which you're not working.

less developed countries (LDCs)—countries with relatively lower standards of living and little industry.

less than truckload (LTL)—loads that take up less than a full truck, which means they must be combined with shipments for other customers for the carrier to maximize efficiency and will not qualify for discounts offered for full loads.

lessee—tenant in a leasing arrangement.

lessons learned—experience.

lessor—owner of property being leased.

letter—formal form of correspondence; literal limits of something; to earn recognition from a school or program for participation in extracurricular activities, traditionally sports (usually symbolized by the initial of the school worn on a jacket or sweater).

letter-quality—computer printout that meets the standards of appearance quality for business correspondence.

letter of credit—document from a bank guaranteeing an individual's or business's credit up to a certain limit, often used in international trade to remove the risk of dealing with unknown partners.

letter of intent—notice of intention to take a course of action, such as a merger or initiation of legal action.

letter of representation—official notification from a legal or accounting firm that it represents a business in certain matters.

letter of reprimand—documentation of disciplinary action that becomes a permanent part of an employee's personnel file.

letterhead—formal paper and envelopes used by the company, containing the company logo and address and sometimes the names of the officers, the company motto, or other information.

level—even, flat, or equal; degree.

level of service—amount of service (self-, limited, or full) provided by a business.

leverage—ratio of debt to equity; advantage based on position; to borrow money using something as equity in hopes that the funds will allow the business to earn more than the interest it will have to pay.

leveraged buyout (LBO)—buying a company with borrowed money that will be repaid out of the purchased company's assets or cash flow.

liability—debts owed; legal responsibility for harm done to another; something that represents a weakness or competitive disadvantage.

liaison—relationship or alliance; someone who acts as an intermediary or go-between in a relationship.

libel—false *and* defamatory statements made in printed words or symbols that injure another's reputation (if you say it, it's "slander"; if you put it in writing, it's libel; if it's true, and you can prove it, no matter how defamatory it is, it's not libel).

license—official permission to do something, usually gained after an inspection or test; unusual freedom assumed to achieve a purpose, such as poetic license; too much freedom.

lien—legal right to hold and in some cases sell property being used as collateral for a loan.

life behind the quality dikes—total-quality guru Joseph Juran's metaphor to describe how life in industrial societies requires high quality of services and products.

life cycle—natural movement of a product through various stages from conception through obsolescence; each company or product has a distinct time period for each stage, and some never reach the obsolescence stage.

life expectancy—actuarial calculation of how long a person at a given age is likely to live, used in setting insurance premiums and estimating payouts.

lifelong learning—philosophy that holds that in the era of information, learning must not stop with the end of formal education, but should continue in an organized way throughout an individual's life.

lifestyle—way in which people choose to spend their money and leisure time, a key consideration in the marketing of products.

ligature—something that ties two things together.

limbo contest—getting contractors to bid against one another to see how low they will go to get the business.

limit—edge or boundary; a restriction on the performance of a product or person.

limit up/down—maximum allowable change in a commodity future's contract price during one day of trading.

limited partner—someone whose liability is limited to the amount invested and who typically is not involved in administration and management of the partnership.

limited warranty—manufacturer's guarantee that covers only specific circumstances.

limp—to survive without improving, as in products that aren't growing or a career that's going nowhere.

line—part of a company's workforce engaged in production-oriented activities ("staff" includes administrative and management personnel); production line in a manufacturing operation or frontline in a service organization; product line of a company; company's official story or explanation; false story that is believed.

line executive—director or vice president in charge of the production line or frontline operations.

line extension—expansion of the number of products offered into areas that don't compete with a company's existing line, such as a soap company introducing shampoos.

line-level—anything having to do with the frontline of a service operation or the production line of a manufacturing operation.

line manager—first-level manager or supervisor who works directly with line employees.

line of credit—preapproved amount of money that can be borrowed from a bank or credit company.

linear—on a straight line.

linear analysis—analysis based on looking at events and statistics from the beginning of a time period to the end of the period.

linear media—tape as opposed to computer and optical disks.

linear sequence—statistics arranged from smallest to largest; list presented according to the order in which activities are performed.

lingua franca—common language used by people who speak a different one (Italian for French; go figure).

lingo—slang.

Lions—nonprofit fraternal organization.

liquid—fluid and therefore capable of flowing or changing form; investment vehicle in abundant supply, where large transactions don't radically change the price.

liquid assets—cash; securities and commodities that can be converted to cash with very little delay or complication.

liquidate—to sell out completely, often at extremely low prices; to settle a debt or other legal action.

liquidity—measure of how easily assets can be converted to cash.

list—short for *list price,* or the published price of an item; to trade a security on the stock exchange or to put a piece of property up for sale.

list segmentation—taking a list of customers, prospects, or consumers and dividing it into any of several categories that reflect their possible interest in a product.

listed—registered for trading on a stock exchange (unlisted securities trade over-the-counter).

listening—neglected half of the communications process (because talking is more fun and can often be done without thinking).

listing—written description of property available for sale or lease.

list management—maintaining contact lists used for direct marketing, media relations, and other purposes by updating, adding to and deleting contract names, addresses and other information.

list rental—renting all or part of a mailing list to another organization interested in contacting prospects with known demographics, addresses, or interests.

litho—print made by lithography.

lithography—printing from a flat plate that is treated to repel ink on nonprinted surfaces.

litigation—process of seeking legal recognition and enforcement of a right or claim.

litmus test—in chemistry, test in which litmus paper turns red when saturated with an acid, blue with an alkaline substance; refers to simplistic determinations of suitability based on such things as beliefs, color, brand name, background, or other narrow criteria.

load—sales charge based on the amount of money invested in a mutual fund (if the charge is applied to the purchase, it's called a "front-end load"; if it's applied when shares are sold, it's a "back-end load"; if no charge is assessed, it's a "no-load fund"); products being hauled from one place to another; to install software in a computer.

loaded—rich; product or program with a lot of expensive options added to it; drunk.

loan—funds borrowed from a lender; to allow a borrower to use property, including money, owned by the lender in return for its return with interest.

lobby—entry area in a business; organized interest group seeking to influence a legislative or regulatory body; to try to persuade someone, often a politician or regulator, to do something that will have a positive effect on your interests or a negative effect on a competitor.

lobbyist—someone registered to lobby.

local—chartered branch of a national or international union representing workers in a specific bargaining unit; narrow geographic area, such as a market; telephone call that does not incur long-distance charges.

local area network (LAN)—several personal computers in one building, or buildings in close proximity, that are linked to share programs and exchange data (if the network involves widely scattered locations, it's called a "wide area network," or "WAN").

lock and load—get ready to shoot (command given on a firing range to load live ammunition and put a round in the chamber).

lock-box service—arrangement in which payments to a company are sent to a locked box (typically in a post office box) that is emptied several times a day by a bank so that funds can be deposited without delay.

locked in—in banking, interest rate that will be honored even if rates change prior to closing a loan; in investing, situation in which an investor doesn't sell a security because capital gains taxes would negate the profit; in commodities, situation in which investors cannot buy or sell because the market has reached its up or down limit for the day.

lockout—management decision to shut down a business while negotiating with the union, bringing financial pressure to bear on employees who need to work.

locus—center or most important area.

locus of control—person or office that controls most operations.

log—official list of events (for example, the captain's log on a ship); to make an entry in a journal; to compile miles of travel.

log on—to enter your name or access code into a computer prior to beginning work.

logo—recognizable, often abstract symbol or stylized type used as a trademark.

Loman, Willy—playwright Arthur Miller's fictional salesman who epitomizes the problems faced by older workers as a result of the introduction of new ideas and new technology.

London Stock Exchange—foremost stock exchange in Great Britain.

long bond—bond with a maturity date at least ten years in the future.

long-term—anything that is measured or occurs over a length of time that is longer than average, as defined by the specific situation; in management, period of time beyond the end of the current fiscal year.

long-term disability (LTD)—insurance that pays a lump sum or periodic payments if you are unable to work for longer than twenty-six weeks.

loophole—blind spot in a law or tax provision that allows an individual or organization to evade responsibility for something.

loss—condition in which expenses are higher than revenue; opposite of *profit*.

loss leader—product that is offered at a loss (or at least at a greatly reduced profit) to attract customers in hopes that they will buy more-profitable products as well.

lottery—form of gambling in which equal chances of winning are sold, with the winner determined by random drawing (if you can enter without buying something, it's a "sweepstakes"); illegal if you run it, legal if the government does.

low—in investing, the lowest price at which a stock has sold in the past year.

low bidder—vendor awarded a job on the basis of submitting the lowest estimated price for completing it.

low-grade—of poor quality; many companies produce both high-grade and low-grade products for high-consumption items such as clothing and toilet paper.

low-tech—early, simpler, or less sophisticated forms of a technology; doing something by hand that a machine can do, such as licking stamps instead of using a postage meter.

lower management—first-level managers.

loyalty—nebulous term describing how willing you are to make personal and professional sacrifices for an organization or person.

Ltd.—abbreviation for *Limited,* used primarily by British and Canadian corporations that have limited liability.

lucrative—extremely profitable.

Luddite—someone who resists new technology or methods, whether because it may eliminate jobs or reduce wages, or just because it makes them uncomfortable (in England in the early 1800s, workers rioted and wrecked new textile machinery in imitation of Ned Ludd, a supposedly feebleminded worker who'd trashed his employer's equipment some thirty years earlier).

lump sum—single payment of total amount due rather than paying in several installments.

luxury—something that isn't a necessity.

M

Maastricht Treaty—basic agreement to begin the economic unification of twelve Western European nations by the end of 1992; however, it had to be ratified by each country before taking effect, and not all ratifications were accomplished by the deadline.

Machiavellian—describes someone who will do anything to get ahead, especially unscrupulous, deceitful acts (derived from the fifteenth–sixteenth century Italian statesman Niccolo Machiavelli and his famous book *The Prince*).

Macintosh—brand of personal computer made by Apple Computer Corp. that introduced the icon-based graphic user-interface system of menu selections.

macro—prefix meaning "large."

macroeconomics—study of a country's or the entire world's economic system.

macroenvironment—world situation.

macroprocess—multifaceted system of conducting and overseeing the most important parts of a company's business.

Madison Avenue—refers to advertising, derived from the street in Manhattan where many major ad agencies have been located.

magnetic strip—magnetic tape, attached to something such as a credit card, containing encoded information (usually read by inserting it into or sliding it through a scanning device).

mahogany row—top executives' offices, usually furnished with desks, chairs, credenzas, and other things made of real (often expensive) wood.

mail—originally referred exclusively to material handled by the U.S. Postal Service, but now applies to any messages sent to an individual by conventional or electronic means; to send a message or package to someone.

mail order—to buy something from a catalog or direct-mail promotion and have it delivered directly to you, though not necessarily through the mail system.

mailbox—place for receiving mail, whether mounted on the porch or a post by the street, contracted for at another location (such as a post office or private service), or accessible by computer.

mailing list—label-formatted list of people who receive publications, financial reports, advertising, public relations materials, and other information on a regular basis, often coded so it can be segmented by specific characteristics such as zip code, job title, or other criteria.

mailroom—literally, the place where mail entering and leaving the organization is handled; "starting in the mailroom" means entering an organization at the lowest level and working toward the top executive ranks.

Main Street—retail and financial interests in a city, state, or region; sometimes applied specifically to banking.

maintenance—department you call when something crucial in your building isn't working right; the reason something you absolutely need access to right now won't be available for several hours.

maintenance fee—charge assessed for maintaining something, such as a building or financial account.

maintenance marketing—marketing activities done to retain a product's position in the marketplace.

major—significant or important; area of concentrated study in a university or college.

major in the minors—to concentrate on trivial or unimportant things rather than the main issue.

majority—more than half (if the largest portion of something doesn't represent at least half, it's a "plurality").

make a market—in investing, what a brokerage firm does when it commits itself to buy and sell a firm's stock to encourage its active trading.

make good—monetary, replacement, or in-kind payment for a defective product or unsatisfying service.

make-work—project or practice with no real value, assigned or required (by a union contract, for example) to keep someone busy who otherwise would have nothing to do.

malarkey—nonsense; nonoffensive form of bullshit.

malinger—to try to get out of work by pretending to be ill.

mall—street or walkway inaccessible to vehicles that connects retail stores and offices; development where several merchants share a common structure and parking area.

malpractice—negligent performance by a professional that provides grounds to seek legal redress.

malpractice insurance—coverage carried by a physician, hospital or other health care provider to protect against legal judgments arising from lawsuits.

Malthusian—idea that population will have to be or should be limited because otherwise it will outgrow the food supply and the ability of economic forces to provide prosperity (named for nineteenth-century philosopher Thomas Malthus).

manage—to take care of business or personal affairs; to cope.

managed care—containing costs in health care through a controlled marketplace where third-party payment sources contract with large provider organizations to provide treatment to groups and individuals, with both insurers and regulators monitoring the way services are provided.

managed obsolescence—plan developed to take a product off the market with the least disruption to company profits and customers' needs.

management—people in an organization responsible for decisions about the allocation of resources and the strategic direction of the business as well as overseeing the people who do the actual work.

management advisory committee—committee of employees and/or outside experts who advise management on actions to be taken on key issues.

management advisory services (MAS)—offshoot of traditional accounting that uses expertise and insight gained from audit and other financial records to advise a business on current and future activities.

management by objectives (MBO)—controversial but enduring technique of trying to motivate people and evaluate performance by setting annual objectives agreed to by the employee and his or her manager, then measuring how well or how poorly they are achieved (the system rises or falls on whether the objectives are truly appropriate and challenging, and aren't rendered pointless by events that take place between the time they are set and the time they are evaluated).

management by walking around (MBWA)—involved, hands-on management style characterized by managers' willingness and ability to leave the safety of their private offices to observe firsthand what people are doing, to listen to their ideas and suggestions/complaints from their customers, and to support rather than dictate activities.

management consultant—someone who provides analysis and advice to management, whether on specific problems or general issues, but does not work for the company itself; often someone with extensive management experience or academic background (too often, as well, someone who simply tells managers what they want to hear for a fee).

management information system (MIS)—originally involved systems and procedures set up to manage the data and functions of a company's mainframe computer system to provide information to management; now applies to any system designed to organize computer resources and records.

management inventory—inventory of the skills that the management team as a whole brings to an organization.

management style—how a manager interacts with subordinates, often described in either/or fashion, such as formal or informal, Type X (controlling) or Type Y (empowering).

management succession—formal plan for replacing top executives as they retire or in case they move on by grooming successors within the organization.

management team—top executives of a corporation.

management training—educational programs designed specifically to improve the management skills of current and prospective managers.

manager—someone who manages; generally refers to those

who supervise white collar workers or, in some cases, manage projects that don't involve other people.

mandate—command or order; the understanding of what people supposedly want done that a politician assumes, however momentarily, by virtue of winning (by extension, new managers often feel they have a mandate from above to make changes); to require.

mandatory retirement—legally dubious requirement that workers retire by a certain age.

Manhattan—"downtown" borough of New York City where commercial and financial enterprises are concentrated; alcoholic drink made with whiskey and vermouth.

manifest—list of goods or passengers being carried; clear or readily apparent.

Manifest Destiny—phrase coined in the mid-1800s to reflect the belief that the United States had a divine right to expand territorially across the North American continent and profit accordingly.

manifesto—written declaration of intent or principles.

manual—book containing instructions, policies, and procedures; something done by hand.

manufacturing—turning raw materials into finished products, whether by hand or machine or a combination of both.

manufacturing resources planning (MRP/MRP2)—see *material requirement planning*.

manhour—one person working for one hour.

manyear—one person employed for one year.

maquiladora—foreign-owned production facility operating in Mexico.

margin—amount of gross profit made on an item; difference between gross and net; in securities, percentage of the amount being borrowed from a broker to buy securities that the customer actually puts up; white space around the edges of a document.

margin account—account set up for a customer by a brokerage firm that allows the customer to buy securities with money borrowed from the broker.

margin creep—common, ultimately suicidal tendency to focus only on top-end products and high profit margins (when the market becomes price-sensitive, the business may not be able to respond).

margin for error—room to be wrong without invalidating or endangering the results of the effort (for example, a research poll finding that 70% of a group agrees with a certain statement might have a margin for error of "plus or minus 3%," which means that refining the study further would most likely find that between 67% and 73% of the group agrees with the statement).

marginal—on the edge; of minor or dubious prospects or value.

maritime—business involving the sea.

mark—basic unit of German currency; grade in a course; indicator of a quality or characteristic; impression; to write on; to pay attention to.

markdown—reduction below the original selling price.

market—current or potential customers or demand for a product; a place or store where retail business is conducted; to sell.

market analysis—research to predict what a market, including the stock market and business markets, will do; research to determine where a company's products fit based on the defining characteristics of the market.

market area—region in which a product is sold or potentially could be sold.

market basket—group of products used to track price changes for such indicators as the consumer price index.

market broadening—expanding the type of customers a

product is suited for either by changing the product or by changing consumers' perceptions of the product.

market evolution—four stages a market goes through during a product's life cycle: emergence, growth, maturity, and decline.

market growth—selling more product to more customers.

market niche—segment of a larger market targeted for a specific product.

market penetration—percentage of sales that a particular product has in a market.

market price—price set in accordance with current market conditions, such as the price of a stock agreed to by buyers and sellers or the price of a restaurant item that changes daily based on supply costs; last reported price at which a security was sold.

market research—studies designed to determine what customers want from products, services, and promotional efforts.

market saturation—state in which no more product could be sold no matter what marketing efforts were undertaken.

market segmentation—division of a major market into smaller groups with specific needs and desires.

market share—percentage of total sales of all products in a market that a company's product accounts for; traditional measure of relative strength in a market.

market stretching—attempting to sell a product to groups on the fringe of the core market group (consumers who feel the product isn't a major need but can be swayed to purchase it with marketing tactics).

market value—actual amount an item can be sold for.

marketability—relative ease with which something can be sold.

marketing—process of conceiving, pricing, promoting, and distributing a product, service, or concept, especially those that do not involve direct contact with a salesperson.

marketing communications—communications with customers that are designed to make them think favorably of a product or a company, especially advertising and public relations activities.

marketing coop(erative)—in agribusiness, joint venture through which independent members market their crops, livestock, and other products.

marketing-driven—company that makes plans for new products and services based on the needs of the marketplace.

marketing manager—person charged with planning the conception, pricing, promotion, and distribution of products or services.

marketing mix—combination of tactics used to market a particular product or service.

marketing plan—specific plan for the amount and type of advertising, public relations, promotional activities, and sales promotions that will be offered to support a product or product line.

marketing strategy—overall marketing goals for a product or product line and general strategies for meeting those goals.

marketplace—market in general rather than a specific location or facility.

markup—amount of money added to the price of an item above and beyond its cost, often expressed as a percentage.

martini—traditional businessperson's drink, at lunch or after hours, made with gin and dry vermouth.

Marxism—communism or socialism as defined by Karl Marx.

Maslow's hierarchy—see *hierarchy of needs*.

mason—someone who works with brick and stone.

Mason—member of the Freemasons (a.k.a. the order of Free and Accepted Masons), a secret fraternal organization.

mass—large body with no shape; weight; large-scale; to gather.

mass marketing—selling products to large markets based on universal appeal, usually supported by advertising in general-interest print and electronic media.

mass media—newspapers, magazines, television, and radio.

mass merchandising—displaying and selling products designed to appeal to a broad rather than niche or specialized market.

mass production—producing a large number of identical products, relying on machines for quality and efficiency.

massage—to fine-tune a message for greater clarity or to make sure it is understood in an advantageous way; to sweet-talk a prospect and give small concessions to gain their business.

master—someone in charge; teacher; tradesperson who has reached a high level of skill, training, and experience as defined by his or her union; to achieve proficiency.

master contract—contract between a union and management.

master craftsman—highest level that can be reached in a trade.

master's degree—designation awarded for completing an advanced course of specialized study beyond a bachelor's degree in a college or university (common types include master of arts, M.A., or master of science, M.S., followed by the field of study, and master of business administration, M.B.A.).

master franchise—license to run more than one franchise location in a region.

master of business administration (MBA)—advanced degree granted for graduate study in business, usually including both general courses and a specialized concentration, such as accounting, finance, marketing, or management.

masthead—list of people who work for a magazine or newspaper and information about its business operations, including ownership, circulation, and advertising.

material—physical resource or substance used to produce a product; fabric; relevant.

materialism—overemphasis on possessions, typically to the exclusion of spiritual things.

materials cost—cost of materials only in producing a product.

material requirement planning (MRP/MRP2)—MRP is a sophisticated online inventory management system based on the application of information management technology; MRP2 is the next generation of the same function, often called "manufacturing resources planning."

maternity leave—time off provided to women who have babies, either paid or unpaid, the term subject to limitations set by the employer, at the end of which the woman is guaranteed the opportunity to return to the same or similar job.

matrix—rectangular tool for displaying statistics or other information in which each item has a unique position based on rows and columns.

matrix organization—organization in which employees belong to two groups: their department and a team working on a specific project; authority runs both vertically (the traditional hierarchy) and horizontally (for project management between departments).

mature—fully developed; no longer growing; due or payable; displaying the desirable characteristics of an adult.

maturity—date when a financial instrument becomes due or eligible to be cashed in; something missing in people you don't like.

maven (mavin)—expert who has an assertive point of view.

maximize—to get the most out of something.

Mc(anything)—slang for large and generic (derived from McDonald's; for example, McPaper is a nickname for *USA Today*).

mealymouthed—describes someone who is unwilling or unable to get to the point, especially if he or she might be criticized or argued with or would have to give clear credit to someone else.

mean—average; exact midpoint between two extremes; evil, wicked, or nasty; slang for very trendy or impressive; of poor or low quality; to convey understanding; to intend; to symbolize.

meaningful downturn—recession.

means—financial resources and personal abilities.

means test—criteria used to decide eligibility for government or other support programs, based on first determining the individual's ability or inability to pay for such services.

media—means of communication via a physical entity, such as television, radio, newspapers, and magazines; plural of "medium" when it refers to an intervening substance. (e.g., magnetic media).

media audit—analysis of the content of specific media in relation to a company or product.

media buyer—specialist in negotiating the purchase of advertising time or space for an agency and its clients.

media event—event designed to draw coverage by the mass or trade media.

media kit—folder containing information on a company or issue, provided to reporters to summarize basic topics involved; the information kit provided to potential advertisers containing rates, specifications, and pertinent information on the audience served.

media plan—schedule and budgets detailing which advertisements will run how often in which media, including the objectives of the campaign.

median—middle element in a list of variables or distribution of values.

mediator—third party who helps to negotiate a resolution to a dispute, but does not have the power to impose a solution on the parties involved.

mediocre—average (literally "halfway up the rock"), but usually implies poor quality or performance.

medium—something in the middle or of intermediate degree; singular of "media."

medium of exchange—money or any other commodity accepted as having common value.

mega(anything)—prefix meaning extremely large; in science, prefix representing 1 million (a megabyte is 1 million bytes of information; a megawatt is 1 million watts of electrical power).

meltdown—slang for a miserable, quick failure; in the stock market, implosion of values.

member—someone or something that belongs or has been elected to a group.

memento—commemorative item or souvenir designed to remind you of a past event or accomplishment.

memo(randum)—informal letter used within an organization and with clients and vendors; basic form of informal communication among business people.

memory—measure of the amount of information a computer can store; first thing to go when you're under stress.

menial—subservient; work that demeans the person doing it.

mentor—experienced, generally older colleague who agrees to help a newcomer learn a job and gain insights into company and business politics.

mercantile—business of merchants.

merchandise—products to be sold; to use marketing tactics and displays to try to influence consumers to buy a product; to gain commercial value from something.

merchant—retailer; someone who buys goods at wholesale and sells them at retail.

mercurial—prone to radical changes in temperament or behavior, especially under pressure (like mercury rising in a thermometer when the temperature increases).

merge/purge—combining two or more mailing lists and deleting duplicate entries.

merger—when two or more organizations become one.

meridian—line that encircles the globe, passing through the North and South poles.

merit—value or worth; characteristics; degree to which something deserves attention; to deserve.

merit contract—contract to perform a specified amount of work for a specified amount of money.

merit pay—regular payment for the work you do or bonus payment for work performed beyond your quota.

merit raise—raise in pay based on superior performance.

message—information conveyed from a sender to a receiver; information left by a caller with a secretary, colleague, or on a voicemail system; in advertising, the point being made, whether obviously or subtly.

message center—area in an office in which one or more people answer phones for those who are unavailable and either hold the messages for pickup or deliver them.

messenger—someone designated to carry a message, document, package, or other small item from one party to another; the person you shoot if you don't like the message.

metamorphosis—change that significantly transforms appearance, behavior, or style of operation.

metaphor—figure of speech that tries to explain something by offering an example or an analogy for figurative comparison (for example, "the Titanic of new product launches"; if it's constructed with the words *like* or *as,* it's a "simile").

meter—39.37 inches in the metric system; device that measures, and often records, changes in information; device that imprints postage on an envelope or label; to measure; to imprint postage.

metric—measurement using the metric system; a measurement or performance standard.

metric system—international system of weights and measures based on units of 10, used by most of the world (with the notable exception of the United States.)

metropolitan statistical area (MSA)—U.S. Census Bureau category for a city of at least 50,000 residents in a region of at least 100,000.

mezzanine—low-ceilinged story of a building sandwiched between two other stories, often with a balcony overlooking the floor below; usually located between the first and second floors.

micro—prefix meaning "small" or "minute"; in metric measurement, one-millionth.

micro/macro dilemma—situation in which something is very good for the immediate future but may have adverse long-term effects, or would be good for a large group but have negative effects on a small one.

microeconomics—study of the behavior of small economic units, such as individuals and families.

microenvironment—small area in relation to a larger area under consideration, usually no larger than a medium-size town or a suburb and often as small as an individual person.

micromanage—to take obsessive interest in detail at the expense of paying attention to the larger context or keeping up with other responsibilities; to closely control subordinates, making decisions for them rather than allowing them to develop and use their own judgment.

micromarket—extremely small subgroup of a larger market, no larger than a few thousand people and often much smaller.

micron—one-millionth of a meter.

microprocess—system that has one or a few distinct tasks, usually performed in one department.

microprocessor—microchip that contains the computer's brain or central processing unit.

middle—where you tend to get caught if you're a manager.

middle drawer statement—formalized but unpublished policy statement for responding to disasters or other sensitive events, so named because it's often kept locked up in the middle drawer of an executive's desk to keep it from being seen unless needed.

middleman—person who delivers messages or performs other services between two parties.

middle manager—someone who supervises people or projects and reports to someone higher in the organization.

midlife crisis—phenomenon, becoming more noticeable as the Baby Boom generation moves through its forties, of realizing your life is (statistically speaking) half over and you haven't achieved the happiness and/or success you thought you would.

migrant worker—in agribusiness, workers, often whole families, who move from region to region as crops come ready for harvest, typically working for minimal wages.

migration path—path of improvements a product or technology is projected to take.

mil—one-tenth of a cent; common term used in tax rates.

military-industrial complex—coined by former U.S. President Dwight Eisenhower to describe the combined power represented by the military and the industries created to meet its needs.

milk—what you get from mother or another female mammal; to get the most out of something or someone; to exploit or take advantage of a situation.

mill—factory; plant containing machinery; place that turns out large quantities of something, such as puppies or graduates, having indifferent or suspect qualities; in agribusiness, facility where grain is processed; to grind or crush.

millage—property tax rate, representing $1 for $1,000 in assessed value.

millionaire—someone whose net worth exceeds $1 million.

mineral rights—rights to exploit resources below the surface of land owned or leased.

minimize—to downplay; to control; to denigrate.

minimum wage—wage floor set by the government (workers who receive tips or who work in agriculture are not covered); lowest wage that can be paid for a job as specified in a union contract.

minion—loyal subordinate, typically one who will follow instructions slavishly and without question.

minnow—in business author Harvey Mackay's analogy, a small player in business who tends to get eaten by larger or more aggressive players ("sharks").

minority—group that represents less than half of a larger population; member of a minority group.

mint—place where money is coined; small candy that improves your breath; having the same quality as when new; unused; to make or produce.

minute—exceedingly small; what you get 60 of in an hour.

minutes—permanent, official written record of a meeting.

mirandize—to warn, derived from the Miranda warning read to criminal suspects.

misery index—measure of inflation's effect on consumers.

misinformation—false information planted deliberately to mislead.

mismanage—to do a poor, inadequate, or careless job of managing, usually with the implication of ineptitude; to waste or squander.

misrepresent—to lie for personal or corporate advantage.

mission—overriding, broad-ranging goal; diplomatic or trade office set up in or sent to a foreign country.

mission statement—organization's official statement of its overriding goals and principles (usually a prolix, pretentious way of saying, "We're trying to make money.").

missionary—salesperson who handles all the details for a new customer, doing anything necessary to keep the customer happy while also presenting all the virtues of the company; representative of a company sent to work with, train, or advise vendors or customers.

missionary work—trying to convert others to your viewpoint.

MITI—Japanese Ministry of International Trade and Industry, the nation's chief architect of industrial policy.

mitigate—to lessen the severity or impact.

mitigating circumstances—in law, factors that partially reduce the onus for doing something illegal.

mobility—ability to move from one situation to another (in terms of the job market, how easily you could change jobs).

mobilize—to gather resources in preparation for an effort.

mode—style or manner; how something is done, often used when more than one choice is available for performing an activity; in mathematics, value that occurs most often (also called "norm").

model—prototype or pattern used to produce or guide; scaled-down representation of a larger object; mathematical construct that explains how something works; someone who poses for photographers or artists; idealized or worthy of imitation; to demonstrate; to pose; to create a preliminary plan or prototype.

modem—computer device used to transfer information via phone lines from one computer to another.

modernization—systematic process of renovating or updating to take advantage of current technology and methods.

modified American plan (MAP)—room, breakfast, and dinner, but no lunch.

modular—consisting of pieces that can be rearranged or replaced.

module—standardized piece of a modular setup; unit in a training course.

modus operandi (MO)—Latin for *manner of operating;* style; typical pattern of behavior.

modus vivendi—Latin for *way of living.*

mogul—extremely powerful person.

mom-and-pop store—small, privately owned retail operation, usually in an industry dominated by large chains.

moment of truth—SAS president Jan Carlson's way of describing (with a phrase borrowed from Ernest Hemingway) the crucial instances when customers come in contact with the organization in any way and have an opportunity to make a judgment about the quality of what's being done on their behalf.

momentum—in business, movement in a specific direction with the implication that it can take on a life of its own and fuel additional movement; in science, mass multiplied by velocity.

momento—Spanish for *moment* (a "memento" is a souvenir that helps you remember something).

mommy track—hypothetical second-tier career track rumored to exist for (and work against) working women who have children.

monetarist—economist who thinks the money supply controls economic activity.

monetary—involving money.

money—as defined by Ambrose Bierce, supportable property; agreed-upon medium of exchange and store of value that measures relative demand for other things, including raw materials, products and services, and time; the thing the love of which is the root of all evil.

money market fund—investment option that buys and sells various forms of short-term debt, paying interest on the amount invested and providing investors on-demand access to their funds.

money order—third-party check purchased for a fee in order to send funds when you don't have a checking account or a personal check is not accepted.

money supply—amount of money in an economy, including both cash and funds on deposit in checking and savings accounts.

monitor—televisionlike device that displays visuals from another source, such as a computer or VCR; to periodically check on something or someone.

monopoly—company, agency (such as a utility), or group that completely controls a product or service.

monopsony—situation in which there is only one consumer of a good, such as military products that are sold exclusively to the country's defense forces.

Moody's Investors Service—financial services company owned by Dun & Bradstreet that rates bonds.

moonlighting—working a second job, usually but not always in the evening.

moral—objectively right or good.

moral suasion—trying to convince someone of a course of action by appealing to higher principles rather than selfish interests or the letter of the law.

morale—informal measure of how happy or confident people are in their work.

moratorium—set time span during which something can't be done.

morbidity—rate of sickness or injury in a population.

mortality—subject to dying; the mortality rate is the death rate per 1,000 people at a given age.

mortgage—loan to buy property, such as a home or commercial building, secured by a lien on the property, which the borrower can continue to use while paying off the balance; to pledge property as security for a loan; to abandon higher principles for commercial gain or expediency.

motel—hotel where you can park your car at the door of your room.

motion study—detailed examination of the physical aspects of performing a job, often used to find more efficient ways of producing a product by spotting wasted or redundant actions.

motivation—inner reason for an action; desire to do something, a major concern for managers trying to find ways to get their workers to work harder.

motivational maintenance theory—theory that people perform well due to factors that directly motivate them, and that they perform poorly due to factors that can only demotivate, but that if taken away do not directly motivate.

mouse—small, hand-controlled device for performing certain functions with a computer.

mouthpiece—corporate spokesperson, often a lawyer.

movement—degree of change in a market; group of people organized around a cause or issue.

movers and shakers—important people.

muckraker—journalist who tries to find out bad things about public officials and celebrities.

mugshot—head-and-shoulders photo of someone.

multichannel marketing—using several types of marketing strategies at once, especially on the sales front, such as direct marketing as well as selling through retail stores.

multifamily housing—building that provides separate living quarters for more than one family, such as an apartment building or townhouse complex.

multilateral—having more than two parties.

multilevel marketing (MLM)—direct sales organization in which sellers in the system recruit others to sell product and receive a commission based on their recruits' sales as well as their own (critics often accuse it of being a pyramid scheme, while proponents say it's the road to riches for everyday people with drive).

multilingual—fluent in more than one language.

multimarketing—when a company sets up two or more semicompetitive marketing channels to reach one or more customer segments.

multimedia—in electronics, computer system that has sound and graphics capability; program involving sound as well as pictures and text; in marketing, presentation or advertising campaign that uses more than one type of media.

multinational—company that has major operations in more than one country and makes its business decisions in a global context.

multiple—product of multiplying two numbers together; in investing, way of evaluating a stock's desirability by dividing stock price by earnings per share.

multiple branding—developing more than one brand of similar products, often to reach different price points, but which compete with each other even though they are made by the same company.

multiple listing service (MLS)—cooperative realty service that lists homes for sale by subscribing realty companies.

multiplier—percentage something is multiplied by to arrive at a new statistic.

multitasking—ability of a computer or other machine to do more than one operation at once.

municipal—involving the government of a city or town.

municipal bonds—bonds issued by a state or local government agency, usually to underwrite construction of infrastructure.

Murphy's Law—"If anything can go wrong, it will," the legendary observation coined in 1949 by a frustrated development engineer named Ed Murphy.

mutual fund—pooled investment fund made up of a diversified collection of stocks, bonds, and other securities and managed by an investment company for several or more customers.

mutual insurance company—underwriter owned by its policyholders.

Muzak—generic music often played in elevators and reception areas.

myopic—nearsighted; refers to someone who can see only a small part of a larger picture, usually the part that directly affects him or her.

mystique—prestige; aura of mystery surrounding something.

myth—something that people state as fact but isn't completely (or at all) true; story that has grown in the telling.

N

Naderite—follower of consumer safety crusader Ralph Nader; by extension, someone prone to think that a business is not operating in the best interest of the public at large or its customers in particular.

nadir—lowest point (highest point is the "zenith").

naive—unsophisticated; hopelessly innocent.

naked—not carrying insurance coverage; not concealed.

naked position—unhedged securities position.

nametag—tag you wear at major events so people can pretend they remember meeting you (hint: it should be worn on the right, not the left, so the person you're meeting can read it as you shake hands).

nano—prefix meaning "one-billionth."

narrowcast—television broadcast to a small geographic area or selected audience.

national—having to do with an entire country.

National Aeronautics and Space Administration (NASA)—government-funded agency charged with the nonmilitary exploration of space and related research.

National Association of Securities Dealers (NASD)—organization of brokerage firms dealing in the over-the-counter market, quotations for which (along with many other listings) are carried on a computer system called the National Association of Securities Dealers Automated Quotations (NASDAQ).

national brand—product or service marketed under the same brand name throughout the country.

national bank—federally rather than state-chartered bank that belongs to the Federal Reserve System.

national debt—amount owed by the federal government from years of deficit spending, now one of the largest components of the U.S. national budget.

National Institutes of Health (NIH)—organizations that use public moneys to fund health-related research.

National Labor Relations Act (NLRA)—1935 federal law outlining collective bargaining procedures and fair treatment of labor; also called the Wagner Act.

National Labor Relations Board (NLRB)—agency established to oversee union relationships with employees and settle conflicts between unions and employers.

nationalize—when a government takes over a private company.

natural—occurring in or produced solely by nature; someone who shows inborn skill for a job; authentic or unfeigned.

natural resources—things occurring in nature that can be used to produce goods (and wealth), such as coal, oil, mineral ores, water, and land.

nazi—add-on used to describe someone with beliefs you consider radical and distasteful, for example drug nazis (people who believe in heavy-handed drug enforcement), femi-nazis (strident feminists), or timeclock nazis (managers who expect you to come in early and stay late).

near money—bank deposits and other highly liquid assets that can be quickly converted to cash.

near term—vague form of "very soon."

necktie—noose that a white collar man ties around his neck before going to work (all it takes is a jerk at the other end to keep him under control); male equivalent of pantyhose.

negate—to deny; to block or counterbalance another's advantage.

negative—something bad; the opposite of "positive"; in photography, film on which a reversed image has been developed and from which a print is made.

negative cash flow—losing money; not taking in enough money to cover expenses.

negative growth—euphemism for declining or going backward.

negative income—situation when costs exceed revenues.

negative income tax—suggested process of helping the poor by using the tax system to provide direct subsidies to people who fall below specified income levels (below a certain level you would receive money from the government, above it you would pay taxes).

negawatt—measure of power generation capacity saved by conservation and other reduction methods.

negligence—carelessness; in law, liability for damages resulting from actions or precautions not taken or systems and safeguards not followed.

negligible—not large enough to be significant.

negotiable—subject to terms to be mutually agreed to; security or asset that can be sold or transferred; what everything is.

negotiate—to dicker over terms and conditions; to settle the specific details of an agreement after both parties have agreed what the major outcome will be; to get through.

neo—prefix meaning "new".

neon—gas used in illuminated advertising signage; bright and colorful; gaudy and cheap.

nepotism—hiring or showing favoritism to family members, a practice traditionally forbidden in many nonfamily businesses, but occasionally encouraged on the premise that desirable work values run in the family.

nest egg—money put away for a purpose, typically for retirement.

net—amount of money left after all debts and expenses have been paid (subtract expenses from the gross); final or actual; to earn; to catch.

net income—income left after accounting for the costs involved in obtaining it (subtract expenses from total sales or income: a positive number equals "net profit"; a negative number equals "net loss").

net price—price actually paid after figuring in allowances, discounts, and other factors.

net proceeds—amount actually received from a sale after deducting commissions and other costs.

net worth—what's left after you subtract an individual's or company's liabilities from assets.

net yield—return on an investment after deducting sales and service fees and other charges.

network—any group of people or machines that produces a result by working together or by passing something such as information from one member to the next; a support group; to make contacts in the business world who can help with a current problem or a future project; to connect two or more computers together.

neurotic—showing erratic or eccentric behavior.

new—according to U.S. product law, the six months after the first production volume sale; something you just thought of (whether or not somebody else had the same idea before).

new and improved—popular advertising oxymoron (if it's improved, it's a variation on something old; if it's new, there hasn't been time to improve it).

new issue—stocks or bonds offered to the public for the first time, whether through an initial public offering (IPO) or the issuance of new securities after an IPO.

new money—money obtained by a new securities issue.

New York Stock Exchange (NYSE)—the nation's oldest and largest stock exchange, located on Wall Street in New York City; securities that meet its requirements are listed on "the Big Board."

news release—short article sent to the press to make an official announcement or statement.

newsletter—small, printed periodical containing information on a specific topic and sent to a relatively small, specific group of people, such as customers or a company's employees.

nibbled by ducks—experience (like being yelled at by your boss) that is unpleasant but not life-threatening and therefore bearable.

niche—sustainable place.

niche market—small or specialized market, often more profitable than the larger market in general, whose customers share similar needs and wants and can be efficiently reached.

nichemanship—business art of designing products and marketing to meet the needs of small, lucrative groups of consumers.

nickel—what a good cup of coffee should still cost.

nickel and dime—cheap or miserly; to reduce or wear down in small increments.

Nielsen rating—measure of how many people watch a specific television show in comparison to other programs, compiled by A.C. Nielsen Co. as a basis for advertising rates.

NIH syndrome—"not invented here," and therefore not worthy of serious consideration.

Nikkei—the Tokyo Stock Exchange.

NIMBY (not in my back yard)—used to describe people who believe something has a right to exist, but not where they have to deal with it.

Nintendo—diversified technology company most famous for its electronic arcade-style games and play-at-home game systems; using technology to meet a need or solve a problem is a "Nintendo solution."

no-load fund—mutual fund purchased with no sales charge (the "load") directly from the company that runs it rather than through a broker.

no-show—someone who makes a reservation for an airline flight or a hotel room but doesn't show up, creating a dilemma for the business which now has empty seats or beds (and resorts to overbooking to compensate, running the risk that now too many people will show up).

noise—in marketing, anything that can distort or disrupt a message.

nolo contendere—Latin for *I don't choose to contest it,* a legal plea that means you do not choose to contest a charge brought in court; cannot be used against you in subsequent legal action as an admission of guilt.

nom de guerre—French for *war name,* a fictitious name adopted to hide your real identity.

nom de plume—French for *pen name,* a fictitious name used when writing articles or books.

nomenclature—system for naming the parts of something.

nominal—minor or insignificant.

nominal group—involved consensus-building exercise in which participants brainstorm options, group and rank them by their importance, then continue to narrow and refine them until a best option emerges.

nominal rate—stated rate of interest on a bond.

nonsufficient funds (NSF)—used by banks to describe the situation in which a check is written for more money than is in the customer's account.

nonaudit services—services provided by an accounting firm that do not involve auditing accounting records.

nonbusiness organization—nonprofit organization.

nonconformity—not doing things the way virtually everyone else in an organization does them; degree to which something does not conform to an established norm.

noncontributory—benefits given by the company at no expense to the employee.

nondurable goods—items such as food that are consumed in one or several uses and thus need to be replaced often.

nonempirical validity—statistics or other information gained through means other than testing.

nonexempt—employee who is not exempt from labor laws, requiring that overtime be paid under specific circumstances (while some white collar workers are nonexempt, based on the type of work performed, most nonexempt employees are blue collar or clerical workers).

nonliquid—describes assets that are not easily convertible to cash.

nonperformance—in law, failure to do something you were

211

legally bound to do, which can be cause for legal action to recover damages; also called "nonfeasance."

nonprofit—organization that meets specific government guidelines for providing educational or charitable services, and operates without offering stock, making it exempt from income taxes; essentially the same as "not for profit."

nonrenewable—resources that, once used, cannot be replaced.

nonstore retailing—sales activities conducted without a storefront, such as vending machines and catalog sales.

nontraditional—different from the usual.

nonverbal communications—body language.

nonvoting stock—class of stock, such as preferred stock, that does not entitle the stockholder to vote on nominations for the board of directors or other proposals.

norm—standard or average.

North American Free Trade Agreement—controversial international business agreement creating free market conditions among the United States, Canada, and Mexico.

not-for-attribution—information provided to a reporter on the condition that it not be attributed to its source.

not-for-profit—see *nonprofit*.

notarize—as a notary public, to verify that you witnessed a person's signature.

notary public—officer appointed by a government agency or other authority who is empowered to legally witness signatures, administer oaths, and certify documents.

note—loan or negotiable certificate; document that sets the terms for repayment of a debt; informal message that calls your attention to something; paper currency; to make a point of noticing or remembering something.

notebook computer—small battery-powered computer that is approximately the size of a notebook.

notice—formal announcement of your intention to leave your employer; formal communication of official or extremely important information; to pay attention to or take note of.

novel—work of fiction; new or different.

novice—beginner.

NOW (negotiable order of withdrawal) account—savings account offered by a bank or savings and loan in which an order of withdrawal is negotiable (like a check), creating an interest-bearing checking account.

nuclear energy—energy obtained by splitting atoms.

nuke—to heat in a microwave oven; to destroy, as with a nuclear weapon.

null and void—something that cannot be enforced.

number cruncher—accountant or statistician.

number 10 envelope—business-size envelope.

O

obfuscate—to confuse or obscure skillfully.

objective—goal; expected results for the organization, work unit, or individual employee, often tied to performance (for example, based on a time period or target for quality defects or production) in order to give direction and purpose; without bias or prejudice; based on things that can be observed and measured.

obligation—debt or duty.

obscene—grossly offensive; sexually hazardous.

obsolete—outdated, usually as a result of technological advances; previous version of a product or document that has been significantly changed.

obvious—readily apparent; that which is known to those to whom it has been explained and never will be known to those to whom it hasn't.

occupant—person or business making legal use of a property or place, whether the legal owner or a temporary tenant; in correspondence, unnamed person at a deliverable postal address to whom mail is sent.

occupation—job or profession; grouping of jobs throughout an industry that require similar skills.

occupational hazard—factor in the workplace or involved in doing a job that increases the chance of work-related accidents, illnesses, or debilitating conditions; slang for an employee who's so good-looking that workers of the opposite sex are distracted.

occupational parity—whether the percentage of minorities or other subgroups in a company's workforce is equal to that of the population in the surrounding community.

Occupational Safety and Health Administration (OSHA)—agency of the federal government charged with setting and ensuring safety standards in the workplace.

odd lot—small number or irregular purchase; in investing, fewer than 100 shares purchased at one time; any amount of product purchased that is different from the usual amount, such as breaking a gross into smaller units.

odd-value pricing—setting prices at other than even-dollar amounts so consumers feel they are paying less for the item, such as gasoline priced at 1.09^9 instead of $1.10 or potato chips at $.99 instead of $1.

off/on the books—information that is (on) or isn't (off) recorded in official accounting records; "off the books" transactions usually involve barter or cash, often to avoid payment of taxes.

off/on the clock—not working or working; employees who receive pay based on the hours they work are on the clock when they are at work and off the clock during lunch or before and after work; short breaks are usually on the clock.

off the cuff—informal, unrehearsed, or extemporaneous remarks.

off/on the record—statements made to reporters that both parties agree are not to be used in an article, but are provided only for background or to lead the reporter to another source (practical rule of thumb: Anything you tell a reporter is on the record).

offer—tentative or firm indication of the amount a prospective buyer is willing to pay for something, subject to negotiation of mutually agreeable terms; in investing, number and price of shares that are available for purchase; request that you accept employment with a company.

offer sheet—official terms and conditions of a sale or financial agreement for acceptance or rejection.

offering—large quantity of an investment security available from a broker at a fixed price.

office—if you're not at work, generic term for the building you work in and sometimes the company as a whole; if you're at work, your workspace, even if it doesn't have a door; any defined workspace for white collar activities.

office automation—machines that make office work faster and easier, such as typewriters, computers, labelers, postage meters, etc.; process of bringing technological tools to office functions.

office holder—elected official.

office manager—senior secretary or administrator charged with organizing the day-to-day running of an office.

Office of Federal Contract Compliance Programs (OFCCP)—office in the U.S. Department of Labor that ensures equal employment opportunity by federal contractors and subcontractors.

Office of Management and Budget (OMB)—agency in the executive branch that prepares the president's budget for presentation to Congress, advises on the development of fiscal programs, and reviews the workings of government agencies.

officer—in a company, person with the title of vice president or higher who shares legal liability for the company's actions; in law, someone who works for the best interests of the court or legal system, including the attorneys involved in a case.

official—authorized.

officialese—long, wordy, overwritten explanation for something simple, meant to make it sound official or legally portentous.

offline—in computers, information stored on disk or tape that must be reloaded into the computer before accessing; unofficial conversation.

offpeak—hours or days in a business that are very slow, especially as a result of natural cycles, such as seasonal changes (derived from offpeak hours of demand for electricity).

offpeak pricing—lower rates offered to stimulate offpeak demand or to shift demand from peak to offpeak hours.

offprice—to sell brand-name merchandise at lower than normal prices.

offset—printing method where an image is transferred to a "blanket," which then transfers it onto the paper or other material being printed; amounts on opposite sides in different accounting ledgers that equal each other; to put equal amounts on opposite sides of an accounting ledger; to counterbalance.

offshore—bank or other organization with headquarters outside the legal limits of the country, allowing it to operate free of U.S. regulations and tax provisions; things that take place at sea, such as drilling.

offsite—business activities that take place somewhere other than on the company's premises, such as a training meeting held in a hotel or conference center.

oligopoly—market dominated by a small number of sellers.

ombudsman—objective third party who handles internal or external complaints about an organization but is not necessarily charged with or capable of resolving them.

omit—to leave out.

omnicompetence—being extremely competent or overqualified to perform a job.

omnipotence—having unlimited power.

on—operating; state of being highly productive and proficient.

on acceptance—work that will be paid for when it is received and found to be of acceptable quality, even if it is not immediately used by the customer.

on budget—project completed for the cost anticipated.

on consignment—goods delivered to, but not paid for by, a retailer until after they are sold; if unsold, they are returned.

on demand—payment due when the holder of the obligation requests it.

on order—something requested but not yet received or paid for.

on-sites—inspection visits of a company's facilities by regulatory personnel.

on spec(ulation)—doing a job without a guarantee of being paid for it, in hopes of winning a client's business.

on the job training (OJT)—learning to do a job by doing it, usually under the supervision and tutelage of an experienced coworker, rather than in a training course or academic classroom.

one—united or uniform; in electronics, half the code set for binary notation (the other is zero).

one hundred percent location—in retail, location where sales would be highest compared to other locations in the marketing area.

one hundred year risk—in insurance, potential hazard that is likely to occur only once in a century, such as a flood in a certain area.

onerous—hateful or burdensome; something you really don't enjoy doing.

online—state of being linked to a computer or electronic information service.

ongoing—computerese for "continuing."

op/ed—opinion and editorial pages of a publication; article or commentary that explains the individual's or organization's opinion on an issue.

open—accessible to customers; unlocked; in investing, price of a stock or level of the market at the beginning of trading; in banking, to set up an account.

open architecture—computer system to which subsystems and upgraded components can be added without a major reconfiguration of the hardware and software.

open book management—information-driven, participative style in which workers throughout the business have access to up-to-date financial and other data traditionally given only to management on the premise that they will better understand the importance and consequences of their work.

open-door policy—style that encourages frequent casual discussions with workers, ideally including those initiated by workers with their superiors, often without regard to the traditional chain of command (figuratively speaking, anyway, the boss's door is always open); in international trade, treating products of a foreign producer the same as those produced domestically.

open-ended—agreement that has no set limit to time or dollars.

open house—corporate party in which outsiders and employees' families are invited to tour new or remodeled facilities; in real estate, sales tactic in which a house for sale is open for casual inspection by potential buyers (sometimes used by realtors to seek leads for additional listings rather than to sell the house itself).

open kimono—Japanese metaphor referring to a long-term relationship between two or more businesses in which nothing is hidden.

open market—competitive market permitting easy entry by new companies or new products.

open shop—company that hires union and nonunion workers for the same job.

open space—land that doesn't have something built on it.

open stock—items in a merchandise line that can be bought piecemeal as well as in a set; merchandise on display in a store.

open up—to broaden or expand access to a market; to enter a new market.

opening—opportunity; point in a conversation where someone who has been listening can speak.

opening bell—bell signaling that trading has begun at a stock exchange or board of trade.

operating—working.

operating expenses—expenses incurred as a direct result of producing a product.

operating manager—someone who manages people directly involved with the production of an organization's products or services.

operating profits—income before deductions minus expenses, excluding income and expenses from unusual or irregular activities, such as the sale of a large corporate asset.

operation—business or unit within a business; in production settings, process or one stage in a large process; mathematical calculation.

operations—area of the company directly responsible for producing product.

opinion—what someone believes is true at a given point in time; in law, a court's decision, interpretation or assessment of the relative legality of an action; in accounting, statement by an independent CPA regarding the state of a company's books.

opinion leader—someone who is respected enough by others that their endorsement or approval may favorably impact your prospects, and their disapproval could have a negative effect.

opportunity—chance to do something under favorable circumstances.

opportunity cost—best-case estimate of how much more you could have produced with the same time and money if you had spent it differently.

optical character reader (OCR)—device that reads printed material and converts it to electronic data; often called a "scanner."

optimist—one who expects good things to happen.

optimize—to get the most out of something or out of a situation.

optimum—best.

optimum capacity—most cost-effective level of production (which is generally not the maximum level possible).

optimum mix—mix of retail goods that give the highest total sales in a given store.

option—choice; something added to a basic product to enhance its attractiveness, value, or functionality, such as a Jacuzzi in a bathroom; right to do something, such as buy or sell a security by a given date for a predetermined amount of money.

oral—verbal.

oral contract—legally binding agreement that may or may not be set down in writing.

oral exam(ination)—test in which you must respond verbally to questions asked by one or more reviewers rather than write your answers out for subsequent review; in dentistry, examination of the teeth, gums, and general health of the mouth.

order—buy or sell directions given to a broker; direction by a court to do something; commitment to buy or trade goods; choice made from a restaurant menu; general neatness or organization; to tell someone to do something; to request a good or service; to rank items by their importance or other system of organization.

order entry—the entering of customer orders for production or fulfillment.

order form—standardized, preprinted form requesting something that must be produced or shipped to order.

order number—device used by a company's computer system and/or people to keep track of orders; what you usually need to have to expedite response to an inquiry, because your order typically isn't filed or accessible by your name alone.

order taker—someone who enters orders but does not sell to or service the account; disparaging term for a salesperson with little initiative to build sales by selling to new customers or to build the firm's business with existing customers.

ordinance—local law (not to be confused with "ordnance," which refers to military ammunition).

ordinary—common or usual.

organic—natural part or characteristic of a substance; derived from living things.

organic capability—how smart or skilled someone is.

Organization of Petroleum Exporting Countries (OPEC)—cartel consisting of countries with significant petroleum resources.

organization—business or firm; ability or process of handling things systematically; way in which a process is structured.

organizational chart—pictorial representation of who re-

221

ports to whom within an organization; sometimes called an "org chart."

organizational development (OD)—planned process of improving the function of an organization through the training and education of its workers and management, and the implementation of supportive systems, using the principles of behavioral science.

organizational dynamics—how the forces in an organization interact.

organizational inducements—benefits and other perks offered by an organization to attract job applicants.

organizational replacement chart—chart that shows both current employees and potential internal and external replacements for any given position.

organizational vitality index—measurement of employees' talents and skills as well as an assessment of who is promotable and who can back up other employees.

organize—to arrange systematically; in labor relations, to build support for a union among workers not yet represented.

organized labor—workers represented by unions.

orientation—introduction to any new aspect of the organization or process within the organization; what you like to do and are good at, such as a technical orientation.

original—first; creatively new and unique; something from which a copy is made, such as a document or painting.

original equipment manufacturer (OEM)—company that makes a product or subsystem that will be marketed by another firm.

origination fee—charge assessed for starting something, such as a loan.

orphan account—customer who currently doesn't have a sales contact.

OUS (outside the United States)—foreign operations or customers of U.S. companies.

out of context—statement or information presented by itself, without the surrounding contextual information that would explain it more completely, in some cases significantly distorting the true meaning.

out of stock—not in inventory.

outbound—leaving; going out to make a delivery.

outcome—result of an action.

outflow—anything leaving the office, such as inventory or information.

outgo—expenditures; opposite of "income."

outlay—money spent.

outlet—store that often sells a manufacturer's products at a reduced price; means of escape for something or someone under pressure; wall-mounted access point to electricity (which you never seem to have enough of in a workplace).

outline—general shape of something; schematic for a long document, such as a book or report; to identify the major parts of a process or presentation without filling in the specific details.

outplacement—services provided to help someone who has been laid off find a new job with another company.

output market—customers who buy finished goods or services from an organization.

outside director—member of an organization's board of directors who is not an employee of the company.

outsource—to give work to another business, such as an independent contractor or subsystem manufacturer, rather than to have it done by your own employees.

outstanding—not yet paid, such as accounts receivable; stock held by shareholders; excellent or praiseworthy.

over the counter (OTC)—in investing, market for stocks not listed on an exchange; in medicine, drug that can be sold without a doctor's prescription or a license by the seller.

over the transom—unsolicited.

overage—surplus; too much of something, or more of it than you're supposed to have; opposite of "shortage"; too old.

overauditing—wasting time and company resources by performing too many audits of a procedure or accounting methods.

overbook—to take more reservations than a hotel, restaurant, or airline can accommodate in the expectation that a certain percentage will be no-shows.

overcharge—to charge (inadvertently or deliberately) more than authorized for a product or service.

overdraft—check written for more funds than are on deposit in an account.

overextended—stretched too thin to hold; unable to meet all financial obligations.

overhang—large number of securities or commodities contracts that would depress prices if released on the market all at once.

overhead—costs to maintain a business that do not directly go to producing a product or service.

overkill—doing something to extremes, sometimes to the point that it produces adverse results.

overload—workers available on a temporary basis; to exceed the capacity of a machine or system.

overprint—amount of a press run that is done in addition to those copies needed for regular purposes, such as those for promotion; to print an image on top of an existing one during the printing process.

override—mechanical function that allows a machine to operate beyond its safety settings; to set aside a veto by a two-thirds majority.

overrule—to reverse the ruling of a subordinate.

overrun—costs beyond those contracted or budgeted for; producing more product than you need to fill an order.

oversight—minor mistake made unintentionally; monitoring by a supervisor or regulatory agency.

overtime—work done in addition to the normal workday or workweek as defined by contract or custom, often compensated at a higher rate (legally "time and a half," or 1.5 times the normal wage, for hourly and nonexempt workers).

overwrite—to replace all or part of existing information with something new, such as a file in a computer.

owe—to be indebted; to be in the process of paying back a debt.

own—to have legal ownership of an asset; to psychologically or physically control something; to admit or confess.

owner—someone who has legal title to an asset; in quality theory, someone who performs a process and/or has responsibility for correcting problems in the process.

owner-operator—someone who both owns and operates a business, such as truck drivers who own their rigs.

oxymoron—words that seem to contradict each other but are used together to create a specific meaning, such as "jumbo shrimp."

ozone—thin layer of oxygen in the atmosphere that filters radiation from the sun but is in danger of being depleted due to fluorocarbons from aerosol sprays; scientifically, a form of oxygen (O_3); in business, nebulous place where people sometimes seem to keep their heads.

P

Pac-Man defense—defending your company from an unwanted takeover by trying to gobble up (like the character in the old video arcade game) the stock of the attacker.

pacesetter—person or product that sets the standard for imitation or competition; leading-edge company in an industry (but not necessarily the largest, best known, or most respected).

pacific—peaceful.

Pacific Rim—growing marketplace for countries bordering the Pacific Ocean.

pack—group that acts together, with or without intelligent leadership; a bundle or package; to put something in a container for transit; to crowd closer together; to attempt to tip the balance of a group by adding adherents to your point of view.

package—container a product comes in; something shipped by delivery service; to put a product into a container for shipment or sale; to combine several products or services.

packaged goods—consumer products delivered in packages from manufacturers to retailers.

packer—company specializing in slaughtering and processing food animals.

packing list—itemization of things in a package that accompanies it to provide a check of the contents.

pad—stack of paper that orders are written on; list of officials being paid bribes; to add unjustified or phantom expenses to an expense account; to add funds to a budget as a hedge against contingencies or to insulate yourself from difficult competitive conditions; to cushion.

page—piece of paper in a book or document; the place everybody is supposed to be on at the same time; to use a loudspeaker system to find someone.

paginate—to put page numbers on a document; in computers, to put page breaks in a document.

paid—settled; reimbursed; obligation that has been met.

palatable—something that can be accepted without leaving a bad taste in the mouth.

palletization—packaging of products so that they can be sold by the pallet load (pallets are wooden or plastic platforms that can easily be moved by forklifts).

palmtop computer—handheld portable computer.

pamphlet—short brochure providing information or instructions.

pander—to play to another's weaknesses or vices.

Pandora's box—potentially adverse and, once let loose, uncontrollable effects that may result from a course of action (in Greek mythology, the goddess Pandora opened a box and let out the ills of the world).

panic—situation in which people lose confidence in the financial system; fear that spreads; to lose control to fear; to make someone suddenly afraid.

pantone matching system (PMS)—system used by designers and printers to specify color tones to be added to a document.

pantyhose—garment combining panties and stockings worn in the workplace; the working woman's counterpart to a necktie.

paper—credit or debt; scholarly report; to pass a number of checks; to cover over a fault or deficiency, as with wallpaper.

paper and pencil test—written test used to measure aptitude for a job.

paper assets—assets that are real insofar as a business's books are concerned but may not be readily usable or convertible to cash.

paper profit/loss—difference between the current market price and the investor's original cost for the asset, even though the asset itself is not being sold at this time.

paper trail—written records that document events.

papers—identification documents.

paperweight—desktop decoration used to hold down a stack of papers.

paperwork—written records that must be kept to record, track, analyze, and validate business activities (may be written on paper or into a computer's memory).

par—equal to the full value; norm or average; equal standing or status; number of shots a good golfer should take per hole or to complete the course.

par value—face value of a security.

para—prefix for *not quite* or *partial*; short for *paraprofessional*.

parachute—negotiated severance package that you receive even if you are fired.

paradigm—model; frame of reference for viewing a situation.

paradigm shift—radical transformation in the way you look at something based on changing your basic assumptions or frame of reference; impressive way to say you've changed your mind.

paradox—contradiction.

paralegal—someone in a law firm trained to perform tasks such as research and filling out legal forms.

parallel processing—simultaneous performance of two or more functions by a computer.

paramedic—someone trained to perform basic medical procedures, such as emergency first aid.

parameter—known value or boundary, especially in the context of a wide-ranging project or perspective.

parasite—someone who takes but never gives; something that attaches itself to and feeds on something else.

parcel post—class of U.S. mail for sending items weighing more than one pound and less than seventy pounds; also called "fourth class."

parens—parentheses.

parent company—company that owns another company.

parentheses—brackets in a written document in which you put explanations or meaningful asides.

Pareto principle—observation by Italian economist Vilfredo Pareto that in any population a relative few contributors account for the bulk of the effect ("the significant few and the insignificant many"); also called the 80/20 rule because, as a general rule of thumb, 80% of an effect (such as sales) tends to come from just 20% of those that can cause it (such as customers).

parity—equality, especially when dealing with unlike items or currencies; farm prices maintained by government supports.

park—what you do with your car when you get to work; peaceful natural place; area set aside for a specific activity, such as an industrial park; to put something somewhere safe temporarily, such as parking money in an internal account while evaluating major purchase options.

Parkinson's Law—C. Northcote Parkinson's observation that "work expands so as to fill the time available for its completion," and that organizations lose their initial efficiency and become stagnant and dysfunctional over time.

parliamentary procedure—rules of order for running a meeting derived from those used in the English parliament, most commonly as described in "Robert's Rules of Order."

part time—working fewer than thirty-two hours a week.

participative management—style in which employees are involved in making business decisions.

partition—repositionable wall, such as those used to define a cubicle; to divide.

partner—any person with whom liability and rewards are shared.

partnership—situation in which two or more participants agree to share capital and liability to various degrees in a nonincorporated business; business owned by its partners, such as an accounting or law firm.

party—participant; social gathering for fun; to make a concerted effort to have fun in the company of others.

party line—official explanation that everyone is supposed to stick to; in older phone systems, line shared by two or more subscribers.

passalong rate—measure of a publication's total readership based on estimating the number of people to whom a subscriber's copy is circulated.

passive investor—person who has a financial interest in an organization but is uninvolved in management decisions.

password—secret access code consisting of letters and/or numbers that allows entrance, most commonly to a computer or building security system.

patch—to fix something temporarily; to connect someone or something to an electronic system or network.

patent—government license of an exclusive right to produce a product exclusively for a period of seventeen years; obvious; to go through the process of obtaining a patent.

patent pending—status of an invention when a patent has been filed but not yet issued while a search of patent records is conducted.

paternalistic—fatherly, taking care of basic needs; connotes a system in which people are treated like children of a benevolent but authoritarian father.

paternity leave—paid or unpaid leave granted to fathers when a child is born or adopted, more common in other nations than in the United States.

pathological—diseased or caused by the conditions or effects of a disease; connotes an action someone can't help doing, such as lying.

patron—customer; benefactor.

patronize—to do business with; to talk down to or treat as an inferior.

patronage—business from customers; in government, awarding of jobs based on political connections.

patter—rehearsed sales pitch; glib conversation lacking substance.

Pavlovian—conditioned response, as demonstrated by the Russian psychologist Ivan Pavlov.

pay—gross salary; to compensate someone for something; to settle an obligation (the "payer" pays to the "payee").

pay as you go—system in which you pay for benefits or services as you use or acquire them rather than in advance or on completion.

pay for performance—compensation system in which employees are rewarded for various levels of job performance, often tied to meeting objectives or production quotas.

pay period—interval between calculation of paychecks.

pay the piper—to accept the unpleasant consequences of an action.

pay to play—to invest money or effort before or as a condition of beginning an activity (such as buying chips before entering a poker game).

payback—compensation; retaliation; point at which an investment has broken even (also called "payout").

paycheck—check from an employer in the amount of net wages earned for a pay period.

payday—day you get paid.

payola—secret and illicit payment received for providing preferential treatment for a product or service, such as playing a record on a radio station.

payroll—total number of employees receiving paychecks; total amount of a company's paychecks for a given period; official listing of a company's employees and the money they are paid.

PDA (personal digital assistant)—handheld electronic device capable of performing basic computer functions.

PDCA (plan, do, check, act)—four steps in the continuous improvement model developed by Walter Shewhart and popularized by W. Edwards Deming.

peak—top or highest; to be at your best; to hit a maximum performance level, perhaps too soon.

peas and carrots—situation in which both options are equal.

pecking order—your position in the corporate hierarchy; informal position you hold among peers.

pecuniary—something that can be valued in terms of money.

peer interview—interview of job candidates conducted by people in the same or similar position as that for which the candidate is applying.

peer review—formal or informal performance review by coworkers.

peg—pin used as a fastener; square things people are always trying to put in round holes; to judge or characterize; to link or attach in order to stabilize.

pencil—handheld data entry device (still the most common business tool); rough drawing preliminary to the final.

pencil in—to add something tentatively or belatedly, such as writing a tentative appointment on your calendar in pencil so that you can erase it if the meeting is rescheduled or your schedule changes.

Pendaflex—common brand of hanging folders used to organize files in a drawer or file cabinet.

penalty—fee assessed for violation of a provision; punishment.

penny stock—stock, usually volatile or speculative, that typically sells for less than a dollar a share.

pension—money you will receive after retirement.

pension fund—investment fund set up and paid into by an organization, employees, or both, from which pension benefits will be paid; typically contributions can't be withdrawn without penalty until retirement, but are tax-exempt until then.

penthouse—luxurious living or office space at the top of a high-rise building; top-quality accommodations or amenities.

peon—servant; originally a Hispanic laborer in the southwestern United States or Latin America, now anyone who works in a low-level position in a company and whose professional services (not to mention personal likes and dislikes) are not considered significant by higher levels of the firm.

peppercorn—slang for *insignificant*.

per capita—Latin for *per head*; average per person.

per diem—Latin for *per day*; travel expenses allotted for each day a person is on the road.

per se—Latin for *by itself*.

perception—knowledge gleaned from the senses rather than formal learning; what defines reality in many businesses today.

perceived needs—needs that customers think they have for a product or service.

perf(oration)—row of holes that makes it easier to detach something.

performance—how well you do your job; presentation in front of an audience.

performance review—formal meeting with one or more of

your supervisors to discuss how well you have been working; may or may not coincide with a pay increase.

period—interval of time; what goes at the end of a sentence; way of adding emphasis ("That's it, period!").

perishable—refers to something that will spoil over a relatively short amount of time, such as food.

perk—short for *perquisite*, a nonmonetary fringe benefit (such as an expense account, company car, or free vacation travel) received above and beyond a wage; how you brewed coffee before drip coffeemakers; to pay or attract attention; to cheer up.

permanent file—any file that is to be kept for a long period of time, usually at least three years.

permanent position—job that has no ending date (which does not, alas, mean it can't be eliminated in a layoff or reorganization).

permit—legal authorization to conduct an activity, such as a building permit; to authorize or allow.

perquisite—see *perk*.

personal—confidential; applying to your life away from your job.

personal computer (PC)—computer that can be used as a self-contained desktop or laptop unit.

personal information—nonjob-related information that cannot legally be asked in a job interview, such as age, marital status, whether you are pregnant, religious beliefs, and so forth.

personality profile—test designed to label your personality type based on how you react to questions about situations.

personal property—your stuff that you bring to the workplace, as opposed to the company's stuff.

personnel—people; all of the people employed by a company; department that oversees the administrative tasks of hiring, firing, maintaining benefits programs, and other activities dealing with employees.

personnel management—activities designed to provide for and coordinate the employees of an organization, including but not limited to such areas as benefits, hiring, and compensation (the favored term today is "human resources" management, or HR).

perspective—vantage point or point of view.

persuade—to convince another of your point of view by force of argument or reasoning rather than by force alone.

Peter Principle—Lawrence J. Peter's observation that people rise in an organization to their personal level of incompetence.

petrodollar—dollar placed in European or U.S. banks by oil-producing countries.

petty cash—small amounts of cash kept on hand to meet everyday expenses.

phase system—defined progression in product development that takes the product from concept to customer in discrete segments or phases with distinct areas defined for business decisions.

Ph.D.—doctor of philosophy, the highest academic degree obtainable.

philanthropy—giving money to nonprofit institutions and organizations that seek to help people.

phone—key means of communication in the business world.

phone home—evaluation tactic in which you call your office or company and, without identifying yourself, ask for something in order to evaluate how people respond to actual customers.

phone room—telemarketing center.

photo—picture or photograph; to make a photocopy of something.

photo shoot—taking of photos for an advertisement, annual report, or other printed piece.

photocopy—to make a copy of something using heat-sensitive photographic imaging technology (the most popular form of which is xerography, hence Xerox).

photostat—high-quality image produced by a lithographic camera used at the final stages of a printing project to check for errors.

physically challenged—person with one or more physical handicaps.

pick—choice; pointed tool used in mining and digging; to choose or select; to assemble an order in a distribution center; to harvest a crop; to open a lock without a key.

picket—demonstrator (also called "picketer"); to demonstrate in front of a facility, typically as a result of a union-management dispute (a "picket" is the piece of wood a demonstrator's sign is attached to).

picket line—line of demarcation around a business that a union asks others not to cross in order to pressure management into negotiating; line of picketers around a workplace.

pickle—dilemma; control that is squeezed.

pie—total amount of something.

pie chart—round chart that shows proportional shares of a whole, resembling a pie cut into sections.

piece—part of a whole; something written or published, whether in print or electronically; to put together one part at a time, often without knowing all the details of the finished project, such as a puzzle.

piece rate—postage for one item, especially when mailing bulk; amount that a person doing piecework makes per piece produced.

piecemeal—put together piece by piece rather than in a unified process.

piecework—getting paid for each product you produce.

pig in a python—metaphor for the movement of the Baby Boom generation through U.S. life.

piggyback—transportation system in which loaded truck trailers are taken to locations on rail cars; to add one program or effort to another to take advantage of resources already allocated or activities already under way.

pilfer—to steal by hand in small quantities, often from your employer (the items stolen come under the heading of "pilferage").

pilot—something that is run as a test; guide; someone in charge of flying an airplane or navigating a ship; to introduce something on a small scale to make sure it works properly before expanding it to a larger audience; to test.

pilot plant—facility that makes small quantities of product prototypes for further evaluation.

pilot project—project designed to see if something will work in the real world.

pink collar—originally, jobs requiring little training that were usually held by women, such as hairdressers (who wore pink smocks); today refers to any position for which there are more women than men, such as banking and nursing.

pink slip—notice that you have been laid off.

pinks—message forms; receipts.

pin money—small amount of money advanced before a trip to be used for incidental expenses; originally, money saved from the household budget by housewives for discretionary spending not subject to their husbands' oversight.

pinstripe—subtle, narrow stripe pattern, typically in a suit; slang for a senior executive or professional who works with money, such as an accountant, stockbroker, or banker.

pimp—often exploitive and abusive business manager of a prostitute; to represent or sell something of dubious character or value.

pioneer—someone who proves that something new can be done; to create a new product or market; in a figurative sense, to explore new territory.

pipeline—any route by which gossip or materials travel; source of information.

pirate—someone who plays outside the rules; violator of a commercial law or regulation; to copy a copyrighted or trade-marked product or design.

pit—trading area at a commodities exchange.

pitch—all of the activities conducted to try to persuade a person to buy your product or hire you, such as a sales pitch.

pitchman—salesperson whose specialty is telling the benefits and advantages of a product.

pixel—dots that make up an image on a television or computer screen.

placement—function of finding jobs for people.

plagiarize—to steal ideas or analyses of others and present them as your own.

plain—flat, generally treeless land surface; simple and unadorned; common; unattractive ("plane" refers to a flying machine, a carpenter's tool, or a level of development or achievement: if it's geography, it's a *plain*; if it's geometry, it's a *plane*).

plain language—written or stated in words that a person with a high school education can understand.

plain paper—basic bond paper; attribute of a machine, such as a photocopier or fax, that does not require special paper.

plain vanilla—simple, unadorned; characteristic of a basic product or service.

plaintiff—person who brings a lawsuit.

plan—detailed outline of what is to be done over a given period, used as a reference point for actions during that period; overhead view of a facility or system; to engage in activities designed to develop, refine, rework, and finalize a plan; to think about what you're going to do before starting to do it.

plane—airplane; carpenter's tool used to flatten and smooth a surface; level of development or achievement ("plain" means simple, unadorned, unattractive, or a level land area with no trees). -

planned obsolescence—practice of designing products to last only a certain length of time so they must be replaced.

planned unit development (PUD)—master-planned area, such as a housing tract or an office park, zoned to assure that overall standards are met while providing flexibility for the developer.

planning—act of setting goals and developing strategies and tactics for meeting those goals.

plant—place where something is manufactured; physical resources of a business, such as buildings and the land they're sitting on, manufacturing equipment, and raw materials (often called "fixed assets"); growing thing, or artificial copy of one, that provides greenery in a workplace; to establish or put in place for future developments; in agriculture, to sow seed.

plaque—commemorative design or inscription mounted on a flat piece of wood or stone.

plat—detailed map or plan of a defined area of land.

plate—what you eat or work from; everything that must be completed in a given time period; to coat something with another substance.

plateau—flat, elevated plain; lofty place; to reach a point where nothing is likely to change, such as sales levels, market movement, or relative place on a career ladder.

platform—list of strategies and ideas that you promote; portable stage on which you stand to make a presentation; raised foundation for a machine.

play or pay—situation in which you have to go along with a strategy you may not agree with or suffer negative consequences such as being fired.

player—someone who has, or is believed to have, a significant role in a project; active investor; someone who dabbles in an activity but is suspected of being not seriously committed to it.

plot—conspiracy; graphic representation of data; to chart something; to conspire.

plotter—machine that mechanically draws out diagrams, blueprints, and other schematics; someone who plots or is involved in a plot.

plow back—to put earnings back into a company instead of paying stock dividends.

plow under—to abandon something and start over, such as a farmer plowing under a bad crop and replanting.

plowshare—blade of a plow; what you're supposed to be able to beat swords into (a metaphor much debated in the military-industrial complex).

plurality—in voting, less than half but more than any other candidate or alternative received; margin by which the highest total exceeds another.

pocket—place in your clothing for keeping things; small, somewhat isolated area; something compact enough to fit in a pocket; to pick up and put out of sight; to take.

pocket protector—plastic or fabric liner that fits into a pocket to keep pens and other materials from falling out or poking through the fabric; legendary wardrobe statement of a nerd.

point—key concept or intent of an action; relative place; unit of credit, literally or figuratively, for doing something successfully ("to score points with your boss"); in finance, fee equal to 1% of a loan amount; in bonds, a 1% change in the face value, or $10, since bonds usually have a face value of $1,000; in stocks, a $1 change in price (a stock that goes up "half a point" now costs 50 cents more than it did before); scout position ahead of a military column.

point of purchase (POP)—place where money changes hands; in retailing, anything visible from the cash register, usually advertising or small products bought on impulse.

point of sale (POS)—anything visible from the cash register, usually advertising or small products; also refers to the point in a salesperson's pitch when the sale is confirmed.

point person—someone designated to take the lead in presenting information, handling problems, or answering difficult questions.

point size—unit of measurement for print type; 72 points equal 1 inch.

poison pill—premeditated action by a company targeted for takeover to make its stock less attractive.

poka-yoke—Japanese term for idiot-proofing a device or process so that it can be done only the proper way, such as making a computer connector with an odd number of pins or shaping a part so it will fit only one way.

polarize—to divide people into being strictly for or against something, suggesting that ideas or positions have hardened and neutrality is impossible (derived from the opposite poles of a magnet).

policy—guideline for taking action in defined situations; in insurance, contract to cover a customer against specific risks under specific conditions.

policy manual—formal list of what can and can't be done in certain situations.

political action committee (PAC)—organization formed by an interest group to provide funding to political candidates.

politically correct (PC)—doing something, such as hiring a minority or recycling, because it looks good, not because it is ethically or morally right; trend toward sanitizing speech and actions and adopting tepid euphemisms for any potentially controversial or polarizing subject (implies attempts to control any potential offense that could be given by thought, speech, and/or actions through public intimidation).

pollutants—by-products of manufacturing or use of products that contaminate the air, ground, or water and may have a negative effect on the environment in general or specific forms of life, including human.

pollution—contamination of air, ground, or water; degrading by reducing quality, such as using inferior components in a device previously made to higher standards.

pollution credit—value system in which a business running cleaner than required by regulations can sell credit for the difference to a firm that does not meet regulatory standards (potentially job- and cost-saving alternative to the second firm being forced to install pollution-control equipment or, failing that, shut down its operation).

polygraph—lie detector.

polymer—compound made of repeating chains of linked molecules (the building-block molecules are called "monomers").

Ponzi scheme—pyramid investment in which the original participants are paid off with funds solicited from new ones, named for Charles Ponzi, the 1920s conman who thought it up; also called "pyramid scheme" (geometric reality dictates that it won't work because each level requires more participants until it runs out of enough new suckers and collapses from its own weight).

pool—group created for a specific purpose, such as investing or sharing high risks; man-made place where you swim; to combine.

pop—short for *popular;* refers to current preferences that may not endure over time; also short for *soda pop.*

popcorn—to generate ideas, especially when brainstorming.

popular—desired or liked by a large number of people in a specific population.

population—large group from which samples are taken or conclusions are made; total number of people in an organization or community.

port—harbor through which shipping passes; to carry.

port of entry—supervised place where people or goods enter or leave a country.

portable—easily movable, such as a computer or television monitor.

portal to portal—literally "door to door," refers to the practice of billing transit and other time and expenses to and from a customer's location.

portfolio—in investing, securities held by a person or institution; file of previous work that an artist, writer, model, or other professional shows to potential clients.

posit—to offer as a hypothesis or explanation.

position—job; financial status of a company or bank; in investing, interest you've acquired in a security; to put something in place; in marketing, to present a product or service in a way that will result in its being perceived in a predetermined and advantageous manner; in printing, to place artwork in a piece about to be printed.

positioning statement—formal statement outlining how a product is to be positioned, used to guide marketing efforts.

post—upright pole or support; place to which someone is assigned; to put a formal announcement, such as a job opening, in a public spot; in accounting, to enter a transaction into the permanent records; to mail; to assign.

post mortem—review of a project or event, usually performed soon after its completion.

post office box (P.O. box)—locked box at a postal facility where mail is received for convenience, security, or to have access to incoming materials on your schedule rather than the mail carrier's.

postage—amount paid in advance to send something through the postal service.

postage meter—machine that imprints a postage amount and date stamp on an envelope or label in lieu of stamps.

Post-it—3M Co.'s trademark for repositionable notes or labels on which to write messages, comments, or instructions.

postindustrial—refers to the period after the age of industrialization, where information replaces mechanized power as the driving economic force.

postdate—to put a date already past on something, such as a check or legal document (illegal in some circumstances).

postpurchase—occurring after the purchase of a product; "postpurchase costs" are those associated with keeping a customer happy after a purchase, such as warranty service.

postscript—short note at the end of a document to provide information not included in the main text.

potential—believed to be there, but not yet developed; latent talent or ability.

poverty—state of being poor or lacking resources.

power—ability to perform; relative stature and force in an organization; energy; electricity; applies to something worn or used to show that a person has (or would like to have) power or prestige in an organization, such as blue suits, BMWs, Mont-Blanc pens, and silk ties; to force; to energize.

power of attorney—legal authorization to act as an attorney or representative on another's behalf.

powershift—futurist Alvin Toffler's term for the period of disruption resulting from a change in how the world defines power (which in his analysis has progressed from violence through wealth to information).

predator—person or company that feeds on weak competition, typically in a brutal or merciless way.

predictive validity—validity that is established by first defining a predictor, such as a test, then correlating the test results with success.

preempt—to act first; to seize or take by prior right or greater power; in television, to replace regularly scheduled programming with a special broadcast.

preemptive rights—right of existing stockholders to buy new shares in the company before those shares are offered to the public.

preexisting—existing before a new term or condition took effect; already there (in which case, it means the same as "existing").

prefab(ricate)—to build of modular components that are manufactured elsewhere, then assembled on site.

preference—choice over other alternatives; advantage; real objective of advertising, but typically contingent on first building awareness.

preferred stock—class of stock that is given priority treatment in the distribution of a corporation's dividends or assets.

premise—underlying rationale or concept for an argument or proposal.

premises—land and the buildings on it.

premium—of higher grade or quality; more expensive; in insurance, amount charged a policyholder for coverage; in marketing, something given as a gift for doing or buying something else.

premium pricing—making a product, such as luxury cars or jewelry, more desirable by selling it at a high price.

prenuptial agreement—contract detailing how personal assets and finances are to be valued, allocated, and handled during a marriage and in the event of a divorce, agreed to by a future husband and wife prior to their marriage; also called "prenup."

prep—to prepare.

prepay—to pay in advance; to pay something before it becomes due, which may or may not incur a penalty.

prepress—in publishing, activities required of a printer or subvendor before a piece can be printed, including screening and separating photos, stripping artwork into position, creating negatives or plates, and miscellaneous other tasks.

presentation aids—visual aids used by a speaker to illustrate a presentation, such as flipcharts, pointers, easels and storyboards, and overhead projectors, but generally excluding more complex audiovisual equipment such as slide projectors and video systems.

president—in a corporation, highest-ranking officer after the chief executive officer (if the president is also the CEO, he outranks the chairman of the board of directors; if the chairman of the board is the CEO, he outranks the president); in other organizations, highest-ranking officer.

presort—to arrange outgoing mailings of more than five hundred pieces by zip code and route order in order to qualify for reduced rates.

press—news media; machine that exerts pressure; to pressure someone for a response or action; to smooth out wrinkles using a hot iron.

press conference—public relations event in which members of the appropriate media are invited to hear an announcement and ask questions of key players.

press kit—folder containing key information on a specific event or product, or a company in general, and either given to members of the press at an event or sent to them.

press release—short announcement, generally no more than two pages in length, sent by a company to the media.

press room—room at a function, such as a convention or annual meeting, set aside for members of the news media.

prestige—renown or influence based on accomplishments, wealth, or prominence; fame.

prestige pricing—keeping a product's price higher than it has to be in the belief that customers think you get what you pay for, and if the price is cheap, the quality must be too.

pretax—before taxes have been deducted or assessed.

pretest—test administered before beginning an activity, such as training or an advertising campaign, to assess current levels of knowledge or understanding; administering a posttest shows what was accomplished by the activity.

preventive maintenance—systematic way of reducing costs and extending life by maintaining equipment in good repair on a regular schedule rather than waiting for something to break and then fixing it.

price—cost asked or received in return for something; assumed value of a good or service that the provider and customer agree on; to put a price on.

price ceiling—formal or informal point above which a product or service can't be priced, usually because of government controls or supply and demand equilibrium.

price/earnings ratio (P/E)—way of evaluating investment prospects and performance of a stock (divide the price of the stock by its earnings per share); also called the "multiple."

price fixing—illegally agreeing with competitors on the price of a product or service rather than letting competitive forces in the marketplace set the price.

price floor—formal or informal point below which a product or service can't be priced, either because it will no longer be profitable to make or because customers will not find the price a credible indicator of quality (see *prestige pricing*).

price pack—specially packaged or labeled products offering savings off the regular price; a "reduced" price pack is a single product sold at a reduced price (two for the price of one); a "banded" pack consists of two related products banded together (for example, shampoo and a hairbrush).

price points—products designed to be sold at specific pricing levels, such as budget, midrange, and top quality, or good-better-best.

price shading—activities conducted to make a price look different than it really is, such as offering a bare-bones price but then charging service fees.

price strategies—tactics used to determine how a product will be priced, including analysis of the competition's pricing, consumers' attitudes toward the product, seasonal demand, and other factors.

price support—money paid to a producer by the government if the price of a commodity falls below a minimum level set by the government, used to protect businesses such as farms.

price war—competition in which businesses lower their prices, sometimes below their cost, to attract new customers or gain market share.

pricey—expensive or overpriced: in investments, extremely low bid price or extremely high offer price.

prima donna—show-off; someone who expects preferential treatment based on personality or position (literally, the female lead soloist in an opera company).

prima facie—Latin for *on first appearance;* immediately obvious or needs no more evidence to prove its validity.

primary market—in investing, market for new securities, proceeds from the sale of which go to the issuer ("secondary market" is where previously purchased securities are bought and sold); in marketing, geographical area or demographic category in which most of a company's products or services are sold (for example, the primary market for textbooks is students).

primary metropolitan statistical area (PMSA)—area with a population of 1 million or more within a consolidated statistical metropolitan area (CSMA).

prime—best; in food, top-quality cut of meat; to prepare for operation.

prime rate—interest rate that banks offer to their best commercial customers.

primer—concise guide or sourcebook.

principal—owner of a company; in finance, amount of money actually borrowed or invested, not counting interest; client of a stockbroker or agent; significant participant; most important or primary.

principle—rule or ethical standard that most people follow.

print—photographic copy; copy of an artist's original painting; publications media; to make a photographic copy; to publish or produce by printing.

printout—paper copy of information in the memory of a computer or other electronic device; also called "hard copy."

prioritize—to arrange things in order of importance.

priority mail—first class mail weighing between twelve ounces and seventy pounds.

privacy—right to be let alone; privacy laws and regulations protect people from having certain information released without their permission, such as mental health counseling records, and require those who rent their mailing lists to tell their customers that they are doing so and delete their names if they so direct.

private—restricted or personal; lowest-ranking soldier in an army.

private label—goods produced by a manufacturer for sale under the name of the wholesaler or retailer; also called "private brand."

private placement—investment offered to a limited number of purchasers under specific terms and generally not subject to the regulations of the Securities and Exchange Commission or state regulators.

private sector—nongovernment part of the economy; also referred to as "private enterprise."

privately held—totally owned by one or more individuals or groups, with no stock available to the public.

privatization—act of taking a public company private.

privilege—special right.

privileged communication—legally confidential, such as information shared between a client and a lawyer.

privileged information—information given only to authorized individuals rather than to everyone in the company or the public at large.

pro—in favor of something; professional.

pro forma—presentation, especially of financial information, in which some information is hypothetical (Latin for *as a matter of form*).

proactive—taking an action before it is necessary because you are anticipating events rather than reacting to them.

probate—process of determining the validity of a will; to process a will.

probationary period—specified period in which something can be canceled without penalty; on the job, the first several months, when you can be fired for any reason if you fail to master the needs of the position.

problem child—product, division, company, or other entity that is not doing well and may be causing a financial drain on resources.

procedure—predetermined way to accomplish something.

proceeds—value received from a transaction.

process—steps taken to meet a goal; repeatable cycle used to produce a product or service and the elements of which they are composed; to deal with or take care of according to established procedures; to think.

process capability—amount that could be produced on an ongoing basis if all barriers to quality were removed.

process chart—chart that shows the sequence of events needed to perform a task.

process design—delineating how a process will be performed.

process engineer—someone whose specialty is designing the most efficient, cost-effective procedures for producing a product.

process map—pictorial representation of a process or interrelationships between two or more processes.

process performance—results of a process.

process redesign—changing a process without changing product quality goals.

process validation—analysis designed to ensure that a process consistently meets its goals.

procure—to obtain or acquire.

produce—fruits and vegetables; to make or manufacture.

producer—manufacturer of a product or deliverer of a service; in film, source of funding for a project; in agriculture, farmer.

product—good or service offered for sale to the public; result of a process.

product deficiency—failure to meet product quality goals.

product design—deciding what a product will be like.

product driven—refers to a company that makes decisions based on the products it has on the market or those it is developing (which is not the same thing as basing those decisions on the needs of its customers).

product liability—legal responsibility to compensate customers for losses or injuries sustained through the use of a product.

product life cycle—stages a product goes through from development until discontinuation, typically introduction, growth, maturity, and decline.

product management—style of management in which individual managers make all major marketing and sales decisions regarding a product or product line.

product mix—variety of different products carried by a distributor or retailer.

product performance—how well a product sells in the marketplace; how well a product meets the needs of end users.

product quality—stated goals for variation within a single product.

product rejuvenation—creating a large surge in sales of a product in its existing market by changing a minor characteristic or by advertising it intensely.

product stretching—selling a product to markets in which it is not a perfect fit by changing minor attributes of it or by advertising it differently.

production—sequence of activities that creates or adds value to goods and services; total output; public presentation.

production cycle—repeated activities performed to create or add value to a product.

productive—useful; valuable; capable of creating or producing.

productivity—measure of process efficiency (divide output by input); measure of individual employee's work (divide output by hours worked).

profession—what you do for a living (technically, an occupation that requires advanced education and ethical behavior); entire field of activity, such as the legal profession.

professional—highly competent; acting according to the standards of a profession; someone working in a profession.

proficiency test—job screening technique in which candidates perform the job or a simulation of it for a few minutes to provide an indication of their ability to master its needs.

profit—gain from a commercial activity (subtract total cost from total revenue).

profit and loss statement (P&L)—description of a company's income and expenses during a set period of time, with the "bottom line" being either a profit or a loss; also called "operating statement" or "income statement."

profit center—part of a company that is expected to turn a profit from its operations by charging internal and/or external customers for its products or services.

profit sharing—common benefit in which the company puts a portion of its year-end profits into a fund for employees to be invested in securities or other savings plans or paid out as a cash bonus.

profit squeeze—narrowing profit margin due to increased costs, price reductions, or both.

profit taking—cashing in short-term securities or commodities because of large price increases (if enough people do this, it usually pushes down prices).

profligate—wasteful.

program—planned event or series of actions; set of instructions for a computer or electronic device; written materials that tell what will be happening during an event; to create a program.

programmed instruction—self-study system in which training or educational materials contain both the text information and the instructions that would ordinarily be provided by a teacher, allowing the student to work independently at his or her own pace.

programmed trading—computer-driven system for trading large numbers of securities, options, or futures based on real-time calculations of favorable and unfavorable conditions for stocks in a program or index, typically by large institutional investors.

programmer—person who writes the code that makes a computer do what you want it to; usually receives direction from a systems analyst but does not formally work for the systems analyst.

programming language—computer languages used only for the purposes of programming computers.

progressive—advancing, increasing, or moving ahead step by step; in politics, someone who generally favors reform.

progressive payment—billing a project in stages rather than entirely in advance or on completion to provide more stable cash flow.

progressive taxation—system in which the tax rate rises

with income, so the wealthy pay proportionately more than the less well off.

project—defined endeavor that has a specific ending or goal; to predict something by using current data and trends as a starting point; to cast an image on a distinct surface.

project team—people working on a project.

prolific—highly productive.

proliferation—rapid increase or reproduction.

prolix—wordy, obscure, pointlessly complex, and difficult to understand, such as prolix prose in a corporate document.

promissory note—written promise to pay a specified sum of money on a specified date; the "note" may be negotiable as a security.

promote—to advance a rank; to advocate; to popularize.

promoter—advocate; someone who brings people together in a new venture; source of financing for a venture.

promotion—moving to a job with more power and/or money; event designed to attract consumers' interest in the company or its products and services.

promotion mix—levels of advertising, sales activities, publicity, and promotional activities used to promote a product.

promotional allowance—cash or goods given to retailers by wholesalers and manufacturers for conducting or participating in promotional activities.

prompt—reminder to proceed to the next step in a sequence; on time; to remind.

proof—data or other information that substantiates a claim; checking copy of something about to be printed; alcoholic content of a beverage, expressed as a percentage of volume; to proofread.

proofreader's marks—symbols used to indicate changes that should be made in a document before finalizing and distributing it.

property—something of value owned or possessed; real estate holding; attribute or characteristic.

property tax—local levy based on the assessed value of property owned.

proprietary—belonging to a company or person, such as a patent; information regarding competitive advantages or of a sensitive nature.

proprietary interest—ownership.

proprietor—owner.

pro rata—proportionately (Latin for *according to the share*).

prorate—to allocate based on shares or proportions.

prospect—someone who might become a customer; possibility; someone who might become your employee or ally; to look for new customers; to look for undiscovered deposits or sources of natural resources.

prospectus—document that gives pertinent facts about a business or commercial venture for those considering buying its shares or securities.

prosperity—sense or state of financial well-being.

prosumer—futurist Alvin Toffler's term for a well-informed customer who expects a beneficial selling relationship, not an antagonistic situation.

protectionism—trade policies and barriers that help a country's producers by restricting or excluding foreign-based competitors.

protégé—someone who shows a great deal of talent or potential and is being mentored or sponsored by someone with more influence or experience.

protocol—formal rules for behaving in social situations; in computers, program that makes it possible for two devices to work together.

prototype—preliminary design of a product before it is manufactured in quantity.

provincialism—old fashioned ideas and/or behaviors.

proviso—caveat or provision.

proxy—someone authorized to act or speak for another; written authorization that creates that status.

proxy fight—in a disputed takeover, attempt to convince the target company's shareholders to assign their right to vote their shares in order to oust the current management and replace it with a slate that favors the acquisition.

pruning—euphemism for selectively laying off people.

psychiatrist—medical doctor (MD) who deals with the prevention and treatment of mental illness (*psychologists* are not MDs).

psychic income—nonmonetary compensation, such as the pride that comes from a job well done.

psycho—prefix that refers to things involving the mind.

psychographics—psychological characteristics of members of a demographic class or category used to try to determine how a population will act; includes activities, personality traits, values, attitudes, lifestyles, and interests.

psychological tests—tests that attempt to measure personality characteristics.

psychologist—someone involved in the scientific study of behavior, emotions, and mental processes.

psychomotor tests—tests that measure a person's strength, dexterity, and coordination.

psychotherapy—treatment by a psychologist.

psychotic—suffering from a severe mental disorder.

public—all people in a society as a group (the public is considered an external or fringe customer); government-owned; out in the open where it can be observed; someplace open to anyone, although it may be privately owned.

public carrier—business that transports goods or people for a fee and by law must offer its services to all.

public domain—something that is available to all without the restrictions of patent or copyright; land and water owned by government agencies at any level, as opposed to that owned by private individuals and organizations.

public employee—government worker.

public offering—offering of an investment to the general public, often only after being approved by a regulatory body such as the Securities and Exchange Commission.

public record—information recorded in publicly accessible places, including property records, court documents, minutes and transcripts of public meetings and the general media; not secret.

public relations (PR)—professional function involved in helping a business or individual develop and maintain a favorable relationship with various interested publics, including customers, legislators and regulatory agencies, communities where the business operates, and the public at large, typically through tactics other than paid advertising (tactics include customer newsletters, press releases, favorable newspaper and magazine articles on a company's products or services, and image-building activities that present the organization or its people in a favorable light).

public sector—government.

public service—working for the government in some capacity.

public service announcement (PSA)—free advertising message broadcast on behalf of a nonprofit organization or activities undertaken in the public interest.

public utility—privately owned company that provides service to the public in areas such as electricity, water, gas, and telecommunications.

public works—projects that benefit the public undertaken by government and paid for from tax revenues and other public sources, such as highways, dams, and government buildings.

publicity—information that attracts public notice to a person, product, company, or event.

publicly held—owned by members of the public as stockholders.

puff piece—written, audio, or video report with very little real content that tries to make you think better of something.

puffing—falsely inflating or misrepresenting the value or merits of something.

pull—amount of influence a person has in a given situation; attraction; what you shouldn't do to a door marked "push."

pull strings—to use influence with a person to get something that you normally wouldn't, often for another person.

pullthrough—ability of a product or service to create enough demand that consumers ask suppliers for it.

pulsing—doing frequent, small-scale, spot surveys of a market.

pump priming—government action to stimulate the economy, such as temporarily increasing spending or reducing taxes.

punch in/out—to begin or end work; derived from the blue collar practice of punching a timecard when entering and leaving the work area.

punitive damages—money awarded a plaintiff in a court case above and beyond the actual damages caused to punish the defendant for the action.

purchase cycle—repeated activities a consumer goes through when purchasing the same product again.

purchase order (PO)—document that confirms a company's desire to buy something from a vendor at a given price.

purchase price—amount actually paid.

purge—to eliminate; in direct mail, to drop names of those who have not done business with the company in a certain time span or no longer meet target criteria.

purvey—to furnish or provide.

purview—scope; range of competence or control.

push marketing—using the sales force to persuade wholesalers to stock the product, who then in turn persuade distributors, who then persuade retailers, who then persuade the consumer.

push money—commissions and incentives on retail sales paid by manufacturers to retail salespeople (as a reward for pushing the product).

put—contract that grants the right to sell a specific number of shares at a specific price by a certain date; opposite of "call."

pyramid—using money from one investment to finance purchases of additional investments; business scam in which the goal is to sell only the franchise, not the product.

Q

Q rating—measure of a celebrity's public name recognition, used by the television and advertising industries to determine who's hot and who's not.

Q.E.D. (*quod erat demonstrandum*)—Latin for *which was to be demonstrated;* used to highlight a conclusion based on facts presented.

Q1-2-3-4—describing the first, second, third, and fourth quarters of the annual business cycle.

qualified—in personnel, capable of doing a job; in an opinion, limited in certain regards; in testing, person or sample that has met or exceeded limits or targets.

qualified lead—someone who has expressed an interest in a product or service and meets general buying criteria.

qualified opinion—in accounting, opinion of an auditor that a financial statement is subject to limitations in the audit process or contingencies that may affect its accuracy or completeness, such as a pending lawsuit whose outcome or consequences for the company cannot be predicted.

qualify—to prove yourself suitable for a task or position, or to be judged so by an employer or potential employer; to certify based on testing; to limit or hedge.

qualitative research—investigations of quality rather than quantity, which may be far less precise in methodology but may yield far greater insight into customer behavior and other concerns (typical tactics include focus groups, live interviews, tests, and observations); opposite of "quantitative research."

quality—conformance to customer standards; fitness for use; level compared to excellence; attribute or characteristic.

quality assurance (QA)—process of inspecting goods for their adherence to standards, traditionally done after production (which can be wasteful or even unreliable if the inspectors don't know what to look for), but increasingly being incorporated into the production process itself and made the responsibility of the workers directly involved.

quality audit—examination of how well quality standards are being met.

quality circle (QC)—usually six to eight employees who volunteer to meet regularly to identify and resolve quality issues in work areas under their control; also called "quality control circle."

quality control—process of inspecting and measuring process performance, comparing it with standards, and taking action to eliminate problems.

quality costs—costs that would disappear if products and processes were perfect.

quality council—group of top managers, sometimes also including line-level employees, who work together to oversee a company's quality efforts.

quality culture—company where all employees, especially top management, are attuned to continuous improvement.

quality engineering—devising ways to continuously improve the quality of products and services.

quality function deployment (QFD)—systematic integration of what the customer wants into the design, production, marketing, and delivery of a product or service (in simplistic terms, if it doesn't add value for the customer, don't do it).

quality goal—specified target defining allowable variation in product quality.

quality house—matrix that provides a graphic representation of the elements and interrelationships in an organization's quality efforts (it tends to resemble a house, and is often deliberately made to look that way); also called "house of quality."

quality movement—catchall term for the many activities surrounding continuous improvement, inspired in large part by the competitive success attributed to Japanese quality efforts.

quality of working life (QWL)—efforts taken by a business to improve the quality of both products and services and the jobs through which they are produced, typically including efforts in such areas as job enrichment, job enlargement, participative management, and greater integration of all employees into the culture and activities of the company.

quality plan—strategies for maintaining and improving product quality once goals have been established.

quality planning—discovering quality problems, setting goals, and designing processes to meet the goals.

quality planning road map—Joseph Juran's universal series of interrelated input-output steps that make up the quality planning effort: (1) establish quality goals; (2) identify customers; (3) determine customers' needs; (4) develop product features; (5) develop process features; (6) establish process controls and transfer to operations.

quality supplier—business-to-business supplier that meets specific tests for product or service quality; supplier that practices continuous quality improvement; also called "quality vendor."

quandary—confusion or uncertainty, such as not knowing which of several alternatives to choose.

quantitative analysis—research or analysis that deals with measurable elements and mathematical relationships; the opposite of "qualitative analysis."

quantity—measurement of numbers or volume.

quantity discount—discount to distributors, wholesalers, retailers, or customers who buy large amounts.

quantum—having to do with energy.

quarter—one-fourth of a whole; applied to a year, basic reporting period for corporate results; twenty-five cents; to cut into four pieces.

quarterly report—official financial report of an organization's operating results for the past three months; also called simply a "quarterly."

quasi—prefix meaning "somewhat."

query—inquiry; letter that offers a service or asks for information; in a document, notation questioning the accuracy or relevance of specific information.

questionnaire—list of questions used in surveys and other forms of data gathering.

queue—line where something or someone is waiting.

queue management—management of waiting, such as the determination of how long a wait customers will tolerate versus how many checkout lines a business can staff without wasting resources when those lines are not needed; also applies to products at various stages of assembly.

quibble—minor objection; to disagree over minor issues; to nitpick.

quick ratio—measure of a company's liquidity without consideration of products in inventory (divide the total of cash, marketable securities, and accounts receivable by current liabilities); also called "acid-test ratio" or "quick asset ratio."

quid pro quo—Latin meaning "something for something"; an exchange of value or actions (what you will do for someone else if they do something for you).

quintessential—purest or highest example of something.

quit—to stop voluntarily or suddenly; to leave a job, whether temporarily or for good; to give up.

quorum—in parliamentary procedure or organizational charters, the minimum number of a group's membership that must be present before official business can be conducted (usually one more than half but sometimes as many as two-thirds, in the case of an executive committee, for example).

quota—an allotted amount; in international trade, the maximum amount of a product that can be imported or exported; production target for a given time period; something that always seems 10% off.

quote—price; what someone else said; to offer a price; to repeat with attribution.

quotation—record of the bid and ask prices for a stock at a given moment.

QWERTY—typical keyboard configuration, named for the first six letters at the top left of the layout.

R

®—symbol for a registered trademark.

race norming—tests and formulas used to match a group's composition with the statistical representation of races in the general population.

racial discrimination—treating people differently because of their race.

racial quota—hiring or promoting a specific number or percentage of people based on race to meet affirmative action or other guidelines.

rack—shelf system on which to display or store things.

rack jobber—full-service practice in which a wholesaler stocks and maintains a product display for a retailer.

rack rate—published hotel rates for transient guests; price for something without improvements, or "straight off the rack."

racket—business that profits from fraud or extortion; illegal activity; what you hit a tennis ball or racquetball with; noise.

racketeering—repeated pattern of criminal activity.

rag—cloth used for cleaning; flag; to abuse or bully verbally; to complain.

rag trade—garment business.

raider—someone attempting to gain a controlling interest in a company against the wishes of its management by purchasing its stock, either to realize a quick financial gain from forcing the company to buy it back ("greenmail") or by actually taking control and running or selling the business for personal gain.

raincheck—commitment by a seller to give you an unavailable item at the advertised price when it is again in stock.

rainmaker—someone whose primary role is to bring in new business or financial support; by extension, someone who can make things happen.

raise—increase in pay; to erect something ("raze" means to tear it down); in agribusiness, to grow or breed.

rally—period of improvement following a decline; meeting designed to encourage and motivate; to gather or encourage; to recover strength.

ramp up—to increase from initial sample quantities to full-scale production.

random sample—research technique in which everyone in a given population has an equal chance of being chosen.

range—variation over time or distance; area of activity; distance something can travel before stopping; in mathematics, span between the lowest and highest value; to travel or wander.

rank—rating or grade; foul; to categorize by importance or other criteria; to outrank.

rank and file—members of a union; sometimes applies to blue-collar workers as a group.

rape—to take advantage of by force; to use something without regard for it or the consequences to others, such as dumping toxic chemicals on land.

rapport—mutual understanding or trust.

ratchet—device with geared teeth that is capable of movement in one direction only; to turn up or down another notch.

rate—measurement of flow or progress against a norm; percentage of a total charged or received, such as an interest rate; to rank or judge; to deserve.

rate card—published costs of advertising in a publication, including mechanical requirements for standard ad sizes.

rate of return—amount realized on an investment, expressed as a percentage of what was paid for it (divide dividends and appreciation by purchase price).

ratify—to approve or confirm something, such as a contract agreement, in order to give it legal force.

rating—rank or place on a scale of value; product of ranking systems; in securities, evaluations of risks provided by third-party services; in insurance, calculation of premium rates based on actuarial tables and other factors; in television, number of viewers estimated to watch a program.

ration—to control the supply of something for which demand significantly exceeds supply.

rationale—basic reason or explanation for something.

rationalize—to find a reason, factual or not, to explain a course of action you've already taken or wish to take.

raw data—data that has not yet been organized or analyzed.

raw material—anything used in the manufacture of a finished good.

read—what most people don't like to do anymore; to scan for understanding; to study written material; to check the measurement on a gauge or display.

reader—electronic system that takes in and keeps track of information, such as an optical character reader; someone who reads; collection of articles on a subject.

ready-fire-aim—taking action before thinking through what you are supposed to accomplish.

Reaganomics—free market theories and practices adhered to or promoted during the presidency of Ronald Reagan (1980–87).

real estate—land and the buildings on it.

real estate investment trust (REIT)—investment company that pays dividends to shareholders based on profits generated from property it buys and sells, operates, and/or holds mortgages on.

real income—purchasing power after adjusting for inflation and other factors.

real needs—fundamental customer needs that motivate action.

real time—computerese for *right now*; calculations that are immediately updated as new data is received.

reality—what perception defines.

reality check—putting aside personal beliefs, preconceptions and the conventional wisdom of others to assess what's really going on; slang for telling someone, including yourself, that their beliefs are out of touch with the real world.

realize—to obtain from a transaction; to be aware of and understand.

realty—involving real estate; anyone licensed to represent property owners in a real estate transaction and who belongs to the National Association of Realtors is a "realtor."

ream—package of five hundred sheets of paper; to criticize abusively.

reasonable person—in law, inexact standard based on the actions a typical person, as defined by psychologists, would take in a given circumstance, as compared to the actions taken by a plaintiff or defendant.

reasoning error—error in logic.

rebate—refund or deduction based on a purchase or tax, sometimes requiring submission of a form.

rebound—to bounce back from adversity, such as declining sales or profits, or being fired.

recall—memory; order that goods be returned to the producer or authorized agent for repair of a potential defect or replacement of defective parts.

receipt—document proving that you've paid for something; act of receiving.

receivables—money owed to the business by customers for products sold or services rendered.

receiver—recipient; in law, nonowner placed in control of a business during the form of bankruptcy called "receivership" to protect its assets, creditors, customers, and employees and manage affairs pending disposition by the court.

recession—economic downturn, usually continuing for at least two quarters; connotes a mild depression.

reciprocal—characterized by an exchange of equivalent or similar value.

reciprocity—relationship in which the parties agree to grant each other the same conditions and courtesies; business relationship in which two businesses agree to buy from each other.

reckoning—to perform simple mathematical functions without a computer; to settle an account; to estimate.

recognize—to give public credit for achievement or success, usually separate from tangible rewards; to identify something that you've seen before; to officially take notice of, such as recognizing a speaker or the new government of a nation; in labor relations, to accept a union as exclusive bargaining agent for all or part of the workforce.

reconcile—to balance a company's accounts; to bring two hostile or disputing parties to a state of agreement and harmony.

recondition—to repair to usable form or original specifications.

record—written evidence or information on an event or transaction; file; to write down; to register legally.

records management—systematic keeping of standardized business records, including collection, storage, security, and eventually destruction when no longer needed.

recoup—to recover completely.

recourse—source of aid or assistance.

recovery—upswing that follows a recession or depression; process of regaining the customer's trust after a mistake has been made; salvage of something lost.

recruit—someone recruited, generally connoting lack of experience or savvy; to seek qualified job candidates or project participants rather than wait for them to come to you.

recycle—to reuse something in whole or in part rather than dispose of it; to get something useful from waste or garbage.

red flag—sign that something is wrong.

red herring—something that distracts attention from the real issue (ironically, red herring was once used to train hunting dogs to follow a scent); in investing, preliminary prospectus, signified by red type on the cover noting that it cannot be sold pending approval by the Securities and Exchange Commission.

red ink—euphemism for financial losses (from the system of recording deposits in black ink, debits in red).

red tape—maze of time-consuming forms and procedures, often imposed by outside bureaucracies, that must be followed in doing something (in the past, public documents were sometimes fastened together with red tape).

redeem—to turn in for cash or merchandise; to regain title by paying off a debt or note; to recover or save.

redeploy—to rearrange or move people or assets.

redevelop—in urban renewal, to remove existing buildings, usually old or in poor condition, and build something new.

redeye—airline flight that leaves very late at night and arrives early in the morning, usually before 6:00 A.M.; whiskey.

redline—in finance, illegal practice of restricting or denying mortgages based on racial and ethnic factors (suggests red lines drawn around certain neighborhoods on a map).

reference—collection of background information; someone who will vouch for the quality of your work on a previous job, or the letter of recommendation they provide; to refer to; to use someone else's work as background for a speech or written document.

referral—directing someone to a business or professional on the basis of your satisfaction with them as a customer.

refinance—to renegotiate an existing debt.

refund—to give money back to a customer due to dissatisfaction; in finance, to issue new securities and use the money received to buy back ("retire") old ones.

refurbish—to clean up or renovate.

regent—member of the governing board of an educational institution; someone who governs in the absence of the proper authority.

region—generally well-defined area, such as a distinct part of the country.

regional mall—large, usually indoor shopping center, typically with at least one hundred stores anchored by several large department stores.

regional office—center of operations within a specific region, either autonomous or closely linked with the company's main office.

register—formal record of events or transactions, such as a check register; the device where sales are rung up and cash, checks and credit card receipts collected during the business day; in printing, to align the negatives in a piece of more than one color; to sign up or make a record of; to show.

registered check—check issued by a bank and paid for in advance by the customer, much like a money order.

registered company—company that has filed a registration statement with the Securities and Exchange Commission prior to releasing a new issue of securities to the public.

registered representative (RR)—someone who works for a brokerage firm licensed by the Securities and Exchange Commission and the New York Stock Exchange to act as an account executive for clients in the trading of securities.

registration—in securities, process of reviewing new issues that are to be sold to the public, conducted by the Securities and Exchange Commission; in a hotel, where arriving guests arrange for accommodations; documentation of a vehicle's ownership and current licensing; process of signing up for something, such as college classes.

regression analysis—method of finding the interrelationship between a dependent variable and one or more independent variables to determine how good a predictor the independent variable is.

regressive taxation—rate of taxation that remains the same no matter what amounts are involved, thereby taking a larger proportion of money from lower-income people than from higher-income people.

regulated industry—industry that operates under government regulations to a significant degree.

regulatory agency—government organization specifically charged with overseeing an industry or commercial activity.

rehab(ilitation)—restoration; treatment for substance abuse and other physical or emotional conditions.

rehearsal—practice before an actual event; in manufacturing, trial run.

reinforcement—psychological theory that people repeat actions that are rewarded and discontinue actions that are ignored.

reinstate—to restore to a previously held position; in insurance, to restore coverage that has lapsed due to nonpayment of premiums.

reinsurance—practice through which one insurance company assumes a percentage of the risk in another company's policies for a percentage of the premium, providing greater stability and insulating any one company against a major loss (in other words, insurance for insurance companies).

reinvest—to use money from an investment to buy more of it.

relative risk—risk of doing something as compared to possible gain.

release—written notification that a debt has been paid or an obligation met; permission to use something, such as your photo in a publication; information provided to the media; to turn loose; to relinquish a claim on.

reliable—person or product that can be counted on; financial records deemed accurate and properly prepared.

reliability engineering—engineering that tries to make a product work as well and as long as possible.

relocation—moving to a new location for business reasons, whether an individual employee or an entire business unit is being transferred.

remedial education—math, English, and other courses taught to bring employees up to minimum standards they should have achieved while in high school (and sometimes grade school).

remedial journey—portion of quality management that begins when the causes of problems are known and ends when processes are in place to solve the problems.

remit—to send payment.

remnant space—in advertising, space left over, because of odd-size ads or stories, ad cancellations, or other circumstances, that is made available to advertisers at reduced rates; in commercial real estate, odd-size areas too small to be desirable to larger tenants leased to smaller firms at reduced rates or on a short-term basis.

remote worksite—field location; temporary or part-time location away from the main office, often in the employee's home.

remuneration—total compensation package, including pay and benefits.

renegotiate—to change the terms of an existing contract.

renewable resource—natural resource that will replenish itself over time, such as trees.

rent—to pay to obtain temporary use of, but not title to, something.

rent to own—conditions under which something rented can be purchased, such as through repeated rentals or long-term rental.

reorganize—to change or rearrange, such as files in a storage system or managers in a department; to restructure debt and operations, usually under the provisions of Chapter 11 of the 1978 Bankruptcy Act, to keep the business operating while unable to settle all of its debts.

rep—representative; repetition of a skill being practiced; to represent; to sell.

repatriate—to bring or send something, such as money or an individual, back from a foreign country to the original country.

repeat business—customers who come back again.

repossess—to legally take something back from a customer who has not made timely payments on it.

repudiate—to refuse to acknowledge or to reject validity or obligation.

repurchase agreement—agreement by the seller to buy back, under certain circumstances and conditions, what it is selling to the buyer.

request for proposals (RFP)—solicitation of bids and plans by a company, government agency, or research institution that wants to evaluate a number of alternatives before awarding a contract or choosing a new vendor.

requisition—written request for something needed; to take something needed by force.

rescind—to take back or repeal.

rescission—to cancel a contract by mutual consent or court order.

research and development (R&D)—process of discovering or creating new products and services and putting them into production.

reseller—company that buys goods or services from an originator and resells them essentially unchanged to a customer (for example, car dealers buy from the manufacturer and sell to consumers).

reservation—advance order, usually not accompanied by payment; doubt or misgiving; area set aside for certain uses.

reserve—funds set aside for required safeguards, possible emergencies, or capitalization needs.

resolution—statement of belief or intent; sharpness of a visual image.

Resolution Trust Corp.—federal agency established to preside over the liquidation of failed savings and loan associations.

resource—asset available to the business, whether concrete (cash, equipment) or intangible (time, intelligence); source of supply or information.

response—answer; level of reaction to an action, such as a survey or advertisement.

responsibility matrix—chart listing decisions and actions necessary to successfully complete a process, as well as which person holds each role in the process.

restitution—compensation for loss or injury; restoring something to its rightful owner.

restraining order—legal order prohibiting an action, either prior to or because of a court hearing or decision on the matter.

restraint of trade—illegal business activities that interfere with free competition.

restricted stock plan—plan that gives or lets employees purchase stock that must be forfeited under certain conditions, such as leaving the company within a short time.

restructure—in bankruptcy law, to reorganize operations

and debt payments to allow an indebted company to meet its obligations and stay in business; in general, to make an organization more competitive and efficient by focusing on operational strengths and eliminating or selling off weaknesses.

résumé—list of qualifications a person has, usually including work experience, education, and volunteer activities.

retail—selling items to an end user.

retail mix—selection of goods, support services, marketing tactics, and physical amenities employed by a retailer.

retail outlet—store.

retain—to keep; to contract for the services of a professional, such as a lawyer.

retained earnings—profits remaining after dividends have been paid, usually reinvested or kept in the business.

retainer—partial fee paid in advance to a professional or firm based on services to be rendered.

retention—keeping; ability to remember; percentage of customers who come back to do business with a company.

retire—to stop working, ideally to do something you consider more fun; to withdraw; to remove a product from the market and replace it with a newer version.

retirement income—money received after someone stops working, including disbursements from pensions and personal savings as well as Social Security.

retrain—to teach workers new skills or prepare them for new jobs because what they have been doing is being eliminated; to train people again because they didn't master the skill or knowledge the first time.

retreat—to back off or withdraw; to leave a market in which competition has become too intense; to let superiors or co-workers have their way when you disagree.

retro—prefix meaning "backward" or "after the fact."

retroactive—policy, contract, or formal agreement that covers a period prior to when it was enacted.

retrospective analysis—analyzing data from past experiences (an impressive way to say "hindsight").

return—profit from an investment; products that are brought back to where they were bought for refund or exchange; tax form; response to a direct mail program; to come back.

return on equity (ROE)—measure of value created for stockholders (divide net income excluding dividends to preferred shareholders by total equity held by common stockholders).

return on investment (ROI)—measure of capital effectiveness based on net gain over a specific period of time (divide after-tax profits by capital employed).

return on sales—measure of capital effectiveness preferred by Japanese businesses (divide profit by total sales).

return policy—guidelines under which a company will refund or exchange a product.

revalue—to purposely change something's value; in monetary policy, to raise the value of the country's currency in relation to others (or a gold standard, where still in effect); opposite of "devalue."

revenue—income or yield.

revenue bond—municipal bond that will be paid off with revenues from what it is used for rather than general tax revenues, such as an issue that funds building a toll road, sports arena, or other public facility.

revenue stream—amount of money coming in from a source.

reverse—dramatic change in direction; setback; in printing, to put white lettering on a dark background instead of dark on light; to change direction 180 degrees.

reverse discrimination—preferential treatment of an individual or group (most commonly racial minorities, women, the elderly, or the handicapped) to compensate for past discrimination against them.

reverse leverage—when the financial advantages of owning something are less than the interest being paid on the money borrowed to buy it.

reverse R&D—finding that consumers are using a product for a purpose other than that which the company envisioned and redesigning the product to fit the new needs better.

reverse split—reducing a company's total shares of stock without reducing the total value of the shares, for example by exchanging one new share for two old ones, with the new share having the same value as the two original shares; opposite of "stock split."

revert—to return to a previous condition or owner.

review—test or inspection; in accounting, brief examination of financial records that does not involve a full audit; journal that covers a profession or specialized field of study; to inspect or evaluate critically; to reconsider; to give an evaluation in writing or verbally; to study material previously covered.

revoke—to cancel or annul.

revolution—complete or major change; one complete turn around an axis (RPM is a measure of revolutions per minute).

revolution of rising expectations—futurist Harlan Cleveland's observation in the 1950s that manufacturing growth and newfound prosperity were causing consumers to expect constant improvement in the products they purchased and the lifestyle those products contributed to; applies to any area where improvement creates an expectation of further improvement.

revolving charge account—line of credit, such as a credit card, the balance on which does not have to be paid in full before further borrowing.

revolving fund—account or budget in which expenditures are constantly replaced.

277

rewards—cash or items of monetary value given to an employee for good job performance.

RGB (red, green, blue)—single-color "guns" that make up a television picture.

riceburner—pejorative term for an imported product made in Japan or the Far East, such as a motorcycle.

rider—limiting clause added to a contract; in insurance, modification to a standard policy that adds or reduces a specific type of coverage; in legislation, unrelated amendment added to a bill; someone who rides.

rifle shot—precisely on target, as opposed to "shotgun," in which you hit a wider target area, but without very much force.

right—legal or moral authorization; correct or proper; in politics, conservative; to bring back to an upright position (such as a boat); to redress.

right-hand (anything)—refers to a trusted associate or ally (in olden days, the person to your immediate right could obstruct your sword arm, so it helped if you could trust him).

right to work—state law that prohibits employees being required to join a union as a condition of retaining employment.

rightsizing—euphemism for laying people off.

ring out—to clear a cash register drawer from the system prior to removing it and counting its contents.

ring up—to make a sale.

ringer—someone who is not what he or she purports to be, usually to obtain some kind of shady competitive advantage, such as a professional brought in to compete with amateurs or an expert on a panel of generalists.

risk—prospect of harm or loss; measurable odds; in insurance, the party to be covered; to venture.

risk averse—seeking to avoid risk as much as possible.

risk management—practice of prioritizing and handling

risks by identifying potential sources, estimating their potential impact, and acting to control them.

rising star—employee who has won the favor of top management and is being quickly promoted; someone or something on the way up.

Robert's Rules of Order—handbook outlining the generally accepted rules for running official meetings.

robotics—using programmable machines to do work that formerly was done by people, especially manual work.

robust—fully developed and healthy; a robust design includes tolerances for unavoidable production variables to provide more consistent quality (or a "healthier" product).

roleplay—training technique in which participants act out potential situations to learn firsthand how to handle them.

rollout—initial large-scale introduction of a new product.

rollover—to renew automatically; to replace one debt with a new one; to put certain types of savings, such as retirement accounts, into a new account without officially withdrawing for use so that no penalties or taxes must be paid.

Rolodex—popular brand of card file in which you keep the names, numbers, addresses, and other pertinent information of your business contacts.

Rotary—nonprofit membership organization of businesspeople who meet to network and discuss community and business issues.

rotating shift—working different shifts in a scheduled rotation, such as going from day to swing shift, then swing to graveyard, then back to days.

rotogravure—process of printing where rollers are etched with the information to be printed and rolled across the paper.

round—circular; to change a number to the next higher or lower level ("rounding off" cents to the next dollars, dollars to the next 10 or 100, etc.); period in a fight; a single bullet.

round file—wastebasket.

round lot—in securities, generally accepted unit for trading on a stock exchange; even amount, such as a dozen, a hundred, or a gross.

rout—to defeat in a demoralizing fashion.

route—path that something takes; road or highway; to pass something along to others; to determine a path or progression, such as routing a shipment.

route sheet—list of who should see a document or publication, usually attached to the item so recipients can initial or cross off their names after seeing it.

royalty—share of proceeds from sale given to the owner of something by the company authorized to sell it; derogatory term for top management or someone prone to expect deferential treatment.

rubberstamp—to approve something without examining it closely.

ruble—basic unit of the Russian currency system.

rule—official corporate guideline, policy, or procedure; something that can take precedence over common sense; to decide; to exercise authority over.

ruminate—to think about something deeply for a long time.

rumor—unsubstantiated information of unknown origin; basic form of communication in the workplace.

run—sudden high demand for a specific product or service, such as withdrawals from a bank or sales of a product; batch of product; hole or snag in pantyhose that causes the fabric to split or unravel; to make; to move rapidly; to operate; in computers, to use a computer program.

run of paper (ROP)—press run for a publication or advertisement in a publication; many publications allow advertisers to run in selected editions, so the ROP for an ad often is different from that for the publication as a whole.

run of schedule (ROS)—radio or television advertising that is run whenever the station's schedule allows, usually priced lower than specific time slots.

run the numbers—to analyze financial data prior to taking action, such as determining how much a customer has spent with you in order to bill the account or how much it cost to produce a given product or project to judge whether the operation is cost-effective.

rundown—summary report; in a poor state of repair; to outline options or results.

run(ning) control—checking the operation periodically to make sure it is within tolerances so you can shut it down as soon as quality problems arise.

rural—outside urban areas; rustic.

rurban—areas surrounding urban areas that are earmarked for urban development.

rust belt—industrialized area of the midwestern United States that fell on hard times as plants aged and more efficient and aggressive competitors emerged around the world.

rustout—situation in which underutilized people corrode on the job and lose their motivation and effectiveness, often misdiagnosed as burnout.

S

S corporation—company with fewer than thirty-six stockholders that is not subject to double taxation as other corporations because it meets the requirements of subchapter S of the corporate tax code; stockholders are protected from liability and report capital gains on their personal income taxes.

sabbatical—leave of absence to pursue a personal project, such as an advanced degree, with the job guaranteed upon return (comes from the ancient Judean custom of leaving the land unplanted every seventh year).

sabotage—deliberate destruction of or interference with an activity, usually conducted clandestinely.

sacred cow—something untouchable or unquestionable; project, product or person that continues because a top manager likes it, even though most people feel it is no longer viable.

safe—locked box for storing valuables; lacking risk or danger.

safety margin—amount that something can deviate or deteriorate before loss or injury; sales in excess of the break-even point.

salable—sellable.

salability—relative ease with which something can be sold.

salary—fixed gross amount of money someone makes in a given time period.

salary survey—survey of people in a given profession done to gain perspective on how different organizations pay people for the same basic services.

sale—exchange of goods or services for money; period when products are sold for less than their regular retail price; formal agreement to purchase a product at a mutually agreeable price.

sales—total products or services sold.

sales analyst—someone who tracks and analyzes sales patterns for accuracy and insight into what can be done to improve them.

sales and marketing (S&M)—activities undertaken to get the customer to buy something; department or departments charged with presenting products and services to customers, including functions such as advertising, public relations, promotions, and direct and indirect sales activities.

sales budget—expected sales in a given time period.

sales charge—fee assessed on a sale, generally as a percentage of the purchase price.

sales-driven—refers to company or function whose highest priority is selling products or services.

sales literature—brochures, pamphlets, and other materials (including videotapes) that provide information on a product or service to customers deciding whether to buy it.

sales meeting—gathering of a company's sales and marketing staff, often annually or quarterly, to discuss past efforts and current plans, introduce new products or strategies, and award past efforts.

sales pitch—prepared presentation that a sales representative gives to a prospective customer.

sales plan—strategies that will be used to try to achieve sales goals for a given time period.

sales promotion—event designed to stimulate sales through reduced product prices, bulk purchase discounts, gifts with purchases, or other tactics.

sales quota—amount of sales needed to reach the company's target (reaching or exceeding it may trigger additional compensation in the form of bonuses and incentives; failing to meet it may have adverse consequences, such as demotion or termination).

sales response curve—graphic representation of the amount of a product's or service's sales at different prices.

sales tax—tax assessed as a percentage of the selling price and collected by the seller.

sales force—everyone who sells.

Sallie Mae (Student Loan Marketing Association [SLMA])—publicly traded government corporation whose stock is based on student loans purchased from the original lenders.

salvage—value derived from something lost, discarded, or destroyed; to save.

sampling—research technique that involves choosing a small group of products or customers as representative of the whole when trying to determine factors such as customer likes and dislikes or product quality.

sampling error—extent to which a small group does not represent the whole, and thus may result in inaccurate information or conclusions.

Santayana review—using data from repetitive cycles of an activity to draw conclusions about the current or future state.

satellite communication—using a satellite to relay voice, audio, or written communications, increasingly common in broadcasting and for such functions as telecommunications.

satellite operation—small work unit of a business that is geographically removed from a larger unit, such as a division or corporate headquarters.

satisfaction—pleasure derived from something that meets needs and expectations; compensation for an injury or loss; payment of a debt or obligation; from a customer standpoint, goal of a product or service.

saturation—filled to capacity; in a business, point above which supply exceeds demand.

savings and loan association (S&L)—financial institution formed by investors primarily to offer home loans and savings accounts to individuals of moderate means; deposits are insured by the Federal Savings and Loan Insurance Corporation (FSLIC).

savings bond—U.S. government security sold for half the face amount and guaranteed to be worth the face amount no later than a specified maturity date.

savings rate—rate at which the citizens of a country, or a large subgroup of a people as a whole, save, expressed as a percentage of income.

scab—pejorative term used by union members for those who cross a picket line to work during a strike.

scale—system of measurement; relationship between a model or drawing and the real piece; wages for specific work, especially when referring to unionized jobs; to adjust by proportion; to climb.

scalp—to buy something in great demand but limited supply, such as tickets to an athletic event or a new stock issue, and resell it at a vastly higher price (generally illegal or quasi-legal at best).

Scanlon plan—1950s forerunner of quality circles devised by Joseph Scanlon that combined participative management tactics with worker incentives based on sharing the gain realized from reduced labor costs; now generally refers to a plan that gives all employees a bonus based on reduced costs or increased productivity, with or without the participative management aspect.

scanner—device that reads and transfers information to another device, such as a computer or electronic cash register; checkout system in many stores in which purchases are rung up, totals and taxes are calculated, and inventory is adjusted electronically.

scapegoat—someone who takes the blame for a failure on behalf of a group (in the Old Testament, Aaron symbolically laid the sins of the people on the head of a goat, which was then driven into the wilderness); to blame someone for a problem in which they had only a minor (or even no) part.

scarcity—in short supply.

scatter diagram—pictorial representation of the relationship between two variables made by plotting values for one variable along the horizontal axis and the other·variable along the vertical axis and placing a dot where they meet; also called "scatter plot."

schedule—printed timetable showing the steps to be accomplished and the deadlines for completion of each; list; tax form.

Schedule SE—federal tax form that must be filled out by self-employed individuals.

scientific management—Frederick Taylor's ideas on organizing work, based on determining the best way to accomplish a task, training workers to use that method, then assuring maximum cooperation between workers and management to achieve the best results (since the early 1900s, efficiency-driven disciples have pretty much ignored the part about cooperation, with dire consequences for all involved).

scoop—in news media, to break a story before a rival does.

scorched earth—destroying that which makes something attractive in order to delay or discourage an adversary (derived from the tactic of burning crops and buildings before an advancing army); in corporate finance, disposing of a company's key assets to make it less desirable for a takeover, at the risk of wrecking the business in the process.

score—to make points with someone or achieve a success or breakthrough; to do something that gains the attention of a senior manager; to mark a piece of paper so that it is easily bent or torn in the area desired.

SCORE (Service Corps of Retired Executives)—voluntary group of retired businesspeople who provide free information and advice to small businesses under the sponsorship of the U.S. Small Business Administration.

screen—something that diffuses or hides; surface onto which a visual is projected; mesh through which something is strained or passed; in printing, block of color overprinted on a page; system used to break a photographic image into a dot structure for printing; to filter, hide, or protect; to show or preview (such as a movie); to reduce to a screen.

scrip—piece of paper given in lieu of currency, often used only for a specific purpose.

script—prewritten words a person uses when making a presentation.

scut work—basic, essential, but far from glorious or respected tasks that nobody really wants to do but somebody (usually the lowest person on the totem pole) has to.

seagull management—Ken Blanchard's characterization of a style in which managers act like seagulls, swooping down, picking up a scrap of something, squawking loudly, crapping all over the people in the vicinity, then flying off; also called "hit and run management."

seal—closure or packaging device that shows that something has not been opened; to enclose within securely; to finalize a deal.

seal of approval—organization's literal and figurative stamp attesting that something has met its standards of quality or reliability.

sealed bid—awarding of business or selling something based on offers submitted in sealed envelopes and opened all at once, without an opportunity for revision.

season—time period during which there is a predictable change in business activity; to flavor with experience.

seasoned citizens—people who have done something or been somewhere for a long time, especially employees who have been with the company through several major changes.

seasonal downturn/upturn—natural, predictable change in business due to time of year, such as the resort industry seeing less business after Labor Day or toy stores ringing up most of their year's sales during the Christmas shopping period.

seat—where you sit or what you sit on; center of power; in brokerage, purchased right to conduct business at a stock exchange.

seats in seats—system of measuring attendance (and sometimes, unfortunately, attention) by physical presence, such as in a classroom.

second class—inferior to first class; discriminated against, such as second-class citizens.

second-class mail—U.S. Postal Service classification for newspapers and magazines, with postage based on the distance mailed and amount of advertising included.

second color—in printing, adding one additional color to a black-and-white piece of literature.

second mortgage—loan subordinated to and in addition to the first mortgage, usually used to fund home improvements and major purchases or to reduce the amount of cash down payment required.

second source—another supplier (many government and other large-scale contracts require a second source to provide assurance of dependable supplies and competitive prices).

secondary issue—public sale of securities held by large investors.

secondary market—buying and selling of securities after they have been issued (in essence, investors selling to other investors); market where money market securities are traded.

secondary syndrome—workplace phenomenon of seeing absolutely no faults or weaknesses in the person hired to replace a previous hire that didn't work out (because if number two doesn't work out, it looks as though the boss is the problem).

secret shopper—someone trained by the business or a third-party organization to pose as a normal shopper and evaluate the quality of service provided.

secretary—officer responsible for maintaining the official records of an organization's activities; head of a government department; clerical support person for an executive, manager, or department; person traditionally responsible for making the boss look good and keeping the place running smoothly by getting all of the scut work done and covering for mistakes.

sector—zone or region; major market category, such as the financial sector.

secular—involving the physical or temporal rather than spiritual or timeless.

secured debt—debt that is guaranteed by collateral.

securities—most commonly stocks and bonds, but technically anything that gives the holder the right to money or other assets.

Securities and Exchange Commission (SEC)—U.S. agency charged with regulating the buying and selling of securities.

security—negotiable document establishing ownership of an asset; collateral for a loan; safety.

seed money—money used to start a new business (literally the money a farmer uses to buy seed to plant a crop).

segment—part of a larger market; to divide something into major, distinct parts so that it can be more easily or effectively addressed.

segue—smooth transition, such as between slides or subject areas in a presentation; to move smoothly and without interruption from one segment to another.

selective distribution—allowing only certain wholesalers or retailers who meet specific requirements to sell a product.

self-addressed stamped envelope (SASE)—time and cost-saving courtesy that involves sending a preaddressed, postage-paid envelope for the reply to your request.

self-central—slang for having self-confidence.

self-control—personal discipline; in quality systems, worker who knows what the goal of the company is, what the goal for his or her performance is, and who has the means of changing either personal performance or the mechanics of a process.

self-directed team—team of workers that makes many of the everyday business decisions within their scope.

self-employed—those who work for themselves; may refer to a business with fewer than ten employees under the owner.

self-fulfilling prophecy—belief that leads to action, such as believing a new program will fail, leading people to give up on it prematurely, and thus making sure it fails.

self-help—activities and information designed to help people improve or control aspects of their lives, such as health and fitness.

self-inspection—situation in which the worker producing the product or service makes the decision about whether it conforms to standards, rather than rely on a separate inspector.

self insurance—putting money aside to pay for costs associated with an event that you could buy insurance for.

self-liquidating—something that pays for itself from sales and may not be replaced or repeated.

self-managed—person or business that is not overseen by someone else.

self-starter—someone who does not need external motivators or supervision to do a job.

sell—to exchange something for money; to persuade.

sell short—to sell a security you do not own in expectation of buying it back later at a lower price to make a profit; also called "short sale."

seller's market—when demand exceeds supply, allowing the seller to raise prices or negotiate more favorable terms.

semi—prefix meaning "half"; truck (also called "tractor") to which a trailer can be attached.

semiannual—twice a year.

semiconductor—material that does not conduct or insulate against heat and electricity very well; key component in computers.

seminal—acting as a source; creative or groundbreaking.

seminar—meeting conducted to give specific information or training to a small group.

senior—older; superior to; someone over the age of sixty-two.

senior discount—price inducement provided to older customers to attract their business (ostensibly because some seniors are on limited incomes, but in many cases because as a class, seniors often have high discretionary incomes and stable tastes, making them very profitable customers to serve).

seniority—rank based on the number of years an employee has worked for a company in comparison to other employees, often used to help determine promotions, first right to something, or who is laid off first.

sensitive—to be dealt with carefully; easily offended or irritated; potentially dangerous or controversial.

sensitive market—unstable product or securities market that is prone to experience dramatic shifts as a result of good or bad information.

sensitivity training—training designed to teach people, such as abrasive executives and managers, how to be nicer to and more supportive of others; mockingly called "charm school."

sensor—device that receives a signal; in total quality, anything that locates information and converts it to data, whether a mechanical device or an employee watching an operation.

separation—in personnel, euphemism for quitting or being fired; in printing, individual negatives that are combined to create a colored piece.

serviceable—usable or durable; easily serviced.

service—work with an intangible or semitangible result; action on behalf of another; repairs or maintenance; to take care of.

service bureau—organization that makes specialized services available to others for a fee.

service center—organization or place where repair services are provided.

service contract—contract under which, for a fee, products are maintained and repaired after or in addition to warranty coverage.

service department—part of the business that takes care of special customer needs, such as complaints, returns and exchanges, special orders, delivery, gift wrapping, and inquiries about proper use or care of a product.

service pin—token gift given to employees to mark so many years of service with the company.

service policy—statement of conditions under which a company will provide specific services, such as repairs or returns.

service sector—all businesses and people working in service jobs (as of 1990, this accounted for more than two-thirds of the U.S. economy).

service year—measurement used in the calculation of benefits, such as vacation time; often rounded off to the first of a month or the first day of a quarter, so it may not coincide with actual time worked.

setback—defeat or delay; in real estate, distance from the curb or lot line to a building.

settle—to finish or consummate; to pay off a debt; to reach a mutually agreeable solution to a legal dispute prior to a court decision; to agree to end a labor dispute; to distribute the assets of an estate; to establish residence or become comfortable in; to sink to the bottom.

settlement—negotiated agreement.

severance—cutting off, such as firing; severance pay is money given to an employee leaving a job beyond salary and vacation pay owed.

Sevareid's law—former journalist Eric Sevareid's observation that "the chief cause of problems is solutions."

seven quality tools—measurement and analysis techniques commonly used in continuous quality improvement: check sheets, scatter diagrams (scattergrams), histograms, run charts, control charts, cause-and-effect diagrams (also called "fishbone analysis"), and Pareto charts.

sexual harassment—uninvited sexual advances, including physical acts of a sexual nature and verbal harassment, that threaten or demean an individual at work or that can alter job status (firing or promotion, for example) depending on the victim's response.

shakedown—dry run to assess quality and spot problems before commencing normal service or production; attempt to solicit a bribe or illegal payment.

shakeout—tightening of a market that forces out the weakest or least committed competitors.

shakeup—sudden and significant change designed to redirect an organization's style of action; rapid reorganization.

share—basic unit of stock; part or allotment; interest in a business venture; to divide or distribute; to hold or experience in common.

share of voice—percentage of radio and/or television advertising given to one product as compared to the competing products.

shareholder—person who owns shares of stock in a company.

shark—aggressive competitor; someone who seeks to take over other organizations.

shark repellent—corporate activity designed to thwart an unwanted takeover.

shark watcher—firm that specializes in spotting initial evidence of takeover activity.

sharks and pilot fish—basic theory behind the layout of a regional shopping mall: large stores (sharks) leave enough behind for smaller, specialized, and noncompetitive outlets (pilot fish).

sheetfed—refers to printer that takes sheets of paper instead of a roll of paper.

shelf—place to display or store something.

shelf life—how long something can be stored before it spoils.

shelf space—amount of space in a retail store given to a specific product or group of products.

shelve—to set aside; to postpone or indefinitely defer a decision.

shift—regular hours for work, usually eight plus time for lunch and/or breaks; to transfer or move.

shift differential—extra money paid to employees who work less-desirable hours; also called "shift premium."

shift gears—to change subjects.

shiftless—lazy; unwilling to work.

shoddy—inferior; of poor quality.

shop—small business or store; work area where something is repaired; to look for what you want to buy; to evaluate purchase alternatives.

shop steward—liaison for unionized workers in an area of a business, usually elected by the workers involved.

shopping center—collection of stores with a common parking area.

short—not very tall; less than expected or required; curt or abrupt; to give customers less than they paid for.

short bond—bond with a maturity of less than one year.

short haul—transportation service for goods traveling a relatively short distance, usually no farther than can be reached in eight hours.

short term—of relatively brief duration, usually less than a year, although it depends on the long-term comparison.

short-timer—someone who will be leaving a job soon and thus has little reason to curry management's favor.

shortchange—to give people less than they should receive.

shortfall—amount by which something fails to meet a target or standard.

shorthand—system used to quickly and accurately write down what is said for later transcription; abbreviated form of something.

shotgun—to scatter broadly, as opposed to focusing on a single target.

shotgun mic(rophone)—rod-shaped directional microphone that picks up sound from a distance.

shotgun plan—plan that provides numerous options in a wide range of areas.

shoulder season—in the hotel business, time of year when business is typically slow.

show time—start of any major event, such as a speech or presentation.

showboat—to show off.

shredder—machine that destroys documents by cutting them into long, thin pieces.

shrinkage—difference between what should be in inventory and what is actually there, generally caused by theft; loss from natural causes, such as the weight lost when grain dries, or unrecorded damage.

shrinkwrap—packaging film that on application of heat shrinks to the shape of what it covers.

shutdown—work stoppage due to lack of work or raw materials, broken machinery, or union action.

shyster—con artist or dishonest businessperson.

sign—display board; something used to predict a future event; to make official by putting one's signature on.

silent partner—technically, limited partner in a general partnership; also applies to any participant in a venture who chooses to remain in the background rather than play an active or visible role.

silicon—nonmetallic element used as a surface in computer microchips.

Silicon Valley—area in northern California between San Francisco and San Jose known for state-of-the-art computer technology.

silkscreen—color printing method in which ink is forced through a fiber screen.

silver—coins as opposed to paper currency.

silver print—print taken directly from negatives or plates of a piece that is to be printed to allow a final check for errors.

simile—comparison of essentially dissimilar things using words such as *like* or *as* (a metaphor is basically the same thing without *like* or *as*).

simple interest—interest that is not compounded but paid only on the principal.

simplified employee pension (SEP) plan—pension fund to which both the employer and employee can contribute.

simulation—small-scale test of a process; using mathematical models to extrapolate future events.

simulator—device that mimics an event, often for training purposes.

sin tax—levy on products and services considered vices, such as cigarettes and alcoholic beverages.

sincere—honest and true.

single-breasted—coat whose edges overlap very little and are fastened with one row of buttons.

single-family dwelling—house.

sinking fund—money set aside on a regular basis to pay back a debt, whether by buying back debt securities or preferred stock, or accumulating the amount needed at maturity.

site—location; to choose a place for conducting an operation.

site visit—tour of a property for a specific purpose, such as planning a meeting or inspecting a manufacturing process.

situation analysis—prologue to a report or proposal that summarizes the current state of affairs.

six-sigma—statistical measure of deviation from perfection that in popular quality applications represents 3.4 defects per million; also refers to the methods used to achieve that statistical goal.

skid—pallet on which product is packed for shipment.

skill—marketable proficiency.

skill-based pay—salary determined on the degree of skill and number of skills brought to the job, not the actual job performed.

skill-intensive—refers to tasks that require a high degree of skill to perform.

skills inventory—list of the formal and informal skills and education held by all company employees.

skimming—continuously stealing a small amount of money or product.

Skinner box—B. F. Skinner's rat maze, used to demonstrate behaviorist principles, such as how sentient creatures can learn; refers to any confusing or intricate system or layout.

skunk works—small, sometimes secretive part of an organization charged with new product development free of the interfering oversight of conventional bureaucrats; also refers to risky, pet, or long-shot enterprise projects being worked on by people without their boss's knowledge or permission.

slack—slow period where demand is low; tolerance or freedom; something that can be tightened if it has to be.

slander—oral defamation of a person or company (as a simplistic rule of thumb, if it's spoken, it's slander; if it's in writing, it's libel).

slap suit—countersuit filed by a large company against parties to a lawsuit against it, a key effect of which is to inflict legal costs on people who may not be able to afford them in order to discourage them from proceeding with their original action and intimidate others from taking similar actions.

sleazy—cheap; immoral or dishonest.

sleeper—someone or something in which there is little interest, but which may well be undervalued and have great potential.

sleeping beauty—takeover target that hasn't yet been noticed.

sleeping giant—large organization capable of squashing a smaller competitor if aroused.

slowdown—in labor relations, deliberate work reduction by employees to protest some aspect of working conditions without resorting to a walkout or strike.

slump—short period of decline or subpar performance.

slush fund—secret amount of money set aside for discretionary uses, often of an illegal nature, such as political payoffs.

small business—by U.S. Commerce Department definition, a company with fewer than 100 employees; by other definitions, a business with as many as 500 employees; sector of the economy made up of small businesses, where most job growth actually happens.

Small Business Administration (SBA)—U.S. agency that offers low-interest loans and other forms of assistance to small business owners.

smoke and mirrors—illusory or not real, such as bluffing or alluding to having capabilities you don't.

smokescreen—something designed to obscure or hide.

smokestack industries—older, large-scale manufacturing businesses, so named because of the smokestacks over the factories.

smuggle—to move by stealth; to import or export without paying duties.

snowball—an effect that magnifies as it continues, like a snowball rolling down a hill.

Social Security—U.S. government assistance for the unemployed, the disabled, and the elderly, funded by taxes on workers' wages.

socialism—government control or ownership of industry; differs from communism in that the market is allowed to control prices to some extent.

sociotechnical—marriage of social and technical issues, such as the effects of computerization on society.

soft currency—unreliable or overvalued currency that cannot be exchanged for the currency of other countries.

soft goods—items made of fabric.

soft market—market with greater supply than demand.

soft money—tax deductible contribution to an investment.

soft sell—telling someone the features and benefits of a product without making an extremely strong case for the purchase of it.

softening—a market that is becoming weaker; a potential customer who is beginning to set aside objections and consider buying the product.

software—computer programs; any kind of programming played in an electronic device, such as video games, videotapes, CDs, and music tapes.

soil bank—U.S. Department of Agriculture's program to stabilize commodity prices and encourage soil conservation by paying agricultural producers to leave land fallow.

sole proprietorship—business owned by one person.

sole supplier—only source of a product or service.

solicitor—person who contacts people individually, often by phone or door to door, to try to sell something or receive donations; in British law, lawyer who does not belong to the bar and can be heard only in lower courts.

solid citizen—employee who is extremely loyal to the company, but whose performance doesn't warrant promotion; customer who pays bills well; product that has good, predictable profits.

solidarism—political-economic system in which the government provides basic social goods, such as housing and medical care, for the poor from funds raised by taxing the wealthy.

solidarity—unity of purpose; rallying cry for labor organizers in Eastern Europe, especially Poland.

solo—alone.

solvent—in finance, capable of meeting obligations; in industry, solution that can dissolve something else, typically used for cleaning.

song—company's official response to a question or criticism that comes up repeatedly.

song and dance—vigorous, ideally interesting presentation designed to be more entertaining than informative, such as a sales pitch based more on style than substance, or an attempt to avoid answering a difficult question without appearing to dodge it.

SOS—international distress signal; call for assistance; slang for "same old shit," a spoken or written notation to alert others that the information is insubstantial.

sound/slide—presentation using slides and prerecorded music or words.

source—someplace revenue comes from; supplier of something, such as goods, services, information, or employees; reference or verification point.

spaghetti—tangle of wires or cables, such as those behind a computer or under a car's dashboard.

span of control—in traditional hierarchies, number of people reporting directly to a manager (seven was considered a maximum for effectiveness); informally, amount of power an employee has in the company.

specialist—person with a great deal of training and experience in a very narrow area.

specialization—area of expertise; strategy that emphasizes specific rather than generalized skills and activities; subgroup of a major area in which an employee or business works.

specialty advertising—use of novelties and premiums, such as balloons or pencils with messages printed on them, to promote a product or service.

specialty goods—subgroup of a larger group of merchandise that is used by a small number of people, such as quilting supplies as a specialty within sewing supplies.

specialty retailer—store selling a narrow but deep niche of goods in one area.

specie—coins.

spec(ification)—detailed requirement for a building, product, system, or purchase.

speculate—to guess based on research; to purchase a property or security with the expectation of obtaining a quick profit.

speculative risk—in insurance, investment that could reap large gains but is extremely risky, making the venture uninsurable.

speed dialer—feature of a telephone or portable device that remembers and rapidly dials frequently used phone numbers; also called "autodialer."

spendthrift—someone who wastes money; prone to extravagance.

spiff—special compensation offered to retail salespeople for pushing the sale of a particular item (also called "push incentives"); to clean up or improve the appearance of.

spike—sharp up-and-down movement in a value, such as a stock price or heartbeat; upright post on which messages or orders are impaled; to hit a high point; to add alcohol to something.

spin—interpretation; different treatment of something common; to tell a story.

spin doctor/master—public relations or issues management specialist skilled at presenting a message or explaining events in the most favorable light.

spinoff—independent company created from a corporate-owned entity; product or service created through a minor change in another offering; in television, new entertainment program based on characters from an old one.

spiral of progress—Joseph Juran's depiction of the sequence of events necessary to put a product on the market.

split—in stock, to break one share into two or more without initially changing the total value of an individual's holdings or total shareholders' equity; many companies adopt this tactic because they prefer to have their stock trade in a specific price range (under $100 per share, for example); a stock trading at $120 per share that splits three-for-one would result in the investor now holding three times as many shares trading at $40 per share immediately after the split.

split commission—agreement by two brokers or agents involved in a transaction to split the sales commission from it.

split shift—working two separate blocks of time in one day with a minimum of two hours in between, such as lunch and dinner in a restaurant.

split 30—30-second advertising spot that has been split into two 15-second commercials.

spoilage—rejected products that fail to meet quality targets.

spokesperson—someone designated to speak on behalf of a company, usually an executive or public relations specialist.

sponsor—someone who lends significant support to an event; in electronic media, advertisers who buy time during a program; in total quality, manager who ovesees specific quality improvement projects; in a limited partnership, general partner.

sporadic quality problems—problems with product or service quality that occur infrequently.

sporadic spike—quality problem that occurs infrequently and has no immediately discernible cause.

spot check—random quality check on product or performance.

spot market—market in which commodities are sold for cash and with immediate delivery, such as the world's oil market.

spot price—delivery price of a commodity.

spread—in banking, difference between what it costs a bank to obtain money and the rate at which it loans money out; in investing, difference between yields on similar investment options with different maturities or different investment options with different maturities; difference between bid and offer prices on a security; difference between high and low prices of one security over a specific time period.

spreadsheet—arrangement of data into horizontal and vertical rows designed to show a relationship between a constant and a variable; most commonly used in accounting, but gaining use as a tool for displaying quality-oriented data.

spur—rail line or highway running from a main line to a specific point, such as a factory's loading dock; to encourage or inspire; to goad to greater effort.

square footage—measure of floor space in a building.

stack—to add benefits, such as in life insurance policies.

staff—assistants to an executive; people who work in a specific department or specialty area, such as the sales staff; employees not involved in making a product for or delivering a service to a customer (in one old bromide, *line* makes money and *staff* spends it).

staff authority—authority to give advice, but not to supervise others.

stage—well-defined step in any sequence of events, such as the stage of product development; to present, sometimes with the connotation of creating a false or controlled impression.

stagflation—inflation combined with stagnant economic growth, coined to explain economic conditions in the U.S. in the 1970s.

stagnation—lack of growth or progress, such as an economy that isn't growing.

stake—interest in something; usually implies partial ownership, but also relates to any situation in which a person can lose or gain something depending on action taken by another individual or entity.

stakeholder—someone who cares about the outcome of events or the actions of an organization because he or she is directly affected: in addition to shareholders, employees, vendors, customers, and members of the community at large are stakeholders.

stale check—check held for a long time before it is cashed or deposited.

stale date—mail run through a postage meter whose date stamper is not current, making it look like it has taken the postal service a long time to deliver it.

Standard & Poor's—investment rating service owned by McGraw-Hill that publishes a popular index derived from the financial performance of five hundred common stocks.

standard AV—audiovisual equipment normally available with a meeting room, including overhead projectors, slide projectors, and videocassette players with monitors.

standard deviation—probability that one piece of data will vary from the mean: one standard deviation includes about 66% of the population, two includes about 95%.

standard industrial classification (SIC)—federal government's numerical system classifying organizations on the basis of their primary business activity; the number assigned to a given category is its "SIC code."

standard of living—measure of relative consumption in an economy.

standard operating policy/procedure (SOP)—usual way in which something is done, often spelled out in a policy or procedure manual, and too often used as an excuse to customers for why something stupid occurred.

standardization—making something in a uniform way or to consistent specifications, a key issue among different manufacturers of similar products (customers need to be assured that all size sevens are interchangeable and all audiocassettes will work in any cassette player).

standing order—authorization for regular shipments of a set quantity of goods at a repeated interval that "stands" until canceled or modified.

Star Wars—sophisticated technology that appears almost magical to the general public (from the whizbang special effects in the popular movie series); space-based missile defense system considered but ultimately abandoned as unworkable and too expensive.

star—high achiever.

start-up company—new business, often one seeking to develop new products and services or markets.

stat—statistic; in medicine, immediately; in printing, photographic image made up of just black and white tones.

stated needs—customer's needs as defined by the customer.

statement—transaction record of an account over a given time period, such as a monthly bank statement; current status of a company's assets and liabilities.

statistical probability—odds of something happening based on past occurrences.

statistical process control (SPC)—using statistical tools, especially sampling, to help maintain the quality of a process within specific parameters instead of inspecting each and every product after it has been produced (the secret of Japan's modern industrial success, originally developed in the U.S. by Walter Shewhart and taught to the Japanese by W. Edwards Deming); also called "statistical quality control" (SQC).

statistically significant—data considered reliable because it was derived from a large sample; statistic that shows a correlation between two elements, even when the margin for error is taken into account.

status—legal condition; relative ranking based on wealth or success.

status quo—current situation.

status report—summary of progress toward a goal, usually provided to those not directly involved in the project.

status symbol—mark of belonging in a prestigious group in the company or society, such as an expensive pen, tie, car, or suit.

statute—legislative act or law.

statute of limitations—period of time within which a statute must be or can be enforced.

stealth—quality of being sneaky or sly; being invisible but powerful, with connotations of being uncontrollably expensive or wasteful, derived from the development of the stealth bomber.

steel-collar worker—computerized robot used on a production line.

steno pad—specialized notepad used by secretaries to take shorthand.

steno pool—in the past, group of employees available to take notes or dictation; today, euphemism for young women who perform low-level office work.

stenographer—someone capable of writing in shorthand, often a lower-level secretary.

step down—to resign from a position, especially a top-level elected position such as president; to take a position in the company that has a lower status level than your previous position.

stet—Latin for *let it stand*; common proofreader's mark meaning material marked for change should be left as it was.

stevedore—someone who unloads cargo from a ship.

steward—someone who has been elected by fellow employees to handle day-to-day union matters in the workplace.

stewardship—representation of a person or group of people; caring for something in lieu of the owner.

stiff—poor performer; to fail to pay or fulfill an obligation.

stipend—allowance or wage paid on a regular basis.

stipulate—to specify or require as part of a contract or other legal agreement.

stock—certificate defining ownership in a company; product in inventory; ordinary or usual; to take product from inventory and put it on a shelf; to keep something in inventory.

stock certificate—printed document of ownership of stock in a corporation.

stock jobbing—illegally manipulating the stock market or selling worthless securities.

stock keeping unit (SKU)—distinct order or inventory control number for everything stocked by a store, usually encoded in scannable numbers or barcode to make best use of electronic cash register and inventory control systems.

stock market—organized system through which stocks and bonds are traded according to predetermined rules.

stock option—in investing, option to buy or sell a stock at a specific price before a certain date; in compensation, option to acquire up to a specified number of shares at a favorable price within a certain period of time, often used as an incentive for executives.

stockbroker—someone who offers advice to and executes trades for an investor and is paid by a commission on the value of the transactions arranged.

stockholder—someone who owns stock in a corporation.

stockholder's equity—invested or working capital (subtract debts from total capital).

stockpile—to accumulate a large reserve of materials.

stockroom—area in a store where goods not on the floor are kept.

stop payment—order to your bank not to honor a check.

stop-loss order—instructions to a broker to buy or sell specific securities when prices reach a predetermined point.

stopover—short stop on an airline, bus, train, or boat trip before reaching the final destination.

store—retail location where goods are stocked and sold.

store brand—product that carries the store's name instead of the manufacturer's and is usually priced lower than comparable name-brand products.

straight commission—compensation based solely on sales commissions.

straight-line depreciation—writing off an equal amount of something's value for each year of its useful life.

straight time—hours worked that do not include overtime.

stranded customer—customer who is not being contacted for new business or who does not have a salesperson to talk to about current transactions because the company has stopped doing business in the area temporarily (until a new employee can be hired, for example) or for good.

straphanger—someone who commutes by train or bus (which used to have straps to hang on to if you had to stand); someone who normally cannot work late hours because of the need to use mass transit.

strategic business unit (SBU)—division organized around its market and operated as a profit center, a decentralizing practice pioneered by General Electric.

strategic plan—plan that seeks to solve a problem or create an outcome, such as increased product sales, through a series of objectives, goals, and tactics.

strategy—plan of action for achieving a goal (tactics are the specifics of how you'll achieve it).

stratify—to divide into layers or segments, often for purposes of testing or further defining a market.

street, the—marketplace; in investing, Wall Street in New York City.

street smarts—intelligence gained from the rough and tumble of experience rather than academic training.

stress—externally induced tension; major cause of poor work performance and absenteeism in the workplace.

strike—job action, often prolonged and bitter, in which workers belonging to a union stop working to try to force management to meet their demands.

strikebreaker—someone hired to replace a worker out on strike; an employee who chooses to cross the picket line and keep working during a strike.

strip mall—small shopping center with outside entrances to each store laid out in one long strip along a parking area, often situated near a larger mall to gain the advantage of traffic moving near it.

Subchapter S—see *S corporation*.

subcontractor—someone hired by a general contractor (or other subcontractor) to perform a portion of a contract.

subdivide—to break a parcel of land into individual pieces to be sold to separate owners, for example in a housing tract (or "subdivision").

subfactor—minor reason for an occurrence.

subjective—personal; judged according to individual rather than universal or objective standards.

sublease—to lease all or part of a property from a leaseholder rather than the property's actual owner.

subliminal—not consciously perceived.

suboptimization—performance that falls short of the optimum or highest level possible, or the normal state of affairs and reason for continuous improvement efforts.

subordinate—someone who works under your direction; to make less important than something else.

suborn—to induce someone to commit perjury.

subpoena—legal instructions to appear in court.

subrogation—taking over financial liability from an original creditor.

subscribe—to sign up to receive a publication; in investing, to sell all the securities in a new issue.

subscript—number or letter used to identify a particular element in an array, usually written below the line or in parentheses.

subsidiary—corporation owned by another corporation.

subsidiary ledger—listing of individual items that comprise the total in a general ledger account; a subsidiary accounts-receivable ledger, for example, would contain a listing of the individual customers' accounts and amounts due.

subsidy—monetary assistance, whether in the form of cash paid or an obligation foregone, to provide economic advantage to a selected business, group, or individual.

subsistence—minimum level at which something can be maintained.

subsystem—system that runs as part of a larger system.

succession planning—formally determining how the business will run when the current officers or owners are no longer involved.

sue—to bring legal action against.

suggestion box—system that allows employees to submit ideas for improving operations (it need not be an actual box).

suit—office attire that includes a jacket and matching slacks or skirt; slang for an executive; legal action.

Sunbelt—states in the southern United States.

supercomputer—computer that can handle immense quantities of information and perform millions of calculations, especially in comparison to standard computers.

superconductor—material that conducts heat or electricity extremely well; key component in computers.

superfund—money set aside by the federal government to clean up hazardous waste deposits.

supermarket—grocery store with more than $2 million in annual sales; said of a market in which consumers have a wide variety of choices.

superscript—number or letter used to modify or identify another element, placed slightly above and to the right of the element it modifies.

superstore—large, typically low-service store that carries a wide variety of general merchandise or an in-depth selection of specialty goods.

supervisor—person who directly reviews an employee's work.

supplier—person or company that provides input for a product or process; also called "vendor."

supply—amount of product held in inventory; to provide something to a company or person.

supply and demand—basic relationship and interaction that determines pricing and activities in a market economy: as supplies increase, prices go down; as demand increases, prices go up.

supplyside—involving theories that if government takes less (in essence, increasing the supply of capital in the economy), it will receive more: that reductions in taxes will stimulate investment by corporations and the wealthy, improving economic performance for all.

surcharge—additional charge.

surety—guarantee against loss or default.

surplus—amount greater than the amount needed to meet current and/or projected needs.

surrender value—amount an insurance policy is worth when turned in for cash by the policyholder.

surrogate—substitute.

surtax—new tax in addition to and levied as a percentage of an existing tax.

survivor—someone left alive after the death of another; someone with a marked ability to outlive other people or events in an organization; in joint tenancy, one who inherits.

sushi—generic Japanese term for rice cakes topped with raw fish; slang for being beaten in a market by the Japanese.

suspend—to stop temporarily; to discipline by barring from work or the marketplace.

suspend trading—temporary halt in trading in a particular security in advance of a major news announcement or to correct an imbalance of orders to buy and sell.

sustained yield—managing a resource to produce a consistent level of production and replenishment, such as replanting forest lands from which timber has been harvested to grow new trees.

sweat equity—work you or your subordinates have put into a product or service before it is completed.

sweatshop—in manufacturing, factory that has poor physical working conditions and pays extremely low wages; by extension, any work setting where long hours and low pay are the norm.

sweepstakes—lottery contest in which everyone who enters has an equal chance to win, often used to enhance interest in a product or service.

sweetener—feature added to a deal to make it more desirable, usually on a onetime basis.

sweetheart contract—agreement between an employer and a union that grants concessions specifically for the purpose of keeping another union out.

swing time—time an employee is at lunch or is otherwise unemployed during the working shift.

swing shift—afternoon and evening work shift, following the day shift and preceding the night or graveyard shift.

switchboard—central system through which incoming phone calls are answered and routed to the correct person.

SWOT analysis—examination of the strengths, weaknesses, opportunities, and threats in a market or situation.

sycophant—boot licker; ass kisser; parasite.

symbiotic—two or more things that must exist together to work.

symbol—something that stands for something else; icon or trademark.

sympathy strike—strike called to show solidarity with another union on strike, not because of a dispute with management.

symptom—sign of a problem or condition.

sync(hronize)—to put in rhythm; to make two things operate at the same rate or time; to think the same way as another person.

syndicalism—economic system in which the workers in an industry maintain control over major decisions.

syndicate—joint venture formed by two or more entities that normally don't work together to tackle a project that none would be able to handle separately.

syndrome—condition or phenomenon.

synergy—energy you get from syn (why not?); literally, two or more things working together to achieve something none would be capable of alone (in other words, the whole is greater than the sum of the parts); commonly used to mean cooperation that leads to improved results.

synthetic—artificial; manmade substance, often intended to be the equivalent of a naturally occurring substance.

system—organized way of meeting a goal; self-correcting form of organization involving input, throughput, output, and feedback.

systematic—according to or using a system.

systemic—involving all parts of a system.

systemic discrimination—institutionalized tendency to discriminate against certain groups in an organization.

systems analyst—someone who directs the writing of the programs needed for a computer system to function.

T

T (treasury)-bill—note issued by the federal government to fund the federal deficit; maturities between one and five years are treasury notes, maturities of longer than five years are treasury bonds.

T&A (tits & ass)—in entertainment, show that relies on watching physically attractive characters in various stages of undress and suggestive situations.

table—place to negotiate; conference table around which members of the board of directors sit during their meetings; to hold over for discussion at another time.

tabloid—half-size newspaper that traditionally contains shorter articles, sometimes of a sleazy or sensational nature.

tacit—unspoken.

tactics—methods or activities (strategy is the goal, tactics are how you achieve it).

Taft-Hartley Act—1947 legislation that requires unions to operate under the same rules of good faith as management and outlines actions that management can take to prevent employees from unionizing.

314

tagline—short slogan used at the end of commercials and on printed materials to identify and position a company or product.

Taguchi Methods—statistical techniques used in design and production developed by Japan's Genichi Taguchi.

take—income from business transaction; profits from an illegal venture; in securities, acceptance of an offer price by dealers or brokers.

take a bath—to lose a great deal of money.

take delivery—to receive or take actual possession of.

take a flier—to speculate on a highly risky investment.

take a hike—to leave (and don't come back).

take home—net income after taxes and other deductions; to close a sale.

take a position—to invest in a security or company.

take private—to buy back all the stock of a public company, making it privately owned.

take public—to offer to the public the stock of a formerly privately owned company.

takeover—acquisition of a controlling interest in the stock of a company by another company or outside investor; if the acquisition is not wanted, it's a "hostile takeover"; if it's accomplished with the support of management, it's a "friendly takeover."

tangible—physically real; essential attribute of a product when compared to a service (which is intangible); physical property, not including real estate.

TARBU (typical activity run by us)—consultant's marginal note for a standard procedure.

tare weight—weight of an empty container or wrapper that is deducted from the weight of an item to determine the content's true weight for shipping or other purposes.

target—goal or objective, such as a sales target; to focus on; to set an objective.

target audience—group to whom advertising is directed; persons or households with common demographics.

target company—company being considered for takeover.

target market—customers for whom a product or service has been created.

tariff—import or export tax levied by the federal government; fee schedule for hauling cargo.

task—job; to assign.

task force—committee or group charged with a specific, short-term assignment.

Taylorism—management approach developed in the late 1800s and early 1900s by U.S. steel industry engineer Frederick Taylor, who recommended dividing work into small component parts that could be handled by a then largely uneducated and low-skilled workforce, with management responsible for planning, training, and overall direction; credited with propelling the U.S. to the forefront of productivity prior to World War II, but since somewhat discredited because, as traditionally applied, it underutilizes and demotivates workers, especially in knowledge-intensive and service professions.

tax—fee charged on a good or activity to help fund government activities; to put pressure or strain on someone or something.

tax bracket—income level at which you are taxed, determined by subtracting deductions and allowances from total income and consulting tables on the tax schedule.

Tax Court—federal court where cases involving the Internal Revenue Service are heard.

tax credit—amount subtracted from taxes owed rather than from income subject to taxes.

tax deferred—income that will not be taxed until a later date or event, such as earnings on a retirement fund that are not taxed until withdrawn.

tax exempt—not subject to taxation.

tax return—official form detailing calculation of taxes submitted to federal, state, or local taxation authorities.

tax shelter—investment or other activity that reduces income subject to taxation.

taxpayer identifying number (TIN)—number used by the IRS to track business activities for tax purposes, generally either a business's federal ID number or an individual's Social Security number.

team—group of people working together toward a common goal or on a common task.

team building—efforts designed to create a feeling of camaraderie and improve cooperation and performance among employees.

team player—unselfish; someone who puts team goals and needs ahead of personal considerations.

team selling—using a group of salespeople rather than a single sales rep to contact and service an account (becoming increasingly common because business relationships often involve multiple contacts in different parts of the client's organization).

teamster—originally, someone who drove a team; generally refers to a member of the International Brotherhood of Teamsters, often (but not limited) to a truck driver.

teaser—advertisement that presents a small amount of information but doesn't reveal either the product or the company, designed to arouse curiosity so that later ads are more enticing.

technical press—magazines and newspapers covering specific technical subjects.

technician—someone who performs an activity related to science, engineering, or medicine.

techno—prefix referring to anything that involves technology or technical proficiency; a techno-illiterate is someone who can't master basic technologies, such as programming a VCR.

technocracy—theoretical system in which experts make the decisions.

technology—application of science to something; machines, systems, and applied knowledge that make it possible to do something better, faster, cheaper, and/or with fewer people than before.

technology-driven—company or activity where the ability to do something takes precedence (even over the need to do it).

technology transfer—movement of technology from the experts to the people or organizations that will actually make use of it; spread of technological knowledge.

tele—prefix meaning "distance" or involving telecommunications.

telecommunications—voice and data signals transmitted electronically through systems such as the telephone and television.

telecommute—to work at home or on the road and send your work to the main office via computer modem or fax machine.

teleconference—business discussion involving two or more locations linked by satellite transmission of visual and audio signals.

telemarketing—selling products by calling people on the telephone.

telemetry—data transmitted from a remote source.

telephony—con artist who works over the phone, such as someone who solicits donations to an organization that doesn't exist or offers a phantom prize package in order to obtain a credit card number.

teleprompter—device that displays a script on a screen so a speaker can look at the text and the audience at the same time; in television, system that projects the script to a screen in front of the lens so the anchors can read their lines while looking into the camera.

telex—system of international telecommunications where messages can be sent from one typewriter to another.

temp—temporary employee, usually office help.

temp(orary) service—business that supplies temporary employees.

template—guide or pattern that can be reused; in computers, a formatted screen or document frequently used as a job aid, such as a purchase order or newsletter layout.

10-K—detailed annual report filed by large, publicly held companies to satisfy Securities and Exchange Commission requirements.

tenant—someone who legally occupies property, whether their own or owned by someone else.

tender—money; bid or offer; small vessel that carries fuel to a larger one; sensitive or delicate; to give (such as to tender a resignation); to pay.

tender offer—in investing, offer to acquire all or a specified number of shares in a company for a specified price by a certain date, often contingent on acquiring the amount of shares specified, usually in an effort to take over the company.

tenet—belief or principle.

tenure—length of time you've been employed by a company; in education, virtual lifetime employment guarantee designed to ensure a professor's independence and freedom from intimidation, but often with adverse effects on motivation and openness to new ideas.

term—period of time covered by a contract; provision of a contract; word or phrase with a particular meaning in certain circumstances.

term life insurance—coverage for a specific period of time only.

terminal—computer workstation, either self-contained or linked to a network or mainframe; facility for handling people or freight; slated to die or be discontinued.

terminate—to fire someone; to discontinue something.

terms—conditions of an agreement.

territory—geographic or industrial area a salesperson covers.

test—process designed to assess quality or nature; to examine or assess; to try out.

test market—small geographic area in which a new product and/or advertising campaign is tried out to determine its likely results before taking it to broader markets.

testate—having a legally valid will.

testimonial—good information about a product from a customer or third-party source, frequently used in public relations and advertising.

think tank—experts gathered and paid to brainstorm a general topic.

theory—explanation for why something happens or exists, usually based on at least a minimal amount of knowledge; front end of practice.

Theory X—Douglas McGregor's generic term for authoritarian companies that believe people need constant supervision and direction or they won't work.

Theory Y—Douglas McGregor's generic term for more empowering companies that believe people are motivated to work and will thrive in conditions that support such motivation.

Theory Z—William Ouchi's attempt to explain how Japanese businesses combine Theory X and Theory Y to create an environment that values both corporate performance and employee involvement.

thermal—working by using heat, such as the way a facsimile machine works by heating spots on film ribbon so that they will adhere to special paper; updraft caused by heat in the atmosphere.

thin market—few buyers or sellers for a stock.

third-class mail—U.S. Postal Service's classification for inexpensively mailed items weighing less than one pound; junk mail.

third party—someone who isn't legally or directly involved in a situation or transaction and hence can be objective in viewing it.

third world—less-developed countries that have a low standard of living and often are in need of aid from developed countries (in the cold war era, Western-style democracies made up the "first world" and the Eastern or communist bloc made up the "second world").

three-martini lunch—symbol of nonproductive business entertainment expenses used by former U.S. President Jimmy Carter to try to persuade Congress to tighten laws for business tax deductions.

threat—anything that may adversely affect business.

Three Mile Island—1979 nuclear power plant accident in Pennsylvania that serves as a symbol of the potential dangers of nuclear power.

threshold—lower frame of a doorway; minimum level or limit, such as a threshold for pain.

thrift—wise use of money.

thrift institution—savings and loan or savings bank.

thrift shop—store that sells low-priced goods, usually used.

throughput—processing stage in a system where input is converted to output.

ticker—telegraphic device that prints information, such as stock prices, on a continuous paper tape; heart.

ticker tape—paper ribbon used for printout from a ticker, traditionally thrown from windows along Wall Street during (ticker tape) parades.

ticket—something that provides guaranteed access, whether literally or figuratively (for example, your father having influential business friends may be your "ticket" to business success); paper record that accompanies a job in progress.

tickler—time-based reminder system; a "tickler file" contains ideas to be reviewed at a later date.

tie—see *necktie*.

tie-in—promotional effort that supports an advertising campaign, such as a fast-food chain putting soft drinks in cups with graphics that coincide with a movie release.

tiger—someone considered vigorous and formidable; one of the rapidly industrializing nations of the Pacific Rim (Asian tigers).

TIGER (topographically integrated encoding and referencing system)—database of computerized census data used in marketing planning and analysis.

tiger team—task force working on new product development.

tight money—time when loans are difficult to get, usually because the Federal Reserve has restricted the money supply.

tight ship—organization in which everyone must follow company policies and procedures to the letter, and unconventional actions and people aren't generally tolerated, based on the classic axiom of naval discipline, "A tight ship is a happy ship" (understandable if the business involves running a battleship, questionable if it relies on people who must act in empowered and creative ways).

tight-assed—anal retentive; someone who insists that the rules be strictly followed.

till—drawer in a cash register; to work the land in order to raise a crop.

till tap—obtaining checking account and credit card information by photocopying checks and receipts from a cash drawer, then returning them before they are noticed missing (gives a white collar thief both current account numbers and a facsimile of your signature).

time—something you trade for money; the most democratic

of commodities, since rich and poor alike get the same twenty-four hours each day.

time and motion study—Frederick Taylor's analytical tool for determining the most efficient way to accomplish a task by timing different ways of doing a job to discover which one produces the most amount of product with the least amount of cost and effort.

time management—art and science of making best use of your time, often involving schedules and time-efficient practices.

time to market—how long a product takes from inception to active sale to customers (as a rule of thumb, the faster the better).

timecard—means of recording the hours an employee is in the workplace; may be inserted into a timeclock, manually recorded by the employee, or recorded by a manager.

timeclock—device that records the exact time at which it is used, providing a record of when an employee arrives and leaves the workplace.

timecode—in video, frame-specific numbers added to the audio track to help editors decide exactly which clips to use in an edited piece.

timesharing—in computers, running two or more programs on the same computer at the same time; in real estate, right to possess or use a property, such as accommodations at a resort, for only a week or two during the year; also called "interval ownership."

timesheet—electronic or paper record of how an employee spends the day, often in increments of as little as six minutes (a tenth of an hour when tracking by computer), for use in billing, time management, and performance evaluation; common in professional service firms, such as advertising and public relations agencies and law and accounting firms.

timetable—schedule of events or activities.

timing—relative knack of having the right person or thing in the right place at the right time.

tip—self-calculated tax on service (from the inscription T.I.P. on containers in olde English coffeehouses, meaning "to insure promptness" in getting a refill); limited-circulation information; to tilt; to knock over.

tirekicking—gathering preliminary information about a possible purchase with no immediate intention to buy (derived from the practice of kicking the tires of a used car to check their soundness).

title—evidence of legal ownership of something; name of a book or program; official job designation.

toaster—something that burns bread in an acceptable way; in video, device that allows desktop editing of video images through a properly equipped personal computer.

Toastmasters—nonprofit self-help organization that provides a semistructured program in which members develop and polish personal speaking skills and critique others as they work on theirs.

tokenism—superficial attempts to meet the letter, but not the spirit, of affirmative action or diversity requirements.

tolerance—degree of acceptable deviation from a standard; acceptance or respect for someone else's behavior or ideas when they don't approximate your own.

toll—cost, usually of a disaster; fee paid for the use of a controlled-access facility or system, such as a highway or long-distance phone network; mournful ringing of a bell.

tombstone ad—text-only advertisement placed in newspapers of record to announce a new public offering of securities (somewhat resembles the headstone on a grave).

toner—heat-sensitive black powder fused with heat to paper to create a copy of something in a photocopier or laser printer.

top-down—cascade style of communication and decision-making in which information and action flow from the top of the organization to each successive layer.

top-line—quick, informal verbal summary of a presentation or document, usually for a time-crunched executive or manager who should have but hasn't found time to study it personally.

top out—end of a period of rising prices or sales, from which point conditions are expected to plateau or begin to fall; to reach the maximum salary level from which Social Security taxes are withdrawn.

tort—private wrong not subject to criminal or contract law for which damages can be sought in civil court; trespassing is a tort.

total quality—catchall term for the movement that attempts to mimic Japan's continuous quality improvement culture, ostensibly to improve ultimate customer satisfaction (although the customer is often forgotten as the object of the exercise); also called "total quality management" (TQM) or "total quality control" (TQC).

tout—to brag; to overpromote something, such as a stock, to the point that it misleads buyers; to make a full-force marketing effort.

toxic waste—by-products of industrial or other processes that are considered harmful to the environment and people; there are very specific rules for disposing of toxic waste and stiff fines for not following the rules.

trace—to try to find something that is lost in transit; a very small amount of something.

track—path that something follows; to follow something closely over a period of time; to proceed logically.

track record—person's job history; product's sales history, especially over several years.

tract—land area developed together for a specified use, such as a housing tract; treatise or explanatory publication.

trade—nonprofessional job that requires a high degree of skill, such as plumber or electrician; to conduct business; to exchange one thing for another; in investing, to buy or sell securities.

trade advertising—efforts aimed at wholesalers and retailers rather than end users.

trade association—organization formed by businesses in a specific industry to promote the industry as a whole.

trade barrier—obstacle put in place by a government or industry to make it harder for products from outside the country to compete with those made inside.

trade corridor—single shipping route through one or more countries.

trade deficit/surplus—amount by which imports exceed exports or vice versa; also called "negative balance" or "positive balance" of trade respectively.

trade name—name by which a product is commercially known.

trade press—magazines and newspapers geared specifically to an industry or profession.

trade school—post–high school institution that provides specific technical or skills training rather than the academic training of a college or university.

trade secret—knowledge essential to producing a product or service that, if a competitor were to discover it, could significantly change a company's competitive position.

trade show—convention centered around a theme in which the major feature is a group of suppliers showing their wares.

trade union—labor organization for workers in a given occupational field, such as plumbers or pipefitters, even though they may work for businesses in different fields.

trademark (TM)—legally registered name or symbol that serves to identify the business, product, or product line (can't be a generic name or picture of the contents; can be exclusively exploited and defended against infringement).

trader—in securities, someone who buys and sells for a personal account, as opposed to a broker or agent, who buys for a client.

tradition—customary pattern of thought or action; respected habit; something that no one has thought to question for a long time.

traffic—in retail, number of potential customers entering a store during a specific period of time; degree of use of a physical or electronic transit system, such as telephone lines or freeways; department that coordinates shipments of incoming and outgoing product; department in an advertising or public relations agency that coordinates a project's movement through other departments.

training—business-oriented education and skills development paid for by the employer and delivered by either an employee of the company or an outside source.

training and development (T&D)—activities designed to fully develop an employee's potential in an organization.

tramp—woman whose morals are suspect; bum or vagrant; in a seniority system, someone who takes the place of others on their days off while earning enough seniority to bid for a permanent slot.

transaction—business exchange.

transcribe—to write out the words from an audiotape or shorthand.

transcript—written text of a speech, interview, broadcast, or other verbal interaction.

transfer—switch in assignments or work locations that does not involve a promotion or demotion; to convey legally from one entity to another, such as a transfer of title; to move to a different part or location within the company; to switch in transit.

transient—moving from place to place; rootless; passing quickly; in hospitality, guest who stays only a short time.

transition—time of change; in a presentation, verbal or visual bridge between two subjects that do not follow in logical sequence.

translate—to convert from one language to another; to simplify or interpret for someone who doesn't get it.

transmit—to send; to pass along motion.

transnational—something that crosses national boundaries; business that operates in several countries.

transportation—business of moving people or goods; how something gets from one place to another.

trash 'n' trinkets—slang for small token gifts given at conventions, sales meetings, and other events.

travel and entertainment (T&E)—reimbursable or company-paid costs associated with traveling for business purposes, usually visiting and/or entertaining customers and potential customers.

traumatic—intensely shocking; having long-lasting negative consequences.

treasurer—someone responsible for overseeing all uses of company funds, usually an officer of the company who can be held liable for actions the company takes.

treasury(T)-bill—note issued by the federal government; notes with maturities between one and five years are treasury notes, those with maturities of longer than five years are treasury bonds.

treatise—formal written presentation on a subject.

treaty—written agreement between nations that sets the terms for trade or other relations.

treble damages—three times the awarded amount, usually as a form of punishment for the action involved.

tree diagram—see *decision tree*.

trend—general tendency or direction of movement; developing phenomenon.

trend analysis—attempt to forecast the future by projecting past actions and movements.

trial and error—learning from your mistakes.

trial and terror—learning from your mistakes under extreme pressure or peril (when you really can't afford to make a mistake).

trial balance—preliminary step in closing the books for a year, listing and totaling all debits and credits to see if they balance.

trial offer—practice of allowing a prospective customer to try the product or service for a limited period of time before deciding whether to buy it.

trickle down—theory that all levels of society benefit when businesses and the rich do well, because they reinvest their wealth to create additional economic activity and jobs; communications dynamic in which new methods or ideas are first taught to managers, who in turn teach their subordinates when and as they deem appropriate; polite way of expressing the first law of organizational physics (shit flows downhill).

trim—to eliminate excess; to take small amounts off or out of something, such as a budget; to get the best of someone in a financial transaction.

triple role—Joseph Juran's theory that employees can be divided into processor teams that carry out three distinct roles: processor, supplier, and customer; the graphic for it is called the TRIPROL diagram.

trolling—cold-calling for new business.

troops—any group of employees, but most commonly the sales force.

troubleshoot—to solve problems by eliminating their source.

trough—low point or gentle depression; tray or tank for an animal's feed or water.

trust—legal structure that holds title to property or administers assets for the good of another party; cartel or other group working together to restrict trade; to have faith or confidence in.

trust company—firm incorporated to act as a trustee, typically operating in conjunction with a commercial bank.

trust deed—title in real estate held by a trust rather than a lender.

trust fund—money and other property or assets held in trust.

trustee—someone who holds title to property that is to be used for the benefit of another (the beneficiary); member of the board of directors of a nonprofit organization.

truth in advertising—federal and state laws that require statements made in advertisements to be factual.

truth in lending—federal and state laws that require lenders to disclose all costs and conditions affecting a loan so the borrower understands what's at risk and what's required in repayment and can compare costs among lenders.

tuition reimbursement—company payment of all or part of the cost of attending school while on the job (either during work hours or on your own time).

turkey—bad investment or endeavor; jerk.

turnaround—significant change from the previous direction, usually involving the transformation of a bad situation to a good one.

turnaround specialist—someone known for revitalizing underperforming organizations.

turnaround time—how long it takes to do something; in transportation, time needed for the process of unloading, servicing, and reloading a truck, train, or airplane so it can go back where it came from or continue on its route.

turning point—decisive movement in a battle or campaign.

turnkey—handling a project from start to finish, with the client only minimally involved before receiving the completed work.

turnover—percentage of employees who must be replaced in a given time period; measure of how often inventory must be replenished in a given time period; percentage of shares of stock traded during a given time period; ratio of sales to net worth.

turnstile—device used to control entry or exit and count people passing through, usually involving rotating horizontal bars on a post.

TVCR—combination television and videocassette recorder in one unit.

twelve-time rate—discounted rate given to companies that advertise in every issue of a monthly publication for one year.

two-color—in printing, job that includes black plus one additional accent color.

two tier—in compensation, system in which workers are paid at two different wage levels for the same job depending on when they were hired.

two-year rule—National Labor Relations Board rule stating that a rival union cannot attempt to persuade employees to switch representation during the first two years of a collective bargaining agreement.

tycoon—powerful businessperson, generally one known for single-minded pursuit of wealth and success.

type—belonging to a common class or category; words in a publication; to use a keyboard to write information onto paper or into a computer system; to classify.

type A—someone characterized by a hot temper, controlling personality, and wide emotional swings, often a workaholic or abrasive individual.

type B—someone characterized by a mellow personality, slow to anger or show anxiety, and not obviously driven by ambition or a sense of immediacy.

twist—in insurance, illegal practice of persuading a policyholder to cancel existing coverage and replace it with a new policy that primarily generates new sales commissions for the agent rather than improves the customer's coverage; to distort someone's words or ideas.

U

U-matic—3/4-inch videotape format once widely used in corporate productions and broadcast studios.

ultra—prefix meaning "extreme."

ultra vires—Latin for *beyond the power*; actions that are illegal for a corporation because they are beyond the scope of the organization's charter; forbidden or unauthorized.

ultimate—furthest extent; conclusive or maximum.

ultimate user—final customer of a product or service.

ultimatum—final statement of terms that, if not met or accepted, may trigger adverse consequences; what you never want to give your employer (because if they lack a graceful way out you may find yourself on the way out).

umbrage—offense.

umbrella—something you use to keep rain off your head; encompassing everything or everyone; protective.

un—prefix meaning "not."

unadjusted trial balance—balances taken from the general ledger at the end of a fiscal period before adjusting entries have been made.

unbundling—charging for separating things that were once packaged together.

unclassified stores—products purchased for onetime special circumstances.

under the counter—sneaky; illegal or dishonest, such as a bribe or payment slipped to someone not entitled to it while no one else is looking.

undercapitalized—business lacking the capital resources to scale up properly.

underemployed—working in a job for which you are over-qualified (like someone with a Ph.D. driving a cab) or that does not make full use of your capabilities and training; measure of how many people in a business or the economy as a whole are overqualified or underutilized.

underground economy—business transactions hidden from the tax collector in particular and the law in general, including illegal activities such as prostitution and drugs, barter, and unre-ported cash payments (so named because its activity doesn't show up in official government statistics).

underpaid—someone not fully or fairly compensated for the true value of his or her work.

understudy—someone learning another person's job so he or she can fill in at a moment's notice; intern.

underutilize—not to use fully or effectively.

undervalued—offered for sale or sold for less than its true worth; in investing, security that, based on statistical assess-ments, should be selling for more than it is.

underwrite—to raise or provide money to assume another's risk; in insurance, to accept liability for a potential loss; to in-sure; in investing, to agree to buy all or part of a new stock issue at a specified time and price for resale to the public.

Underwriters Laboratories (UL)—business that certifies the minimum design and operating safety of electrical devices and other equipment.

undocumented worker—someone from a foreign country, whether in this country legally or not, who does not have docu-mented permission to work; see *green card*.

unemployable—lacking the skills or temperament to be gainfully employed.

unemployment—number of people out of work who are qualified for and actively seeking employment, usually expressed either in raw numbers or as a percentage of the population; official figures typically do not count those who are not looking for work because they have become discouraged or have no wish or ability to find employment.

unemployment compensation—money paid to people for a period of time after they lose their jobs to help them meet their obligations while they look for new jobs.

unequivocal—without doubt or conditions; clear.

unfair labor practices—actions by an employer or union that are forbidden by federal or state labor laws.

uniform—clothing worn on the job chosen by the employer rather than the employee; something that brings or increases conformity; identical or consistent.

unilateral—one-sided; a unilateral agreement obligates only one party.

union—organization of employees that represents workers' concerns and negotiates formal contracts with management regarding working conditions and pay.

union checkoff—fee that union members pay to the union to offset administrative costs.

union label—tag or imprinted icon signifying that the item was made entirely or largely by union labor.

union local—chartered branch of a national or international union representing workers in a specific bargaining unit or area.

union shop—workplace where all workers must join the union after a period of time as a condition of continued employment.

unique selling proposition (USP)—idea, popularized in advertising, that every product or service should have unique value to a customer and be sold in such a way that the customer can readily perceive that value.

uniquely abled—politically correct term for *disabled* or *handicapped*.

unisex—showing no visible distinction based on gender.

unit—part of a whole; subsidiary or operating area; measure of production in a given time period, such as units per hour; in commodities, basic measure of quantity on which contracts are written; in hospitals, intensive care unit.

United Nations Education, Scientific and Cultural Organization (UNESCO)—U.N. organization charged with promoting scientific and cultural exchange.

United Way—nonprofit umbrella organization that raises funds, often through organized corporate contribution campaigns, and dispenses them to a variety of local and national nonprofit organizations.

universal life insurance—adjustable policy that provides earnings on funds invested beyond the actual cost of coverage, as opposed to *term life insurance*.

universal product code (UPC)—machine-scannable barcode for numbers that identify a product, used for totaling bills, updating inventory, and other purposes.

universe—entirety of a group being studied.

unleaded—decaffeinated coffee.

unload—to get rid of, such as unwanted stock or merchandise; to remove cargo or people from a conveyance; to criticize forcefully.

unrecorded liability—liability, such as a debt, that is not recorded in a company's official financial statement.

unsecured debt—debt for which there is no collateral.

unskilled labor—workers who lack the skills needed for even the lowest-paying jobs.

untimely—premature or inopportune; what time it is whenever someone dies.

up front—cash to finance initial activities provided at the time an agreement is reached; lobby in an office where the receptionist sits and guests check in; to be completely honest.

update—timely supplement to something previously published or reported; to bring someone up to date on recent developments and current conditions; to enter new information into a record or file.

upgrade—to replace something with something better; to improve; in computers, to change to a newer, usually more powerful version of a software program or add expanded system capabilities.

uplink—beaming a transmission to a satellite, from which it will be sent to a downlink.

upper management—top and near-top executives in a company, usually vice presidents, division presidents, the president, and assorted "chiefs" (CEO, CFO, etc.).

upscale—top-of-the-line products or services geared to the wealthiest 20% of the population.

upside—good news or potential for good developments (opposite of "downside"); price increase expected of a security.

uptick—small incremental increase.

uptime—amount of time a piece of equipment or an entire production line is running.

urban—involving cities.

useful life—number of years over which an asset can be depreciated.

user—someone who uses a product or service, not limited to the customer (for example, the customer's children); someone who takes advantage of or abuses a person or substance.

user friendly—designed to be easily understood and operated.

user group—in computers, group formed by people who use the same type of hardware or software to exchange ideas and information.

usury—lending money at an exorbitant interest rate or a rate higher than permitted by state law.

utility—company that provides a public service as a regulated monopoly, such as water, telephone, or electricity; in computers, very small software program or command built into a larger program designed to accomplish a small task or processing need, such as converting a file to a different format; usefulness.

utilize—unnecessarily big word for *use*.

V

vacation—paid time off from a job, usually earned in proportion to the number of years or hours worked.

valid—legally binding; sound or well reasoned.

validity—accuracy of a predictor.

VALS (Value and Lifestyles Program)—analysis originated by the Stanford Research Institute that classifies adult behavior according to lifestyle: need-driven (11% of consumers), inner-directed (20%), outer-directed (67%), and integrated (2%).

valuation—estimated worth; appraisal.

value—measure of what something is worth to an individual, not necessarily monetary value; merit; principle or standard of conduct; to estimate something's worth; to consider important or desirable.

value-added—making something more desirable or worth more to the customer by adding a component or enhancement to the basic product or service.

value-added dealer (VAD)—business that buys a basic product from a manufacturer and adds value to it either before or in the process of selling it to a customer; also called "value-added reseller" (VAR), or collectively "VAD/VARs."

value-added tax (VAT)—tax (common in Europe) assessed at each point in a process where something is made more valuable, based on the increase in value.

vaporware—product announced but never brought to market, derived from the computer industry penchant for publicizing new hardware and software that never gets out of the lab; by extension, seemingly formidable strength or advantage that isn't real or substantive.

variable—data that changes as a result of a stimulus; anything that changes periodically or has no fixed value.

variable interest rate—interest on a loan assessed at different rates over the life of the loan, usually in keeping with a schedule or index, or outside economic factors such as inflation or a changing prime rate.

variable pricing—changing the price depending on the customer and the situation.

variation—inconsistency; deviation from a norm or standard; amount that a process or piece of data changes from one period to the next.

velocity—speed of flow or movement; indicator of economic activity based on how often money is spent in a given period of time.

vendor—supplier or seller.

veneer—thin coating with the appearance of high quality glued or bonded to an inferior foundation; superficial appearance or gloss.

venture—risky business enterprise; to take a chance; to attempt.

venture capital—money provided to fund start-up operations of new companies that often are entering risky businesses, but have the potential for high profits; people who provide such funding are called "venture capitalists."

venue—location; in law, court in which a suit must be brought because that's where the crime was committed or the issue arose.

verbatim—word-for-word; verbatims are transcripts of research interviews.

vernacular—common language, peculiar usages, and inside jargon of a country or business.

vernacular engineer—writer.

vertical—going up and down (horizontal means "sideways.")

vertical analysis—item on a financial statement that other accounts are compared to.

vertical marketing—selling to all people in one category, such as all dairy farmers, no matter what size their operation.

vertical union—union that represents employees of different skills within a common industry.

vertically integrated—owning or controlling the entire spectrum of operations from raw materials through finished goods delivered to a customer.

vested—degree of ownership based on length of service, such as a retirement account into which an employer has deposited funds in your name.

vested interest—in law, right to present or future enjoyment of something; informally, selfish interest.

vestibule—lobby or small area at an entrance.

vestibule training—method of training in which a mock worksite is set up away from the regular work area.

Veterans Administration (VA)—federal agency that provides benefits and administers programs for those who have served in the nation's armed forces; a VA loan is a home mortgage whose repayment is guaranteed by the VA.

vicarious—experienced through another, such as enjoyment gained from watching another person's activities.

vice president (VP)—someone who reports to the president and has responsibility for a specific area of operations; as a corporate officer, a vice president can be held liable for the company's actions.

video—system for recording, transmitting, and displaying visual images magnetically rather than photographically, such as on film; short for *videotape*.

video display terminal (VDT)—computer screen device.

video magazine—news and feature program produced on video and sent to people periodically.

videodisc—laser-read optical storage medium, informally called a "platter."

videographer—professional title for someone who operates a video camera.

videotape (VT)—taped video program; cassette and magnetic tape on which a video signal is recorded.

videotext—electronic information transmitted via telephone lines from a computer system to a television screen.

vigorish—bookmaker's charge for accepting a bet; interest paid to a lender.

VIP (very important person)—someone deserving of special treatment due to status, contribution, or other qualifications.

virtual—almost; in essence but not in reality.

virtual corporation—coalition of businesses that function as a unified enterprise on a specific activity but retain their independence and autonomy in all other regards.

virtual reality—electronically generated images that approximate reality for training, entertainment, and system control.

virtuoso—exceptionally skilled performer.

vision—broad perspective or foresight; sense of what something is to become; dream or hallucination; something extraordinarily beautiful or wonderful, although not necessarily practical.

vision statement—official, written statement that outlines and sometimes discusses the broad goals for the organization and the values by which it will purportedly operate (usually the vision isn't that visionary and the values aren't that valued).

vitae—short, detailed résumé (short for *curriculum vitae*, which is Latin for *course of life*).

vital statistics—literally, numbers relating to births and deaths; by extension, essential numbers for understanding something; called "vitals" for short.

vitriol—in chemistry, salts formed from sulfuric acid; emotionally caustic or bitter abuse, usually verbal rather than written.

vocation—profession or calling.

vocational counseling—advice to help people choose careers that fit their personality type, interests, and desires.

voice recognition—electronic systems that translate verbal commands into action.

voicemail—centralized system for leaving personal messages on tape accessible through the telephone.

voiceover—spoken narration on a video program, as opposed to both hearing and seeing what people are actually saying.

void—no longer legally in force; unoccupied or empty; to legally invalidate as though it never existed; to discharge or empty completely, such as body wastes.

volatile—subject to or capable of sudden and rapid changes; not fixed or certain.

volume—measure of three-dimensional space occupied; in

investing, total number of shares traded in a given period; in publishing, a book, or one publication in a series; sound intensity.

volume discount—price reduction based on the amount purchased.

volunteer—someone whose work is done freely and not for compensation; what people who have been in the military know you should never do; to offer.

voodoo economics—disparaging term applied to Reaganomics.

vo-tech—vocational technical school that provides post–high school training geared toward preparing people for specific fields of work, usually in programs lasting two years or less.

voting stock—class of stock that entitles its owners to vote on corporate issues and membership on the board of directors; generally the same as common stock.

voucher—document legally entitling someone to something, often the payment of a debt.

vouching—providing evidence or assurance, such as vouching for the character of another person.

wage—how much money you receive for doing a job.

wage and price controls—controversial technique for trying to control inflation by temporarily freezing or limiting increases in wages and prices.

wage bracket—pay range for a job, established by the human resources department or union contract.

wage curve—chart depicting the relationship between the importance of jobs to an organization and their pay rates.

wage-price spiral—inflation caused by rising wages that lead to rising prices and vice versa.

wage-push inflation—increased prices in response to wage increases without corresponding increases in productivity.

wage survey—compensation paid to employees in an organization compared to employees in similar organizations or among people in a profession.

Wagner Act—see *National Labor Relations Act.*

waitron—unisex term for a waiter or waitress.

waive—to relinquish a right voluntarily; the document through which that is done is called a waiver.

waiver of premium—in insurance, conditions under which a policy will be kept in force, even though the policyholder is unable to pay the premium, such as disability.

walk the line—in labor relations, to picket; in the workplace, to do what you're told to do, especially if you don't agree; to avoid getting in trouble.

walk the talk—do what you say or tell others to do, especially germane for those in management positions when dealing with interpersonal issues.

walking papers—what they give you when you get fired.

walkout—impromptu, unauthorized strike by union employees to attempt to force management to meet demands; also called "wildcat strike."

wall—permanent divider between workspaces, becoming scarce in many modular office landscapes; vertical surface to which to stick things you don't want to bury on a desk or horizontal surface; what you hit when you burn out.

Wall Street—collectively, the U.S. investment community;

literally, street in Manhattan where many investment firms are located as well as the New York and American stock exchanges.

wane—to decline gradually; opposite of *wax*.

warehouse—storage facility for goods, raw materials, and other company possessions.

wares—commercial goods or products; what you have for sale.

warrant—in finance, evidence of a debt or obligation; in investing, option to buy a specified amount of a security at a specified price; in law, judicial instruction to search, seize, or take some other action; to attest to quality or accuracy; to guarantee.

warranty—legal limited guarantee.

wash—situation when two things cancel each other out; to clean out; to run something through a system or process; to stand up under scrutiny or use.

waste—useless material left over from producing a product (if it is toxic or dangerous to people or the environment, it's "hazardous waste"); products that are not up to quality standards; time, money, and effort lost due to inefficiencies; to use up carelessly; to pass up an opportunity.

watch list—securities that a brokerage house or exchange has highlighted for extra attention because of irregularities in trading or other conditions that may lead to sudden changes in price.

watchdog—person or group that looks out for the interests of others by trying to uncover illegal or unethical activity.

watering place/hole—bar favored by businesspeople.

WATS line (wide area telephone service)—network used to provide commercial enterprises reduced rates for high-volume long distance service.

wave theory—see *Kondratieff cycle*.

wax—to grow gradually; opposite of *wane*.

weak market—market with more sellers than buyers.

wear and tear—normal deterioration due to use.

weight—what something weighs; emphasis or force; importance; in paper, thickness; to assign different importance or emphasis to something.

weighted application form—employment application that assigns different values to each question.

welfare—general health and well-being; support provided by a public agency.

welfare state—government assumption of primary responsibility for people.

wetback—illegal immigrant from Mexico, so named because many waded or swam across the Rio Grande to get into the United States.

whet—to stimulate something, such as an appetite.

whine and dine—meal with co-workers, especially one where everyone complains about work.

whiteboard—presentation aid with a white surface that can be written on with special dry-erase markers for more colorful visuals than were possible with a traditional blackboard.

white collar—people who don't do manual labor, primarily those working in offices.

white collar crime—financial crimes such as embezzlement, electronic fraud, and other nonviolent but potentially very expensive and embarrassing activities.

white elephant—something rare but not so valuable, often costing more to keep or maintain than it is worth; formerly prized possession no longer desired.

white flag—sign of surrendering, giving up, conceding an argument.

white goods—large household appliances (which used to be white, but now come in every color of the rainbow).

white knight—friendly suitor for a company who rescues it from a hostile takeover attempt.

white paper—in-depth, ostensibly unbiased investigatory report on something, such as an incident, issue, or technical subject, whether prepared by a company, a third-party source, or the government.

white sale—periodic sale of nonclothing articles made of fabric, such as sheets and towels.

white space—open borders and other areas in a document or publication where nothing is printed, designed to make the piece more attractive and easier to read.

whiteout—correction fluid used to cover up mistakes on a typed document (an essential tool for correcting paperwork at the last second); blizzard in which visibility drops to zero; to eliminate or cover over.

whiz kid—as positive, someone who has achieved recognition for being smart or successful at a relatively young age; as negative, putdown connoting someone brash or inexperienced.

whiz on—propensity to change another's work just to leave your mark, not because the work needs changing (like a dog whizzing on every tree, bush, fire hydrant, and lamp post he passes).

whole life—insurance coverage that provides both a death benefit and a cash value that builds up over the life of the policy at a premium that does not increase with age.

wholesale—in bulk, as it came from the manufacturer.

wholesaler—someone who buys large quantities of goods from a producer and resells them to distributors and retailers, but not end users; the legendary middleman.

wholistic—using nonintrusive methods to solve a problem or cure a disease (favored spelling is "holistic").

widget—hypothetical product used when talking generically about manufacturing or to illustrate a business concept (originally a variation on "gadget").

wildcat drilling—high-risk oil exploration in areas not known for proven deposits.

wildcat strike—impromptu, unauthorized strike by union employees to attempt to force management to meet demands.

will—legal document stating disposition of personal property and financial assets after death.

win-win—resolution in which all parties realize some advantages rather than one benefiting to the exclusion of others (when your boss says this, it means you aren't going to get your way).

windfall—sudden, unexpected financial advantage or good fortune.

windfall profits—embarrassingly high profits, usually resulting from favorable circumstances, but arousing the suspicion of price gouging.

window—workstation where someone transacts business with customers over a counter, such as a teller window; opening in a wall that lets light (and occasionally fresh air) in and allows people inside to see out; in many businesses, the corporate caste system is readily visible by comparing people's proximity to a window and a window's proximity to a corner, especially one with a view.

window of opportunity—narrow time frame in which to take advantage of a situation.

window treatment—how retailers prepare displays in their outside windows to entice customers.

wine and dine—buying meals and drinks for prospective customers or employees, sometimes lavishly, to try to build a relationship in a more relaxed setting; to entertain for business reasons.

wing it—to do something on the spur of the moment and without having the background to know if you are proceeding correctly (for example making a presentation in which some information is missing or for which you are unprepared).

wire—telephone wire; electronic information service; to send or order something electronically; to install electrical or telephone wire; to hook up a telephone or complex electrical device.

wish list—list of items (or prospective employees) you'd like to have under your control.

withholding—amount of money deducted from your paycheck to pay taxes.

word—knowledge of what's going on ("What's the word?").

word of mouth—recommendations, good or bad, from past customers to prospective customers, the most powerful form of advertising.

word processing (WP)—writing with the aid of a computer (if what you're writing includes graphics, it's called desktop publishing); clerical function of inputting and producing documents.

work—effort; in science, transfer of energy by force (work of one joule is accomplished when a force of one newton acts over a distance of one meter); your job and/or the place where you do it; result of your efforts, such as a work of art; anything you have to do when you'd really rather be doing something else.

work ethic—moral compulsion or motivation to work; informally, willingness to put work above personal desires: "strong" when you put your job before your need for family, friends, and recreation, "poor" when you put other desires first, have undependable work habits, or are content with lackluster quality in your performance.

work order—document authorizing or requesting completion of a specific task.

work permit—papers that give a nonresident permission to work in the country.

work simplification—process of studying and reorganizing work so it can be done faster and more time-efficiently, ideally making it more productive and cost-effective as well.

work slowdown—intentional slowing down of time it takes to produce a product or provide a service, used as a signal to management that workers are unhappy with working conditions.

work standards—criteria for what happens in the workplace or the quality of a final product.

work stoppage—walkout, strike, or other organized refusal to work by employees.

work-study—going to school to learn a job or profession and working at the job at the same time.

worker's comp(ensation)—coverage provided under state laws for job-related injuries and conditions that make it impossible for someone to work.

workers—those who do the work, as opposed to those who have supervisory responsibilities.

workforce—entire group of employees in a company or geographic area.

workhorse—someone who takes on or consistently handles a heavy workload without complaining; basic machine such as a photocopier that doesn't break down very often.

working capital—funds a company has to work with, typically the sum of a company's cash, accounts receivable, goods in inventory, and other assets (for net working capital, subtract current liabilities from current assets).

working papers—certificate that verifies a person is old enough not to be subject to child labor laws.

working poor—people in low-wage jobs who, although employed, are still living in and likely to stay in poverty.

workload—amount of work you have to do.

workplace—overall environment in which you work, including both physical and intangible aspects.

worksheet—place for rough or preliminary calculations.

workspace—how much room you personally have to work in.

workstation—specific place or area in which you work, especially if you're a clerical or factory worker; full-featured computer.

workstyle—personal idiosyncrasies and habit patterns a person brings to performing a job, such as organizing, dealing with other people, and preferred ways to supervise or be supervised.

World Bank—originally the International Bank for Reconstruction and Development, a bank that loans money to second- and third-world countries.

worth—value; how much something costs or means to the person who wants it.

writ—written order issued by a court demanding that the recipient do or stop doing something.

write—to put words on paper; to record in a computer's memory; in insurance, to start a policy.

write down—to record something; to take a loss on paper; to package or revise information or instructions so workers at a simple reading level can understand and act on them.

write off—to decide that something is not worth pursuing; in finance, to deduct an expense for tax purposes.

X

X factor—unknown element in a process or equation.

xerography—technical name for photocopying.

Xerox—business machines company that first marketed photocopying.

Y

Yankee peddler—unscrupulous salesperson.

yardstick—any standard measurement that can be used for comparison.

year—twelve-month period that in business may or may not conform to the typical January-to-December cycle.

year-end—something that happens at the end of a business year, such as payment of a dividend or bonus.

year-to-date (YTD)—running totals of transactions from the beginning of the year to the present.

yellow-dog contract—illegal agreement that workers will keep their jobs only if they don't join a union.

yen—basic unit of Japanese currency; wish or desire.

yield—return from an investment, usually expressed as a percentage; in agribusiness, amount produced per acre; in manufacturing, amount of product produced in a production run; to give up or surrender.

yuppie—marketing designation for young urban professionals, now synonymous with white collar Baby Boomers, often living beyond their means, who have trapped themselves with superficial lifestyles and values.

Z

zero-based budgeting (ZBB)—determining a budget by starting from zero every year and justifying each expense for the upcoming year.

zero defects (ZD)—defect-free; motivational goal or slogan for corporate quality campaigns.

zero population growth (ZPG)—point at which a country's births and deaths are in balance.

zero sum—interaction in which the result is zero: whatever is gained by one side is equivalently lost by the other side.

zero tolerance—policy of accepting no excuses or mitigating circumstances for improper actions or failures, such as drug use.

Zip + 4—nine-digit zip code originally designed to be used voluntarily by bulk mailers, but becoming increasingly common due to electronic mail sorting.

zone—division of a larger area; level of high performance ("she's in the zone today"); to divide into areas.

zoning—land-use classifications enacted by local governments.

Acronyms and Abbreviations

AA—Affirmative Action; Alcoholics Anonymous; Associate of Arts

AAA—American Automobile Association

AAP—Affirmative Action Plan

ABA—American Bankers Association

ABC—American Broadcasting Corp.

ACE—Active Corps of Executives

ACI—Advertising Council, Inc.

ACRS—Accelerated Cost Recovery System

ADA—Americans with Disabilities Act; American Dairy Association

ADEA—Age Discrimination in Employment Act of 1967

ADR—Asset Depreciation Range; American Depositary Receipt

AE—Account Executive

AFL-CIO—American Federation of Labor–Congress of Industrial Organizations

AI—Artificial Intelligence; Artificial Insemination

AICPA—American Institute of Certified Public Accountants

a.k.a.—also known as

AMA—American Medical Association; American Management Association

AMEX—American Stock Exchange

AMS—Academy of Marketing Science; Analytical Marketing System; Administrative Management Society

ANI—Automatic Number Identification

ANOVA—Analysis of Variance

ANSI—American National Standards Institute

AP—Associated Press

APB—Accounting Principles Board

APR—Annual Percentage Rate

AQL—Acceptable Quality Level

ASAP—As Soon as Possible

ASO—Administrative Services Only

ASQC—American Society for Quality Control

AT&T—American Telephone and Telegraph

ATM—Automatic Teller Machine

AV—Audiovisual

BA—Bachelor of Arts

BARS—Behaviorally Anchored Rating Scale

BAU—Business as Usual

BBA—Bachelor of Business Administration

BBB—Better Business Bureau

BC—Blind Copy; Before Copiers; Before Christ

BFOQ—Bona Fide Occupational Qualification

BFP—Bona Fide Purchaser

BOC—Bell Operating Company

BOHICA—Bend Over, Here It Comes Again

BPI—Buying Power Index

BRC—Business Reply Card

BS—Bachelor of Science

C&F—Cost and Freight

CAD—Computer-Aided Design

CADAM—Computer-Aided Design and Manufacturing

CAD/CAM—Computer Aided Design/Computer-Aided Manufacturing

CAE—Computer-Assisted Education

CAI—Computer-Assisted Instruction

CAM—Computer-Aided Manufacturing; Certified Administrative Manager

CBD—Central Business District

CBS—Columbia Broadcasting Service

CBT—Computer-Based Training

CC—Copy

CCTV—Closed Circuit Television

CD—Compact Disc

CD-I—Compact Disc–Interactive

CD-ROM—Compact Disc–Read Only Memory

CEA—Council of Economic Advisers

CEBS—Certified Employee Benefits Specialist

CED—Committee for Economic Development

CEO—Chief Executive Officer

CETA—Comprehensive Employment and Training Act of 1975

CEU—Continuing Education Unit

CFC—Chartered Financial Consultant

CFO—Chief Financial Officer

CFP—Certified Financial Planner

CFS—Chronic Fatigue Syndrome

CFTC—Commodities Futures Trading Commission

CG—Character Generator

CIA—Central Intelligence Agency; Cash in Advance

CIF—Cost, Insurance, Freight

CIO—Chief Information Officer

CIS—Customer Information System

CLU—Certified Life Underwriter

CMO—Chief Marketing Officer

CMP—Complete Meeting Package; Certified Meeting Professional

CMSA—Consolidated Metropolitan Statistical Area

CNBC—NBC's Cable news channel

CNN—Cable News Network

COD—Cash on Delivery

COLA—Cost of Living Adjustment

COMECON—Council for Mutual Economic Assistance

COMEX—Securities and Commodities Exchange

COO—Chief Operating Officer

COPQ—Cost of Poor Quality

COQ—Cost of Quality

CPA—Certified Public Accountant

CPCU—Chartered Property and Casualty Underwriter

CPI—Consumer Price Index

CPM—Cost Per Thousand; Critical Path Method

CPS—Certified Professional Secretary

CPSA—Consumer Products Safety Administration; Consumer Products Safety Act

CPSC—Consumer Products Safety Commission

CPU—Central Processing Unit

CRS—Can't Remember Shit

CRT—Cathode Ray Tube

CSD—Credited Service Date

CSI—Customer Satisfaction Index

CSPI—Center for Science in the Public Interest

CSR—Customer Service Representative

CU—Consumers Union

CYA—Cover Your Ass

D&B—Dun & Bradstreet

D&E—Debits and Expenditures

DAT—Digital Audiotape

DBA—Doing Business As

DBS—Data Base Services; Date Base Search

DCT—Data Cartridge Tape

DEC—Digital Equipment Corp.

DJI—Dow Jones Industrial Average

DMU—Decision Making Unit

DOS—Disk Operating System

DOT—Department of Transportation

DP—Data Processing

DSS—Decision Support System

EAP—Employee Assistance Program

EC—European Community; Economic Community

ECOM—Electronic Computer-Originated Mail

ECR—Efficient Customer Response

ECU—European Currency Unit

EDI—Electronic Data Interchange

EDP—Electronic Data Processing

EEC—European Economic Community

EDLP—Every Day Low Pricing

EEO—Equal Employment Opportunity

EEOC—Equal Employment Opportunity Commission

EFTS—Electronic Funds Transfer System

EIR—Environmental Impact Report

EIS—Environmental Impact Statement

EMS—European Monetary System

EOM—End of Month

EOQ—End of Quarter; Economic Order Quantity

EP—European Plan; Extended Play

EPA—Environmental Protection Agency

EPS—Earnings Per Share

ERA—Equal Rights Amendment; Earned Run Average

ERISA—Employee Retirement Income Security Act

ERSOP—Employee Retirement Stock Ownership Plan

ERTA—Economic Recovery Tax Act of 1981

ESOP—Employee Stock Ownership Plan

ESQ—Esquire

EVP—Executive Vice President

EXIMBANK—Export-Import Bank

FAA—Federal Aviation Administration

FAB—Features, Advantages, and Benefits

FASB—Financial Accounting Standards Board

FAX—Facsimile

FCC—Federal Communications Commission

FDA—Food & Drug Administration

FDIC—Federal Deposit Insurance Corporation

FEMA—Federal Emergency Management Agency

FHA—Federal Housing Administration

FHLMC—Federal Home Loan Mortgage Corp.

FICA—Federal Insurance Contributions Act

FIFO—First In, First Out

FIN—Federal Identification Number

FLRC—Federal Labor Relations Council

FLSA—Fair Labor Standards Act

FMIIA—Farmer's Home Administration

FMI—Food Marketing Institute

FMOC—Federal Open Market Committee

FMRR—Financial Management Rate of Return

FNMA—Federal National Mortgage Association

FNN—Financial News Network

FOB—Freight on Board; Free on Board

FOIA—Freedom of Information Act

FOK—Fill or Kill Order

FPC—Federal Power Commission

FRB—Federal Reserve Board

FSLIC—Federal Savings & Loan Insurance Corp.

FTC—Federal Trade Commission

FTS—Federal Telecommunication System

FTZ—Free Trade Zone; Foreign Trade Zone

FUD—Fear, Uncertainty, Dread/Doubt

FYI—For Your Information

GAAP—Generally Accepted Accounting Principles

GAO—General Accounting Office

GATT—General Agreement on Tariffs and Trade

GAW—Guaranteed Annual Wage

GDP—Gross Domestic Product

GI—Government Issue

GIC—Guaranteed Income Contract

GIGO—Garbage/Gospel In, Garbage/Gospel Out

GIS—Geographic Information System

GNMA—Government National Mortgage Association

GNP—Gross National Product

GOB—Going out of Business

GPO—Government Printing Office

GS—Government Service

GTC—Good Till Canceled

HMO—Health Maintenance Organization

HOW—Homeowners Warranty Plan

HP—Hewlett-Packard

HRD—Human Resources Development

HRDIS—Human Resources Development Information System

HUD—Housing and Urban Development

HUHA—Head up His/Her Ass

HVAC—Heating, Ventilating, and Air Conditioning

IBM—International Business Machines

IBM PC—IBM Personal Computer

IBRD—International Bank for Reconstruction and Development

ICC—Interstate Commerce Commission

IMF—International Monetary Fund

IMM—International Monetary Market

I/O—Input/Output

IPO—Initial Public Offering

IR—Industrial Relations

IRA—Individual Retirement Account

IRR—Internal Rate of Return

IRS—Internal Revenue Service

ISO—International Organization for Standardization; Insurance Service Office; Incentive Stock Options

ITT—International Telephone and Telegraph Co.

JC—Junior College

JD—Juris Doctor

JEC—Joint Economic Committee of Congress

JIT—Just in Time

JUSE—Union of Japanese Scientists and Engineers

LAN—Local Area Network

L/C—Letter of Credit

LBO—Leveraged Buyout

LCD—Liquid Crystal Display

LDC—Less Developed Country

LED—Light Emitting Diode; Lighted Electronic Display

LIFO—Last In, First Out

LTD—Long Term Disability; Limited

LTL—Less Than Truckload

MA—Master of Arts

MAP—Modified American Plan

MAS—Management Advisory Services

MBA—Master of Business Administration

MBO—Management by Objectives

MBWA—Management by Walking Around

MCI—Microwave Communications, Inc. (now MCI Tele-communications Corp.)

MD—Medical Doctor

MD&A—Management's Discussion & Analysis

MIS—Management Information System

MIT—Massachusetts Institute of Technology

MITI—Ministry of Industrial Trade and Industry (Japan)

MLM—Multi-Level Marketing

MLS—Multiple Listing Service

MNC—Multinational Corp.

MO—Modus Operandi

MRP—Material Requirement Planning; Material Resources Planning

MS—Master of Science

MSA—Metropolitan Statistical Area

MSU—Making Stuff Up

NAFTA—North American Free Trade Agreement

NASA—National Aeronautics and Space Administration

NASD—National Association of Securities Dealers

NASDAQ—National Association of Securities Dealers Automated Quotations

NBC—National Broadcasting Co.

NCR—National Cash Register; Non-Carbon Receipt

NIH—National Institutes of Health; Not Invented Here

NIMBY—Not in My Back Yard

NLRA—National Labor Relations Act

NLRB—National Labor Relations Board

NOI—Net Operating Income

NOL—Net Operating Loss

NOW—Negotiable Order of Withdrawal

NPV—Net Present Value

NR—Not Rated

NSF—Non-Sufficient Funds

NYSE—New York Stock Exchange

O&I—Office and Industrial

O&T—Office and Technical

OAG—Official Airline Guide

OASI—Old-Age and Survivors Insurance

OCR—Optical Character Reader

OD—Organizational Development

OEM—Original Equipment Manufacturer

OFCCP—Office of Federal Contract Compliance Programs

OJT—On the Job Training

OM—Operating Manager

OMB—Office of Management and Budget

OPEC—Organization of Petroleum Exporting Countries

OR—Operations Research; Operating Room

OQM—Operational Quality Management

OSHA—Occupational Safety and Health Administration; Occupational Safety and Health Act

OTB—Open to Buy

OTC—Over the Counter

OUS—Outside the United States

P&I—Principle and Interest

P&L—Profit and Loss statement

PA—Professional Association; Physician's Assistant

PAC—Political Action Committee

PAL—European equivalent of VHS

PC—Personal Computer; Politically Correct

PCS—Personal Communication Service

PDA—Personal Digital Assistant

PDCA—Plan, Do, Check, Act

PDSA—Plan, Do, Study, Act

P/E—Price/Earnings ratio

PF—Programmable Function

Ph.D—Doctor of Philosophy

PIK—Payment in Kind

PIRG—Public Interest Research Group

PIMS—Profit Impact of Marketing Strategies

PITI—Principal, Interest, Taxes, and Insurance

PM—Post-Mortem; Post Meridian

PMA—Primary Marketing Area; Positive Mental Attitude

PMS—Pantone Matching System

PMSA—Primary Metropolitan Statistical Area

PO—Post Office; Purchase Order; Piss Off

POP—Point of Purchase

POS—Point of Sale

POTS—Plain Old Telephone Service

PPO—Preferred Provider Organization

PR—Public Relations

PS—Postscript

PSA—Public Service Announcement

PUC—Public Utilities Commission

PUD—Planned Unit Development

PVC—Poly-Vinyl Chloride

QA—Quality Assurance

QC—Quality Circle

QFD—Quality Function Development

QM—Quality Management

QWERTY—standard keyboard (top row keys from left)

QWL—Quality of Work Life

®—Registered

R&D—Research and Development

RC—Reply Card

REIT—Real Estate Investment Trust

RFP—Request for Proposals

RGB—Red, Green, Blue

RHIP—Rank Has Its Privileges

ROA—Return on Assets

ROC—Regional Operating Center/Company

ROE—Return on Equity

ROG—Receipt of Goods

ROI—Return on Investment

ROP—Run of Press; Run of Paper

ROS—Return on Sales; Run of Schedule

RPM—Revolutions Per Minute

RR—Registered Representative; Railroad

RTC—Resolution Trust Corporation

S&L—Savings and Loan Association

S&M—Sales and Marketing

S&P—Standard & Poor's

SAR—Stock Appreciation Right

SASE—Self-Addressed Stamped Envelope

SBA—Small Business Administration

SBU—Strategic Business Unit

SCORE—Service Corps of Retired Executives

SEC—Securities and Exchange Commission

SEP—Simplified Employee Pension Plan

SG&A—Selling, General, and Administrative Expenses

SIC—Standard Industrial Code; Standard Industrial Classification

SKU—Stock Keeping Unit

SLMA—Student Loan Marketing Association

SM—Service Mark

SMSA—Standard Metropolitan Statistical Area

SNAFU—Situation Normal, All Fouled/Fucked Up

SOB—Souls on Board; Son of Boss

SOP—Standard Operating Policy/Procedure

SOS—Source of Supply; Save Our Ship; Same Old Shit

SOW—Same Old Way

SPC—Statistical Process Control

SQC—Statistical Quality Control

SQM—Strategic Quality Management

STD—Short Term Disability

STERR—Select, Train, Empower, Recognize, Reward

SWOT—Strengths, Weaknesses, Opportunities, Threats

T&A—Transportation and Administration; Tits and Ass

T&D—Training and Development

T&E—Travel and Entertainment

TAN—Tax Anticipation Note

TARBU—Typical Activity Run By Us

TARP—Technical Assistance Research Programs Institute

TBA—To Be Announced

TI—Texas Instruments

TIGER—Topographically Integrated Encoding and Referencing System

TIN—Taxpayer Identifying Number

TL—Truckload

TM—Trademark

TO—Turnover

TQC—Total Quality Control

TQM—Total Quality Management

TVCR—Television/Video Cassette Recorder

UCC—Uniform Commercial Code

UL—Underwriters Laboratories

UN—United Nations

UNESCO—United Nations Education, Scientific and Cultural Organization

UPC—Universal Product Code

UPI—United Press International

UPS—United Parcel Service

US—United States

USDA—United States Department of Agriculture

USITC—U.S. International Trade Commission

USP—Unique Selling Proposition

VA—Veterans Administration

VAD—Value-Added Dealer

VALS—Values and Lifestyles Program

VAR—Value-Added Reseller

VAT—Value-Added Tax

VCR—Video Cassette Recorder

VDT—Video Display Terminal

VHS—Videotape format

VIP—Very Important Person

VMS—Vertical Marketing System

VP—Vice President

VT—Videotape

VTR—Videotape Recorder

WAN—Wide Area Network

WATS—Wide Area Telephone Service

WIIFM—What's In It For Me

WORM—Write Once, Read Many

WP—Word Processing

WPI—Wholesale Price Index

WSJ—*The Wall Street Journal*

WYSIWYG—What You See Is What You Get

YEC—Young Executives Club

YPC—Young President's Club

YPO—Young President's Organization

YTD—Year to Date

YTM—Yield to Maturity

YUPPIE—Young Urban Professional

ZBB—Zero-Based Budgeting

ZD—Zero Defects

ZPG—Zero Population Growth

Computer Appendix

access time—how long it takes a computer to find information in its memory or on a peripheral storage system such as a floppy disk or data cartridge drive.

active—working; applies to one computer, a network, or the area within a computer program that will be affected by the next keystroke.

active printer—printer currently used or designated to be used by a computer.

adapter—device used as an intermediary to make a computer work with a device it isn't designed to work with.

alphanumeric—numbers and letters on a standard computer keyboard.

Alt—The Alt key on a standard keyboard, often used to activate software commands.

analog—modulated electricity flow; analog (AC power) transmits in waves, digital (DC power) in on-off spurts; computers "talk" in digital while analog power is what most electrical instruments function on in the United States.

ANSI (American National Standards Institute)—organization that determines U.S. standards for computers as well as noncomputer equipment.

ANSI character set—8-bit character set containing 256 characters, including those found in the English alphabet as well as fractions, foreign alphabet characters, and miscellaneous symbols and lines.

APL ("A" Programming Language)—outdated interactive

language used to program computers to run complex operations; requires special symbols and a special keyboard.

Apple—California-based computer company noted for its user-friendly personal computers; the name also applies to any of the company's computers.

application—specific task to be performed by a computer; software program for a specific type of work.

archive—to store information permanently offline, usually on a tape or disk.

argument—variable that can be assigned a value.

arrow keys—keys on a computer keyboard that are used to move the cursor.

artificial intelligence (AI)—computer-driven smarts; use of computers to mimic human thinking, incorporating creative problem solving as well as strict logic.

ASCII (American Standard Code for Information Interchange)—standard code (the first 128 characters of the ANSI character set) used to exchange data between all types of computers and software.

assembler—software program that translates assembly language into binary code that a computer can understand.

assembly language—low-level programming language that must be converted to binary code before the computer can use it.

async(hronous)—type of data communications in which the time interval between characters being transmitted changes.

attribute—feature of a computer; feature of computerized information; way a computer handles a specific function.

auto execute (AUTOEXEC)—program, series of programs, or files that run automatically when the computer is turned on.

aux(iliary)—device that is not a standard part of the computer; port to which to connect a peripheral device.

background activity—function that is being worked on by

the computer while it is working directly with the user on something else, such as printing a file while working in another one.

backup—copy of a file that is kept on a disk or tape; organized data security system in which the user regularly makes or updates an offline backup copy of all files in a computer's memory as a safeguard against a disk crash, theft, catastrophic power surges, viruses, and other data-endangering hazards.

backup sites—remote site linked to a mainframe where copies of all computer records are kept.

bad sector—portion on a disk that is not working correctly.

band width—bits of information transmitted per second; the higher the band width, the faster the transmission.

base address—location of specific information in the computer.

base memory—region of memory containing the first software instructions the computer executes when it is turned on.

BASIC (Beginner's All-Purpose Symbolic Instruction Code)—one of the easiest programming languages, often included in many computers.

Basic Input/Output System (BIOS)—peripheral that allows a user to enter or retrieve information from a computer; software in an IBM or compatible PC that communicates with the computer's devices.

batch (BAT) file—series of instructions or commands that are written into one file identified with the suffix "bat."

batch processing—group of files or jobs that are to be run in a specific order; opposite of "interactive."

baud—number of bits per second that can be transmitted by a modem or other electronic data transmission device.

Bernoulli disk—form of portable hard disk offering large storage capacity, making it easier to move large job files between computers.

binary—using two numbers, 1 and 0, to signify on and off signals for the storage and transmission of digital information.

binary file—file that is written in base two so it can be read by a computer.

bit—binary digit, either 1 or 0, represented by electricity as on or off; eight bits make up one byte.

bitmap—image stored as a pattern of bits, usually a graphics file.

block—section of data that is coded to be moved or in some way changed.

board—short for *circuit board*, where a computer's chips are installed; a board added as an enhancer or extender is often called a "card."

boot—to start the computer or to restart it, loading the operating system.

branch—in directory systems, subset of a major grouping, such as a subdirectory; in programming, potential course of logic in the program.

buffer—device that temporarily stores information going from one device to a device that works at a different speed (for example, a printer works slower than a computer, so the information is moved to a buffer before it is printed).

bug—problem with a computer program or in the computer's electronic functions (the name comes from the havoc wreaked by a real bug that got into one of the vacuum tubes used in the first computers).

built-in font—font stored in the permanent read-only memory (ROM) of a printer; also called "resident" or "hardware font."

bulletin board—interactive computer network where people with common interests can "converse" electronically or exchange information.

bus—path that electronic signals travel; computers and peripherals must have the same bus in order to communicate.

byte—group of eight bits that the computer works on all at once.

C—popular programming language.

cable—power cables and communication cables that transmit electricity differently: AC (analog) power goes through a power cable, DC (digital) goes through communications cables; to connect computer devices together with cables.

cache—RAM used to store frequently used data from the disk drive so the computer can access it from the faster memory the next time it is needed.

canned program—prewritten program sold for use by many people.

card—removable computer component containing electrical components and circuitry; also called "board."

carriage return (CR)—command written by the Enter or Return key on the keyboard to move the cursor to the start of a new line (similar to returning the carriage of a typewriter to the left to start a new line).

cartridge font—device containing information telling a computer how to print a specific typeface that physically plugs in to a printer.

cascade—arrangement of overlapping open windows on a computer screen.

cathode ray tube (CRT)—device used for computer screens in which magnetic fields direct a spray of electrons onto the screen.

central processing unit (CPU)—actual brain of the computer.

channel—path an electronic data transmission takes from one point to the next.

characters per second (CPS)—measure of band width.

chip—thin piece of silicon, usually square or rectangular, on which the circuit elements of a semiconductor device are mounted.

clear—to erase or replace information.

click on—to tap the keys on a mouse.

clipboard—temporary storage location used when transferring data from one file or document to another.

clock speed—base frequency (in megahertz) at which a computer runs; the higher the clock speed "ticks," the faster the computer works.

clone—product that is a copy of a more popular brand.

close—to stop working on a file or document.

cluster—several linked workstations that together function like a low-end supercomputer.

code—computer instructions; the complexity of a computer program is often measured in lines of code.

coding—writing computer programs or instructions.

cold boot—restarting the computer by turning the power off and on (a "warm" or "soft" boot involves restarting the software without turning the power off).

color graphics adapter (CGA)—early video card.

COM—serial port where an auxiliary device can be plugged in; numbered sequentially (COM1, COM2) if the computer has more than one.

command—word or phrase chosen to carry out an action.

Common Business-Oriented Language (COBOL)—programming language often used to write business programs, such as those for accounts payable and receivable.

Compact Disk–Read Only Memory (CD-ROM)—laser-read, high-capacity data storage disk whose information can be read but not changed.

compatible—two devices that work together or two computers that can run the same programs.

compiler—program that takes higher-level programming language and converts it to binary code.

CompuServe—one of the first companies to provide computerized libraries of information that can be accessed through the phone lines.

computer-aided design (CAD)—graphics-based computer that shows images on a screen to help design items or buildings.

computer-aided design and manufacturing (CADAM)—converting images to a robot that physically stamps out or cuts out what is shown on the screen; also called computer-aided design/computer-aided manufacturing (CAD/CAM).

computer conferencing—meeting in which the participants communicate by computer.

computerese—language and jargon used by people who are familiar with computers.

con—short for *conference*.

configure—to make hardware and software work together exactly as you'd like.

control character—symbol that appears on the screen, but is not printed when the file is output, to indicate an embedded command, such as underlining, superscript, or font change.

control menu—first choices displayed while working in a file or directory; also called "system menu."

conventional memory—original memory that comes with a computer.

coprocessor—auxiliary processing unit used to perform time-consuming processes, such as mathematical functions, while leaving the central processing unit free for other functions.

copy—to duplicate information or files from one part of the computer to another location, such as a temporary file, or to another storage device, such as a floppy disk.

core—main memory (the name comes from the first computers, which used a doughnut-shaped device to store memory information).

CP/M—outdated type of operating system.

crash—program error or hardware breakdown that makes the computer inoperable, usually a result of the read/write head of the disk coming into contact with the disk.

Cray—supercomputer built by Cray Research.

Ctrl—Control key on a standard keyboard, often used to activate software commands.

current directory—directory of the file that is being worked in.

current drive—drive that a computer is operating on at the moment (typical PCs will have up to four drives).

cursor—position indicator used on the computer screen to show where the next user entry will appear.

cut and paste—moving information from one place to another in a document or between files.

daisy wheel—printer that uses a rotating wheel as a typeface element.

data—any information stored in the computer, although it most frequently refers to numbers or groups of names that are to be analyzed in some way.

data acquisition center (DAC)—terminal for inputting and receiving information from another computer.

data acquisition system (DAS)—network of terminals for inputting and receiving information from another computer.

database—collection of data that can be accessed in multiple ways as needed; the compiling and updating of the information in a database is called database management.

data cartridge—hard-shelled cassette with a metal baseplate containing magnetic tape on which data is stored, usually for backup purposes; data cartridge tape technology often uses the acronym DCT.

data compression—software function that manipulates data being stored to reduce the amount of physical storage space needed; the amount of compression is expressed as a ratio, such as 2 to 1.

data entry—job in which someone inputs data, such as orders, into a computer system.

data file—computer document containing raw or sorted data.

data integrity—safeguarding of a business's computer information and systems from losses or hazards stemming from fire, theft, sabotage, or unauthorized access or use; likelihood that the data in offline storage is identical to that on the computer's hard drive.

data interchange format (DIF)—way to change data from one format to another that can be interpreted by both machines.

data processing (DP)—sorting data so it can be analyzed; usually refers to business processes such as payroll, billing, and recordkeeping.

data security—protection of computer systems and their data from hackers through the use of passwords, encryption systems, and other safeguards; also applies to tactics to make sure data is safe from hazards such as high heat or electrical surges.

data tape—magnetic tapes of different sizes and shapes on which data is stored for offline backup.

data transfer rate/time—how fast the hard disk can save and retrieve data to internal memory or an offline storage device; how fast a peripheral device can stream data into a computer system.

data transmission—sending or receiving information from one computer to another.

dBase I-II-III—popular business management software that combines graphics, spreadsheet capabilities, and other data management abilities.

dead time—time a computer can't be used because it is malfunctioning; time a user must wait to perform a function because the computer is doing something else, such as sending information to a printer.

debug—methodically checking a computer program or array of hardware to discover and fix problems.

dedicated—piece of hardware reserved for special use.

default—mode that the computer or auxiliary equipment will use if you don't command it to use something else.

default printer—printer that a computer automatically uses when the print command is given; a computer can have only one default printer and it must be an active one.

de-mux—to take information from a multiplexer and break it into its original number of signals.

density—how closely together data is packed on a diskette (high density [HD] and double density [DD] are the most common); disk drives can effectively record information in only one density, but may be able to read information in more than one.

desktop—visual display on the computer screen of a system using a graphic user interface that acts as a vertical counterpart to the standard horizontal surface where work is spread out; also refers to any piece of hardware that easily fits on a desk.

desktop publishing—PC software and hardware capable of producing finished materials of such high quality that they can be used as originals for printing; word processing program with extensive graphics capability.

destination directory—directory to which a user intends to move one or more files.

device—hardware used with a computer, but not the computer itself.

diagnosis—finding problems in computer hardware or software.

diagnostic—computer program or hardware tool that helps locate bugs.

dial up—to connect via modem.

digital—information encoded as a series of binary bits rather than modulated electrical signals.

digital audio tape (DAT)—type of magnetic tape used to store data.

Digital Equipment Corp. (DEC)—major manufacturer of mainframes and minicomputers.

direct access—being able to retrieve data in any order, not just the order in which it was stored; also called "random access."

direct memory access (DMA) controller—microchip that manages requests for memory access from peripheral devices without using the central processing unit.

direction keys—four arrow keys on a computer keyboard that control the movement of the cursor.

directory—collection of subdirectories and/or files.

disk/diskette—most common device for magnetic storage of data: a "hard" or "rigid" disk usually is built right into the computer and provides high capacity; a "floppy" disk (or diskette) is inserted in a floppy drive for reading and writing, then removed and stored outside the computer.

disk drive—device used for storing and retrieving data on disks; can be built in to (internal) or separate from (external or peripheral) the computer.

disk operating system (DOS)—most common personal computer operating system.

documentation—written explanation of how computer hardware or software works, usually available as a printed manual, sometimes also on disk.

dot matrix—printer that uses many small dots to create the image.

dot pitch—sharpness of the image on a computer screen, literally the distance (in millimeters, such as 0.29) between the dots that form an image; the lower the number, the sharper the screen image.

double click—two quick clicks on a mouse button, usually to give a different command from a single click.

double-sided disk—floppy disk that can store data on both sides (early floppies recorded on only one side).

download—to import information from another computer, diskettes, or online information service.

drag—to hold down the mouse button while moving the mouse to highlight the command desired or information to be worked with.

drive—see *disk drive*.

driver—program or set of computer programs that let the computer system recognize and communicate with devices such as a printer or disk drive.

dual in-line package (DIP) switches—small switches in many computers and computer peripherals used to set up or ad-. just the equipment by setting them to On or Off.

dumb terminal—monitor and keyboard with no resident memory that is attached to a mainframe computer.

dump—to download data for later reading or processing.

duplex—ability to transmit and receive data at the same time.

EBCDIC—binary character representation similar to ASCII used by large IBM computers.

echo—graphic representation on a screen of what a user has just input, often turned off when typing a password (so that people can't see it on the screen).

electromagnetic interference (EMI)—problems that can result when a magnet or electronic device is used near a computer.

Enhanced Expanded Memory Specification (EEMS)—informally known as "expanded memory," a way of providing a computer with additional storage area for data.

enhanced graphics adapter (EGA)—an older form of video graphics card.

E-mail (electronic mail)—system for typing a message on one computer and sending it to a user on the same mainframe or network.

emulation mode—mode in which a device such as a computer or printer can imitate the behavior of a different device.

enable—to turn on a computer or peripheral; to prepare a system to receive or send information or execute a command.

encryption—data security technique that puts a message into code that can be decoded only with a decryption device at the receiving end of a transmission.

environment—physical location and specifications needed for a program to operate properly, such as a minimum memory, access to a mouse, graphics capability, and other requirements.

EPT port—port on some printers that requires special software to allow the printer to run.

erase—to delete data permanently from system memory, disk, or tape.

error—deviation from what should occur; faulty reading or writing of a data bit.

error checking (EC)—function performed as part of data transmission from one computer or peripheral system to another to ensure that data is received error-free.

error message—computer's diagnosis of an error, often including a prompt or choices for how to fix it or what to do next.

escape—to abandon a command before executing or before it has been completed; function that allows a user to leave a menu or secondary document without saving changes; Esc(ape) key on the keyboard, used in conjunction with other keys to perform specific functions, such as warm booting the computer.

exchangeable disk pack—portable hard disk that can be moved from computer to computer.

exclusive application—application that takes the computer's full attention so that nothing else can be done at the same time; application that runs only on certain kinds of computers.

expand—to add memory or functionality to a computer; to show hidden information on the computer screen.

expanded memory—permanent memory physically added to a computer or printer in the form of a board or card.

Expanded Memory Specification (EMS)—type of expanded memory available on systems that conform to the Lotus-Intel-Microsoft expanded memory specification (LIM EMS).

expansion boards—cards or small boards that physically contain the chips or hardware necessary to add memory, series ports, network hardware, or other functions to the computer.

expansion slot—physical location in which special boards are placed to increase memory or provide other additional functions to a computer.

extended memory—special type of expanded memory available only on some lower-end DOS machines; it cannot be addressed with all applications.

extension—period and three symbols used after a file name in DOS and some other operating systems to tell what type of information is contained in the file (.DOC = document, .BAT = batch, etc.).

female—end of a cable or device into which another piece fits (the source of the name is obvious, we hope).

file—single document that has been named.

file attribute—any characteristic of a file.

file folder—document file in an Apple system.

file format—structure of data in a file.

file name—name, including extensions, used to call the file onto the computer screen or perform other functions with it.

file server—central computer or disk that contains software or information that allows other computers to access or store software or files.

filter command—command that modifies information or a file so it can be used by another command or device.

first generation—first draft or iteration of anything, whether equipment or a document.

fixed disk—nonremovable memory storage system; also called "hard disk."

fixed-width font—font in which all characters have uniform widths (like typewriter characters).

flaming—sending obscene or abusive E-mail from computer to computer, typically to the dismay of the recipient.

floating operations per second (FLOPs)—measure of how fast the computer can do complex mathematical functions.

floppy—removable magnetic diskette used to store information, so named because larger sizes were flexible; includes plastic-shelled 3.5-inch diskettes (even though they're anything but flexible), but does not include CDs.

floptical—hybrid diskette technology combining magnetic data storage with optical tracking functions.

flowchart—chart that shows the logic flow a computer program uses to perform specific functions.

flow control—handshake used to regulate data transmission from one device to another.

font—graphic design or style applied to all numerals, symbols, and characters in the alphabet; fonts usually come in different sizes and provide different variations such as boldface, italics, and underlining.

footer—text that appears at the bottom of every page of a document when it is printed, such as page numbers.

format—any method for arranging information and making it look a desired way; to prepare a disk to store information.

FORTRAN (FORmula TRANslation)—computer programming language that uses mathematical formulas, developed in the 1950s and still widely used today.

fragmented file—file that is stored in several parts of the computer's hard disk, making it slower to access.

front-end system—small computer that receives information, then translates or works with it before sending it to a larger computer, freeing the larger computer from routine tasks so it can handle more complex or specialized functions.

function key—row of keys at the top or to one side of a keyboard used by software programs for specific processing commands.

fuzzy logic—programming term meaning the program isn't well structured or documented.

garbage/gospel in, garbage/gospel out (GIGO)—theory that the analysis of data is only as good as the data itself or the program performing the analysis.

gate array—transistor matrix on a chip whose logic can be customized by a programmer.

gender changer—piece of hardware that changes a port or cable end from female to male or vice versa.

gigabyte—1 billion bytes, called a "gig" for short.

glitch—similar to a bug, but usually smaller.

global search—method of searching a large amount of data for specific items, whether in one file, several files, or all directories.

graphic resolution—description of how clear and crisp graphics appear on the computer screen and/or when printed.

graphic user interface (GUI)—using icons or graphics to select functions instead of words or alphanumeric commands.

graphics—illustrations, symbols, and special type treatments used to add visual interest and explanatory detail to a document.

gray scale—degree of contrast in a graphic display.

gremlin—slang for a bug or glitch that isn't consistent.

hacker—someone extremely good at understanding the programming and running of computers; someone who uses that knowledge to break in to large computer systems for fun, mischief, or profit.

half duplex—transmitting data in only one direction at a time.

handshake—flow control or "go ahead" signal sent from one computer to another to activate a communications program.

hard copy—printed form of a document.

hard disk—usually nonremovable memory storage device in a computer; also called "hard drive."

hardware—physical parts of a computer, including accessories.

head—device that reads and writes information on the disk; also called "read/write head."

header—text that appears at the top of every page of a document when it is printed, such as a page number or title.

helical scan—way of recording magnetic tape, commonly used in videotape systems.

help desk—support service provided by a software or hardware supplier to help users figure out how to set it up and run it properly or solve operating problems.

high band width—refers to high-speed transmissions of a large volume of data.

high level language—computer programming language that is very close to English.

high memory area (HMA)—area of extended or expanded memory.

Hewlett Packard (HP)—major manufacturer of computers and other electronic devices.

host—main computer, typically the one controlling other computers and devices or providing central memory.

hub—in a computer network, central location serving other locations in some way.

Hypercard—Macintosh program to manage relational databases.

Hypermedia—multimedia; using more than one type of media at a time.

icon—graphical representation (picture or symbol) on the screen that you can select to activate an application, command, software program, or other function.

IDE—a type of bus used in IBM PCs.

impact printer—device that prints images using the impact of a key or dot matrix head on a ribbon.

import—to bring information into the computer from an outside source, such as a file or database; to move information from one file to another.

inboard memory—memory built in to the computer, as opposed to extended or expanded memory.

initialization (INIT) programs—housekeeping programs that prepare the computer or a larger software application for use when power is first turned on.

initialize—to format a disk (using the disk operating system) so it will accept data from the computer.

input—data that is put into a computer's memory, generally by way of the keyboard, but also from another computer.

input device—hardware, such as a keyboard, that enables a user to put data into a computer's memory.

instruction—command from the user or in a computer program.

intelligent terminal—self-contained personal computer or a terminal that is attached to and uses a larger computer, but can also perform some functions independently.

interactive—system that provides the user immediate control of separate input and output operations, as opposed to batch mode, where a series of instructions must be completed by the computer before control is returned to the user.

interface—process of making two pieces of hardware work together; device or code that allows two systems to work together.

International Business Machines (IBM)—major computer manufacturer spanning the spectrum from mainframes to portable PCs, used as a compatibility standard for personal computers.

I/O—input/output, usually to or from the computer's processor and memory.

ISO—designation for a standard published by the International Organization for Standardization, an international clearinghouse, based in Geneva, Switzerland, promoting common standards in electronics and other fields.

jack—single-pole plug or plug opening used to connect peripherals to an electronic device.

joy stick—control device used with video games and other interactive systems.

jumper—two pathways (for example, bus, cables, or circuits) that are connected as opposed to one longer pathway; also called "tie line."

Kermit—popular communications software program used to transfer information between computers using telephone lines and modems and to allow one computer to act as a terminal to another; see also *XMODEM* and *ZMODEM*.

keyboard—typewriterlike device used to enter data and control functions activated by keystrokes rather than a mouse.

keypad—mathematical-function keys on a computer keyboard.

kilobyte (K/KB)—1,024 bytes equals 1 kilobyte.

kludge—bug; temporary fix within a program or piece of computer hardware; computerese for junk; also spelled "kluge."

landing zone—area on a disk that the heads touch when the disk is parked (contains no data).

landscape—print mode in which the page is turned sideways, making it $8^1/2$ inches high and 11 inches wide; see also *portrait*.

language—programming software used by a computer and to write programs for the computer, such as FORTRAN, COBOL, Pascal, and others.

laptop—portable personal computer about the size of a small briefcase with both AC and battery power options, making it easily transported and used away from an office.

laserdisc—optical data storage system read by a laser light; a CD-ROM is a laserdisc, but the term usually refers to larger disks used for movies and other sound-and-video programming; also called "platter."

laser printer—fast, quiet, high-image-quality printer that works by fusing toner powder to paper with heat.

light emitting diode (LED)—display component commonly used in computer indicators, such as a light that indicates when power is on.

LIM (Lotus, Intel, and Microsoft)—three companies that have designed systems for expanding a computer's memory.

line printer—fast, midquality device that prints an entire line of type at once (like an automatic typewriter).

link—to put two or more microcomputers into communication with each other by physically running cables as well as using special networking software; in a spreadsheet, to connect two files together so that changes in one will be reflected in the other.

liquid crystal display (LCD)—technology that forms an image by using a liquid that becomes darker when electricity is passed through it; commonly used in laptop and other small computer screens.

load—to put information, such as a computer program, into a computer's active memory.

local area network (LAN)—direct cable link of two or more computers in a small geographic area, such as a building or adjacent buildings, to share data and operations; if the network covers a wide area, it's called "WAN."

local device—computer linked to and in control of another computer or device (the controlled device is the "remote" system).

location—address in a computer's memory where specific information is stored.

log on/off—to sign on and off the computer or keep a record of having used the computer.

lo-res(olution) graphics—low-quality graphics.

Lotus 1-2-3—popular business management software that combines graphics, spreadsheet capabilities, and other data management abilities.

low-level language—computer programming language that uses symbols and shorthand instead of words, making it difficult to read by the casual computer user.

LPT port—connector or plug on a personal computer used to connect parallel devices, usually a printer.

machine language—instructions written directly to the computer in binary code.

Macintosh (Mac)—major product line of Apple Computer, best known for their ease of use, graphics abilities, desktop publishing capabilities, and icon-style instructions.

MacOS—Macintosh Operating System

macro—programmable series of instructions stored in a special keystroke sequence, usually to perform frequently used complex actions.

mailbox—memory area in the computer where E-mail messages are received and stored.

mail merge—function that combines mailing-list management and word processing software.

main memory—memory storage that is in the computer before any extensions or expansions.

mainframe—large computer that can support several hundred users at once.

male—port or end of a cable that fits into a socket.

malfunction—major failure in the operation of a computer or auxiliary device.

management information systems (MIS)—systems that organize computerized information for management functions.

MCI mail—system that allows a user to send messages over the phone lines.

mean time between failures (MTBF)—average life expectancy based on laboratory testing.

mean time to repair (MTTR)—average time it will take to have something fixed.

media—physical substance on which data is stored, such as magnetic tape, optical disk, even paper.

megabyte (MB)—1,048, 576 bytes or 1,024 Kbytes.

megahertz (mHz)—1 million electrical cycles per second, a measure of operating speed for computer CPUs.

memory—internal storage area used most often by the CPU; RAM can be changed, ROM can't.

memory chip—semiconductor chip that stores information as electrical charges; RAM is stored on memory chips.

memory-resident—software that is loaded into a computer's memory and is available for use even when another application is being performed; also called "TSR software."

menu—on-screen list of available commands or functions.

menu-driven—using a pointing device, usually the cursor

(whether moved by mouse or keyboard), to select a command or function.

merge—to combine two or more files.

microcomputer—computer with a single integrated circuit as a central processing unit; most PCs are microcomputers.

microprocessor—small semiconductor chip with circuitry to perform logic functions, such as executing software arithmetic; CPUs are microprocessors.

milliseconds (ms)—one-thousandth of a second, the common measurement of the time a computer needs to execute a command or accomplish a function.

minicomputer—outdated term for a computer sized between PCs and mainframes.

MIPS—millions of instructions per second, measure of how fast the computer can process software; also, popular RISC-based computer chip used by various personal computers and workstations.

mode—form or condition of an operation, device, or variable.

modeling language—programming language that closely resembles English, usually used to work on a specific problem, such as one general type of business analysis.

modem (MOdular DEModulator)—device that links two computers (or a dumb terminal and a computer) via phone lines so data can be transferred; a modem is required at both ends of the link.

monitor—screen on which a user views the work being done on a computer.

monochrome display adapter (MDA)—board that displays only monochrome (one-color) graphics.

monochrome monitor—monitor that displays just one color, usually amber, green, black, or gray.

motherboard—microcomputer's main circuit board, containing the major controllers, operating units, and expansion slots; also called "system board."

mouse—handheld tool for making choices and giving commands to the computer by moving the cursor or highlight bar.

MPP—massive parallel processing.

MS-DOS (MicroSoft Disk Operating System)—variation of DOS that runs on most IBM-compatible PCs.

Multics—type of operating system; predecessor of UNIX.

multilevel filing—systematically subdividing the information stored in a computer to make it easier to find, most commonly involving directories, subdirectories, and files or similar hierarchies.

multimedia—combination of sound and full-motion graphics, such as video, with text and still graphics.

multimedia personal computer (MPC)—PC that meets the minimum standards established for basic multimedia operations.

multiplexer—unit that receives signals from several devices and merges them into one signal for transmission to another on a single line; a demultiplexer on the other end changes the combined signal back to its individual components.

multiprocessor—computer with more than one processor chip.

multitasking—ability of a computer to perform more than one activity at a time; breaking up a task into smaller parts and letting each processor within the computer do a separate portion of the task.

mux—to send to a multiplexer.

network—several computers connected by cables or satellites and using special software that allows them to share equipment such as printers as well as exchange information.

network architecture—physical layout of a network of computers, such as a ring or bus.

network disk drive—disk drive that can be used by any network user, often used to store data files for people working on the same project.

notebook—small, portable personal computer that is approximately the size of a notebook; usually designed to operate on battery power only.

numeric keypad—separate keypad containing the keys 0–9 and decimal point on a computer keyboard, arranged as they are on an adding machine to facilitate mathematical entries.

numeric processing unit (NPU)—optional co-processor that facilitates complicated mathematical functions; also called "arithmetic processing unit" (APU).

OEM (original equipment manufacturer)—company that makes subsystems intended to be sold with or added to a computer sold under another brand name; devices made by subcomponent manufacturers.

offline—data storage physically outside or away from the computer, such as on diskettes or computer tape; disconnected from an online information service; not immediately accessible by the computer.

online—immediately accessible by the computer; connected to another computer or an information service.

open—to tell the computer to make a file ready to be worked on.

open architecture—computer system designed so other devices can be added to it.

operating system—group of central programs that boots the system, translates commands, manages devices, and performs other system functions; application software programs such as word processors and spreadsheets typically work within an operating system.

optical character reader (OCR)—device that scans typed information and translates it into online information; also called a "scanner."

optical disk—data storage device that uses laser technology for read and write operations instead of the physical head-to-media contact common in magnetic data storage systems.

option—choice presented to the user when entering a command or using a device.

Operating System/2 (OS/2)—IBM's multitasking, multiuser operating system for personal computers.

outboard memory—memory added to the computer via a board or card that was not part of the original equipment.

output—end product of a software function, such as an analysis or printout.

overwrite—to erase what is written as new information is added.

page—process through which computers using virtual memory moves "pages" of different software to the hard disk because they don't all fit in system memory at the same time.

page up/down—command that moves the screen display to the next screen-sized increment above or below the user's current location in the document.

paint program—software that allows graphic images to be created and modified.

palmtop—handheld microcomputer.

parallel—when used alone, usually refers to parallel processing.

parallel interface—interface between a computer and a device in which the computer sends multiple bits of information simultaneously; see also *serial interface*.

parallel port—port used to connect a parallel device, such as a printer.

parallel processing—ability of a computer to execute more than one part of a program at the same time, providing greatly enhanced speed and power.

parameter—in programming, variable that usually has a consistent value.

park—command that locks the read/write head, used to protect it from being damaged or knocked out of alignment if the computer is moved.

Pascal—common high-level programming language.

password—private word or set of symbols that must be entered before the computer will allow a user to log on and use the system.

paste—to move information to a new spot in a file or document.

path—drive, directory, subdirectory, and file designations for stored data.

personal computer (PC)—originally, IBM Personal Computer, but now refers to any single-user microcomputer.

pels (Picture ELements)—smallest graphic units on the screen; also known as "pixels."

pen-based—computer device that allows a user to input information and control functions with a special pen that draws on the computer screen or pad.

peripheral—device in its own housing attached to a computer, such as a mouse, printer, data cartridge drive, or other add-on.

personal digital assistant (PDA)—handheld portable organizer and fax machine.

phase-of-the-moon dependent—only explanation left for why a computer is acting the way it is.

pi character—scientific or other specialized symbol.

pins—small, signal-carrying probes sticking out of the male ends of communications cables and ports or on a computer chip that plugs in to a circuit board; cables and ports are sometimes labeled by the number of pins they accept: 9-pin, 25-pin, etc.

pipe—UNIX command that tells the software to send its output into another software program or device.

pirate—to illegally copy software in violation of copyright.

pixels—smallest graphic units on the screen; also known as "picture elements (pels)."

PL/I, PL/1—high-level programming language for IBM mainframes.

Plato—computer-based education programs developed by Control Data Corp.; forerunners of interactive video training.

plug—end of the cable; connector.

plug and play—ability to connect a computer or other device, turn it on, and have it work immediately.

point and click—common mouse command where an arrow is moved to data that is to be worked with.

point size—measure of type size; 72 points is approximately one inch, 10-and 12-point faces are the most common for computer text.

pop-up—menu or choice that can be superimposed on a screen and allows the user to elaborate on a specific selection; see also *pulldown menu*.

port—connection on a computer where a cable that carries data to another device is plugged in.

portrait—standard vertical format, usually 8½ inches wide and 11 inches high, the dimensions of a standard sheet of paper; see also *landscape*.

power down—systematic process of exiting software, turning off peripheral devices, then shutting down the computer itself.

power surge—sudden increase in electrical power that can damage a computer or other electrical device; also called "spike."

print—to send information from a computer to a printer to produce a hard copy; to display file information on the screen.

print driver—software that tells the computer and devices such as printers how to work together.

print to disk—to transfer information from the computer to a disk location rather than hard copy.

printer—device that transfers computer output onto paper.

printout—hard copy of a computer file.

PRN port—common printer port on many PCs, compared to COM ports used to connect a modem, mouse, or other peripheral.

process—smallest amount of functional activity occurring in the operating system of a computer.

professional graphics adaptor (PGA)—high-resolution graphics card.

program—software application or function provided to tell a computer how to perform a specific task.

programmable read only memory (PROM)—ROM that can be changed.

prompt—symbol used by the computer to tell the user it is ready for input.

proportional font—typeface that can be printed in a wide variety of sizes and in which individual characters occupy only as much space as they need (compare "i" and "m" in this book versus on a standard typewriter).

protected—file or disk set up so it can't be changed without using a password or removing the protection.

protocol—set of rules that defines how computers communicate with each other.

public domain—information that is not protected by copyright and may be copied and used without permission from the creator.

pulldown—menu or choice that can be superimposed on a screen from a graphic bar at the top to allow the user to make or elaborate on a specific command or selection; see also *pop-up*.

purge—to get rid of unnecessary information, such as deleting backup files or using a merge/purge function to combine two lists of information so duplicate items are eliminated.

QIC (Quarter Inch Compatibility/Committee)—standard-setting cooperative industry group for the use of quarter-inch magnetic tape in computer applications.

queue—list of files sent to a particular printer, including the file currently printing and those waiting to be printed; also called "print queue."

random access memory (RAM)—basic form of computer memory that can be changed, used to load and run operating systems and software programs.

read—operation in which a head finds and accesses information recorded on a disk or other storage device.

read only memory (ROM)—nonchangeable memory that is used to store the computer's basic input/output operating instructions as well as other information key to its basic operations.

real time—computer calculations that are immediately updated as new data is received; measure of how long an operation actually takes to complete, not how long it should take to complete before factoring in delays and downtime; also called "real mode."

reboot—to restart the computer system.

reconfigure—with software, to revise commands to the computer that affect how the hard drive operates or how it interacts with peripheral systems; with hardware, to replace or rearrange the devices hooked up to the computer, such as reconfiguring the floppy drive connections to add an additional device.

redirect—to change the mode by which the computer receives or delivers information, such as redirecting input from a keyboard to a scanner.

remote—computer or other device being controlled by another computer (the controlling computer is the "local" device).

resolution—measure of the quality of a visual display.

response time—time it takes a computer to react to a command (anything over a second is unbearably slow).

rewritable optical—magneto-optical disk that can be erased and rerecorded.

RISC (Reduced Instruction Set Computing)—type of computer architecture that reduces the number of instructions the computer needs to translate to perform a function, greatly increasing processing speed; a growing number of PC workstations use RISC technology.

root directory—basic or default directory of a disk created when the disk is formatted; other directories branch off the root directory.

RS-232—common serial protocol for communicating information between a computer and slower devices, such as printers and modems (disk drives are faster and commonly use parallel communications protocols).

run—to use an application.

scalable—refers to type or graphics that can be produced in different sizes.

scanner—input device that translates printed material to digital information that can be transferred to computer memory.

scroll—to move information on the computer screen up or down in a continuous stream rather than a screenful at a time; can also apply to moving left or right.

SCSI (Small Computer Systems Interface)—popular bus standard (pronounced *scuzzy*).

seek time—time it takes the hard disk to find requested information.

semiconductor—material such as silicon that neither conducts electricity efficiently nor insulates well against its flow; basic material in computer chips.

sequential access—retrieving data in the order it was stored, such as from a tape device; disks are faster because they provide direct access (the computer can go immediately to the location desired rather than having to wind through the information in sequence).

serial interface—connection in which the computer sends information to a device such as a printer in series, one piece at a time; see also *parallel interface*.

serial port—connection on a computer, usually COM1, where you plug in the cable for a serial printer or another serial communications device, such as a modem.

server—networked computer whose major function is to serve other computers linked to the network.

shareware—software in the public domain obtained free from another user or user group.

simulation—representation of a real-world function or system, such as landing an airplane, emulated by a computer's software.

smart terminal—terminal attached to a mainframe computer than can perform some functions without the use of the mainframe.

soft boot—see *warm boot*.

soft font—file that contains the information for producing a type font.

soft keys—programmable function keys.

software—coding that tells the computer how to perform specific functions.

source directory—directory that contains information you want to work on or move; directory in which you store software.

SPARC—type of RISC processor made by Sun Microsystems.

spell check—software function that compares words in a document to a dictionary of correctly spelled words to identify those that may be misspelled.

spool—to print a document while working on something else.

spreadsheet—software that manages rows and columns of numbers or other information, typically used to calculate mathematical records such as expenses.

Sprint Mail—electronic mail service offered by U.S. Sprint.

standalone—hardware that does not need extra support to work.

standard mode—operations programmed into a computer or other piece of hardware when it is manufactured, subject to modification by reconfiguring the hard disk.

standards—agreements by manufacturers and suppliers that products will conform to certain quality parameters or physical designs, usually identified by the standard-setting organization's catalog number (ANSI, ISO, etc.).

stream—to input or output a continuous high volume of data without stopping to work on any part of it until the entire transmission is completed, such as backing up information from a hard disk to a peripheral device.

string—group of symbols usually used to give commands to the computer.

stroke font—series of dots connected by lines that can be scaled to different sizes, used by plotters; also known as "vector fonts."

style sheet—set of instructions that define the appearance of text or graphics created by a software program, such as default margins, typeface, page dimensions, and other aspects.

subdirectory—directory that branches off another directory; all directories are subdirectories of the root directory.

supercomputer—powerful computer that can perform billions of operations simultaneously (the definition changes constantly, but is always reserved for the world's most sophisticated and largest computers).

surge protector—electrical buffering device that protects computer equipment from damaging power surges, whether caused by normal variation in the current supplied to a building or extraordinary hazards, such as lightning strikes.

SVGA (super video graphics adaptor)—high-resolution graphics card common on most current-generation PCs.

swapping—function that allows several users to share main memory even though each user's program requires more than half of the computer's total memory; the computer constantly balances the load by emptying memory onto a disk and working a small part of each user's project before going to the next; also applies to running a program that requires more memory than is available.

switchbox—data management system that provides two or more devices access to a single device by switching or blocking current so only one can communicate with it at a time; used to link several computers to a single printer, for example.

synchronous—communications handshake or interaction in which information is transmitted at regular intervals and usually not checked as it's transmitted.

system—computer as well as all attached devices.

system disk—disk that contains the operating system.

system folder—on an Apple, file that contains the basic operating system.

system program—major program used to operate the computer's internal functions.

system time—time according to a computer's internal clock.

system analyst—someone who directs the writing of the software programs needed for a computer system to function.

task—specific function in a software program.

template—predefined parameters for formatting something, such as a letter style or newsletter layout.

temporary file—file deleted when the program is finished working on a project.

terminal—user access point to a computer system or network; workstation.

terminal emulators—software program that makes a computer act like a terminal so it can talk to another computer through a modem or network connection.

text—words.

text file—file containing only ASCII characters.

throughput—measure of the amount of work performed by a computer system in a set amount of time.

tie line—see *jumper*.

time bomb—passive virus that is activated at a certain time in the future.

time sharing—see *swapping*.

tool—utility or small computer program with a very specific purpose.

tower—personal computer configuration in which the CPU, disk drives, and other components are contained in a housing that sits vertically, usually beside a desk rather than on it.

TPI (tracks per inch)—measure of the number of tracks on a disk.

tracball—peripheral device that moves the cursor and performs other functions by rolling a ball under the palm of the user's hand; also called "turbomouse."

track—linear area on a data storage device where information is stored.

transfer rate—how fast an input/output device can read and write data.

transistor—microsized semiconductor used to store 0s and 1s in computer memory.

tree—visible representation of the directory structure on a disk; software design scheme that arranges information in superior and subordinate groups to show the relationship between items.

TSR (terminate and stay resident) software—see *memory-resident software*.

turbomouse—see *tracball*.

tutorial—instructional software provided with a program to help the user learn basic functions and commands.

unerase—idiot-saving function that allows a user to restore data that has been deleted by mistake.

UNIX—multiuser, multitasking operating system.

upgrade—to replace existing components or software with newer versions that perform better.

upload—to send information from a local computer to a remote computer.

user—someone working on a computer (no matter how competent they may be).

user friendly—easy to use.

user group—people who use similar hardware and/or software and meet periodically to exchange information and ideas.

utility—program that helps a user analyze or work with other programs or perform simple housekeeping functions.

video display terminal (VDT)—see *CRT*.

video graphics adaptor (VGA)—standard high-resolution graphics card.

version—release number on a software program; the higher the number, the more recent the release.

videodisc—laser disc, usually in a large format used for movies and interactive training programs; also called "platter."

videotext—pictures and text seen from a computer disk, usually from a laser disc.

virtual—almost.

virtual disk—system memory that acts like a separate floppy or hard disk.

virtual machine—computer that allows several functions to be run at once, as though each were using a separate machine.

virtual memory—extending a system's functional memory beyond its physical limits; see *swapping*.

virtual reality—ability of computers with high-speed graphics to create an illusion of reality by allowing the user to move in and out of the various connected images shown on the screen.

virus—malicious program introduced into a computer system, often by way of a contaminated diskette, that has the capability to instruct the computer to take destructive actions, such as erasing or scrambling files.

virus detector—software program that can detect the presence of known viruses in a computer's memory or on floppy disks.

volume label—programmable name that identifies a specific disk.

VRAM—special memory for a computer screen.

wand—pen or stick used to draw or make choices on the computer.

warm boot—rebooting the startup software by pressing a combination of keys (usually Ctrl, Alt, and Del) instead of turning the power off and back on; also called "soft boot."

wildcard character—symbol such as * or ? that represents unknown characters in a command or instruction.

Winchester disk—old name for "hard disk."

window—segment of a split screen in which work can be done.

Windows—Microsoft's multitasking operating system for personal computers, known for its graphical user interface; generic term for being able to perform multiple activities ("do windows").

wipeout—inadvertent, often permanent erasure of a large amount of data.

word—smallest number of bytes a computer works with.

word processing—software program that handles typewriter-like and simple desktop publishing functions on a computer.

word wrap—function of word processing programs that displays words on the next line when the margin is reached, eliminating the need for a carriage return at the end of each line.

workstation—more powerful version of the personal computer that can operate faster, has more memory, and can sometimes process programs from several users at once.

WORM (write once, read many) disc—optical disc that can be recorded once, but once recorded cannot be changed.

write—to record information to one of a computer's data storage systems.

write protect—mechanical method of preventing the inadvertent overwriting or erasure of a file, disk, or tape.

WYSIWYG (what you see is what you get)—display that accurately shows how a document will look when printed out.

Xfer—short for *transfer rate*.

XMODEM—software package used to transfer information file by file over telephone lines between computers and let one computer act as a terminal to another.

ZMODEM—software package used to transfer information between computers over telephone lines and let one computer act as a terminal to another; provides more functionality than XMODEM software.

Sports Appendix

ace—in baseball, best pitcher on the team; in tennis, serve that cannot be returned.

agent—someone who negotiates player contracts, usually for a percentage of the contract's value, and advises professional athletes on financial and career matters.

air (anything)—outstanding; powerful.

airball—in basketball, poor shot that does not hit the backboard or rim (often provoking a mocking chant from the other team's fans).

air it out—in football, to throw a long pass (a more wide-open style of attack).

Air Jordan—Nike shoe advertising campaign featuring former Chicago Bulls basketball star Michael Jordan.

all star—voted or selected the best at a position; all-star teams are made up of the top performers in a given sport.

around the horn—in baseball, throwing the ball from catcher to third base, second base, and first base in succession, involving all or most of the infielders.

assist—statistical category that keeps track of the team member who sets up another player: in basketball, given to the player who passed the ball to the one who scored; in hockey, to the one or two players who handled the puck before the player who scored, provided that no opponent touched the puck in between; in baseball, to the player who threw the ball to the base where an out (or putout) was recorded.

athletic director (AD)—official in charge of sports programs at a college or high school.

back—in football, player on offense or defense who lines up behind the line of scrimmage.

back up—to position yourself behind another player in case that player is unable to make the play.

backboard—in basketball, glass or wooden board to which the basket is affixed; a shot that hits the backboard and then goes in is called a "bankshot."

backcourt—in basketball, opposite half of the court from the basket you are shooting at (once across the midcourt line, the offensive team cannot take the ball into its backcourt unless it has been knocked there by an opposing player); also refers to the two "guards," usually the smallest players on the court, who typically handle the ball more and shoot from the "outside" (farther away from the basket).

backstop—in baseball, screen behind home plate that stops balls from going into the seats; also slang for "catcher."

balk—in baseball, illegal movement by the pitcher with a runner on base, allowing the runner to advance one base.

ballpark figure—estimate.

bare knuckle—early form of boxing without gloves.

barnburner—exciting game.

base—in baseball, one of the three white bags at the corners of the "diamond" ("home plate" is the fourth corner).

base hit—in baseball, ball hit into the field of play that is not caught before it hits the ground and allows the batter to reach first base safely.

baseline—in baseball, white line that stretches from home plate, past first and third base, to the outfield foul poles and defines the field of play; in basketball, painted line from sideline to sideline under each basket that separates what is in bounds from what is out of bounds.

410

basket—in basketball, goal hung ten feet above the floor at each end of the court; also, a shot from the floor that goes in ("he made a basket").

bat—in baseball, wooden or aluminum stick used to hit the ball; also, what an umpire is as blind as.

bat around—in baseball, when all nine players bat in the same inning.

batter—in baseball, player whose turn it is to try to hit balls thrown by the other team's pitcher.

batting average—in baseball, ratio of base hits to official at bats (excludes walks and being hit by a pitch, counts errors as outs).

batting order—in baseball, order in which the nine players in the lineup take turns at bat.

beanball—in baseball, pitch that hits the batter in the head.

benchwarmer—reserve player good enough to make the team but not good enough to play on a regular basis.

bench strength—measure of a team's reserve potential; becomes important when skilled players are lost due to injuries and other problems, or in a long, physically grueling game.

big league—highest professional league in a sport (most commonly refers to baseball); minor leagues, and sometimes high school and colleges, serve as a training ground for its future players.

Billyball—in baseball, scrappy style of play embodied by the late (and usually controversial) Billy Martin, a manager with a number of teams.

birdie—in golf, getting the ball into the hole in one less shot than is established for par.

blackout—tactic used in professional sports to protect ticket sales for the home team by forbidding free local television coverage unless the game is sold out.

bleachers—in baseball, cheapest seats, usually behind the outfield fence; refers to bench-style seats in any sport, especially those farthest from the action.

blind side—in football, area behind or to the side of a player where visibility has been cut off by the player's helmet or the way he is standing; a hit from the blind side is unexpected and hence often devastating.

blitz—in football, aggressive and sometimes risky defensive tactic in which players in addition to the linemen rush the quarterback.

block—in football, what an offensive player does to keep a defensive player away from the player with the ball, or what the defensive team tries to do to a punt or field goal; in basketball, painted marker along the side of the key used to position players during foul shots where players able to score from close to the basket try to position themselves during regular play ("he gets the ball in the blocks") or the statistical category that tracks shots blocked by individual players; in bowling, area of oil laid across the lane to enhance scoring by making the ball slide farther and break better when it reaches the pins.

blue line—in hockey, line that defines the offensive zone at each end of the rink; offensive players cannot enter the zone before the puck does.

boards—in hockey, wooden walls that define the rink; in basketball, slang for "rebounds."

bogey—in golf, getting the ball into the hole in one more shot than is established for par; two shots over par for the hole is a double bogey.

bomb—in football, long pass intended to score a touchdown on one play.

bookie—someone who makes or manages odds and accepts bets on sporting events; sports betting, though a multibillion-dollar pastime throughout the country, is officially legal only in Nevada and Atlantic City, NJ.

boot—in football, to kick the ball (positive connotation if the kick is deliberate and done well); in baseball, to kick the ball instead of catching it (negative connotation).

booth—where the sportscasters sit during the game; place where you buy tickets.

breaks—lucky things that do or don't happen in the course of a game or season.

brick—in basketball, poor shot ("he threw up a brick from ten feet").

bring it—in baseball, to pitch the ball very fast ("he can really bring it").

bring rain—in basketball, high-arching shot; said of any high-trajectory ball that (whimsically speaking) could hit the clouds and cause it to rain.

brushback—in baseball, pitch thrown threateningly close to the batter to make the batter back away from home plate.

bucket—slang for *basket*.

bullpen—in baseball, area (usually separated from the playing field) where pitchers prepare to come into the game.

bunker—in golf, low-lying area along the fairway or green, usually filled with sand to make it difficult to hit the ball out of it.

burner—someone who runs fast; in baseball, a fast pitch.

bush league—very low-level minor league, often with an unsavory reputation; said of tacky plays or players.

cactus league—in baseball, spring training games played by teams that train in Arizona and Southern California.

call—referee's or umpire's decision ("what's the call, ref?"); in baseball, specifically refers to the umpire's calling of balls and strikes (a player who does not swing at the third strike takes a "called third strike" and is "called out on strikes"); also refers to the broadcast description of the game or event ("calling the game").

call up—to move a player from a minor league team to the major league team, or from a lower minor league to a higher one.

can't hit his hat size—in baseball, player with an extremely low batting average.

Casey—Mudville's Babe Ruthian hometown hero who strikes out in "Casey at the Bat."

center—in basketball, typically tallest and most physical player who plays in the center of the defensive and offensive alignments; in football, offensive lineman who hikes the ball to the quarterback; in hockey, playmaker in the center of the forward line; in baseball, area of the outfield between right and left fields.

chains—in football, official measuring device brought onto the field to determine whether the offensive team has gained the ten yards needed for a first down.

changeup—in baseball, slower (or "offspeed") pitch thrown periodically to surprise a batter whose swing is geared for a faster pitch.

cheap shot—in football and hockey, physical contact designed more to injure or intimidate an opponent than to stop him under the rules of the game (someone known for such tactics is called a "cheap shot artist").

checkered flag—in auto racing, flag that is waved when the winning car crosses the finish line.

chin music—in baseball, ball pitched at the batter's head.

chip shot—in golf, short putt with little apparent difficulty and a very high probability of success; in football, short field goal.

choke—to lose an apparently overwhelming advantage (or game) due to nervousness or lack of confidence.

clean-up—in baseball, fourth spot in the batting order, usually occupied by the most powerful hitter; to win money betting ("she really cleaned up").

clear waivers—in most team sports, to be released as a free agent after being offered to every other team without being claimed.

clinch—to win a championship before the last games or matches (which still must be played) by building a statistically insurmountable lead (for example, a four-game lead with three games left in the season).

clip—in football, illegal block from behind a defensive player by an offensive player.

closer—in baseball, relief pitcher who is called on to pitch the last inning or two in close games; connotes a very reliable performer in high-pressure situations.

clothesline—in football or hockey, vicious hit that results when an unsuspecting player runs into an opponent's forearm held at neck level (the effect is like running into an unseen clothesline).

clubhouse turn—in horse racing, last turn (typically toward the track's clubhouse) leading into the "home stretch" to the finish line.

color man—broadcaster, often a former player, who supports the broadcaster doing the play-by-play with analysis and anecdotes.

comeback of the year—award won by a formerly high-performing player who, after dropping off substantially for one or more seasons, rebounds to previous or higher levels.

coordinator—in football, high-level assistant coach, usually in charge of the planning and coaches for either the offense or defense.

count—in baseball, number of balls and strikes already thrown to the current batter (balls are always tallied first: 3-and-1, 0-and-2; a "full count" is three balls and two strikes); in boxing, 10 seconds counted off by the referee after a boxer is knocked down (if he cannot get up by the count of 10, the fight is over).

crackback—in football, blocking technique in which an offensive player turns around quickly and blocks a player, often unsuspecting, coming up from behind him.

crunch time—period of several minutes, often shortly before an intermission or the end of the game or season, in which the outcome of a close contest or season-long competition is decided.

curveball—in baseball, pitch thrown to rotate in such a way that it will curve before reaching home plate, making it harder to hit.

cutoff man—in baseball, defensive player positioned to take a throw from the outfield and relay it to another base.

daily double—in horse racing, special bet in which you must pick the winners in two designated races to win higher stakes.

defenseman—in hockey, the two players positioned closest to the goalie.

defensive back—in football, player who defends against passing plays and backs up the defense on running plays ("cornerbacks" line up closer to the line and toward the outside of the formation, "safeties" play deeper and more down the middle of the field).

depth chart—in team sports, list of players by positions, with the best players (starters) listed first, the second best players second, and so on down the line; used to illustrate the organization's specific strengths and weaknesses, also to motivate players to try to move up the list.

designated hitter (DH)—in major league baseball's American League, the individual (usually a power hitter who does not play well defensively) who bats in place of the pitcher but does not play in the field; in the National League, the pitcher must bat for himself or be removed from the game; in business, refers to a specialist brought in for crucial presentations or negotiations who typically will not be part of the business team that services the account.

diamond—the part of the baseball field defined by home plate and first, second, and third bases.

dime—in football, defensive formation with six defensive backs to protect against a pass (four is typical, five is called a "nickel" formation).

dinger—in baseball, home run.

disabled list (DL)—list of players who will miss enough games that a replacement player is added to the roster until they are able to play again.

don't beat yourself—sports philosophy that argues for taking few chances and playing extremely conservatively to avoid mistakes that an opponent might take advantage of.

double—in baseball, two-base hit.

double header—in baseball, playing two games on the same day.

double play—in baseball, play on which two outs are recorded.

double team—putting two of your players on one of the opposing team's players.

down—in football, one of the four successive plays on which the offensive team must advance the ball ten yards.

down the pipe—in baseball, pitch thrown across the middle of the plate; strike.

downtown—to score or try to score from a distance: a home-run in baseball; a three-point shot in basketball; a long pass in football (reflects the fact that sports facilities are often built in suburban and fringe areas, far from the heart of the city).

draft—technique used to divide up new players coming into a professional sports league, usually by allowing teams to select new players in the reverse order of their finish in the preceding season; in this system, players are not "free agents" and thus have no choice (other than refusing to play) in what team owns the right to sign them to a contract.

dribble—in basketball, to move the ball while bouncing it with one hand or the other, but not both simultaneously (once a player stops or "picks up" his dribble, he must shoot it or pass to a teammate); in soccer, to move the ball while kicking it.

drive—in football, sustained advance by the offensive team (if it leads to a score, it's called a "scoring drive"); in baseball, hard-hit fly ball; in basketball, to dribble straight toward the basket.

dugout—in baseball, protected area where players and coaches sit when not in the game.

dunk—in basketball, basket scored by a player who jumps above the rim and puts the ball directly in.

eagle—in golf, getting the ball into the hole in two fewer shots than is established for par.

earned run—in baseball, run that scores because of a hit, walk, or hit batsman (not on or because of an error).

earned run average (ERA)—in baseball, ratio of earned runs allowed by a pitcher for every nine innings of play (multiply the number of runs allowed by nine, then divide by the actual number of innings pitched; carry to two decimals only).

end run—in football, play in which the ball carrier attempts to run around one side of the defense to avoid the strong players in the middle of the field; connotes getting around an obstacle rather than fighting through it.

end zone—in football, the ten yards between the goal line and the end line where a player must take or catch the ball to score a touchdown.

error—in baseball, statistic assigned to a player who touches the ball but fails to catch it, or throws the ball to a teammate who cannot catch or control it, allowing an opponent to reach or advance a base safely when he would otherwise have been out (a run that scores because of an error is said to be "unearned").

exacta—in horse racing, bet in which you must pick the horses that will finish first and second in their order of finish (also called "perfecta").

418

extra innings—in baseball, additional innings played when the score is tied after nine innings (baseball games cannot end in a tie); connotes prolonged processes.

face-off—in hockey, possession after a stoppage of play is determined by dropping the puck between two players, one from each team; connotes a head-to-head confrontation with an opponent.

fair ball—in baseball, ball hit between the baselines that extend from home plate to the outfield foul poles.

fairway—in golf, open area of the course between the tee and the hole.

fan—someone who watches the game rather than plays it.

fantasy football—hobby league in which fans draft players and compile game scores based on how their players perform in real games.

farm team—subsidiary team, often remote from the parent team's hometown, where new players are trained and developed; in baseball, farm teams originally were located in small, rural towns.

fast break—in basketball, play on which the team with the ball attempts to go quickly the length of the court and score before the opponent's players can fall back and take defensive positions; connotes rapid effort.

fastball—in baseball, relatively straight pitch that is hard to hit because of the velocity at which it is thrown.

favorite—team that oddsmakers think will win the game.

field goal—in football, ball kicked between the uprights of the goal post (worth three points); in basketball, ball shot through the hoop from anywhere on the court (worth two or three points depending on the distance involved).

field position—in football, relative advantage or disadvantage based on how close a team is to its own or the opponent's goal line.

Final Four—in college basketball, last four (of sixty-four) teams remaining in the season-ending tournament; connotes final competition among elite organizations.

fireballing—in baseball, said of a pitcher who throws the ball extremely fast.

fireman—in baseball, relief pitcher who takes over from a tiring or faltering pitcher in a difficult or dangerous part of the game.

flag—in football, what the referee throws to indicate that he is calling a penalty on the play.

fly ball—in baseball, ball hit in the air to the outfield.

forty-yard dash—in football, timed test used to predict an individual's quickness over short distances; times between four and five seconds are expected ("he runs a 4.4 40").

forward—in basketball, the two players closest to the basket on either side of the center ("3" designates the "small forward," whose primary task is scoring, "4" the "power forward," used primarily for defense and rebounding).

foul—in basketball, rule infraction resulting from illegal physical contact between players on opposing teams; in high school and college, players who "commit" five fouls cannot play for the rest of the game, while professional players are allowed six fouls.

foul ball—in baseball, ball hit outside the baselines that extend from home plate to the outfield foul poles; counts as a strike if not caught before hitting the ground, but cannot be counted as the third strike except when a bunt attempt is fouled off with two strikes.

foul line—in basketball, line fifteen feet from the basket from which foul shots are taken.

foul shot—in basketball, shot or shots (also called "free throws") awarded to a player who has been fouled by an opponent; each is worth one point if it goes in; the shooter (who cannot be guarded or interfered with) stands at or behind the foul line, opponents and teammates must stand outside of the "key" between the foul line and the basket.

four corners—in basketball, ball-control and time-consuming offensive scheme (used toward the end of a half or game when a team has a comfortable but not insurmountable lead); players move away from the basket and attempt to move the ball around the four corners of the offensive zone rather than get close to the basket and attempt to score.

free agent—player who has the right to negotiate his own contract with any team.

full-court press—in basketball, playing close defense over the entire length of the court instead of just in the half closest to your own basket; connotes maximum effort under pressure.

fullback—in football, running back (usually the heavier of the two in the standard formation) used primarily for power running and blocking.

fumble—in football, ball that is dropped to the ground during a play (fumbles are "recovered").

game plan—in team sports, plan for playing a specific opponent, reflecting how the team wants to exploit or counter the opponent's particular strengths and weaknesses.

game point—in tennis and volleyball, point on which one team can win the game or match.

general manager (GM)—team official responsible for player contracts and other administrative matters.

get the gate—in hockey, to be sent to the penalty box for two or five minutes due to a punishable infraction of the rules; in baseball, to be taken out of the game, usually for a fresher or better player.

glass—in basketball, backboard (providing it's made of Plexiglas, not wood).

glove man—in baseball, a player valued more for his fielding than his hitting.

go for it—in football, to try to pick up the yardage needed for a first down or touchdown on fourth down (failure at which means turning the ball over to the opponent at that spot on the field, and perhaps giving the opponent a significant competitive or emotional advantage); connotes determination to succeed.

go for the gold—to compete to win; refers to Olympic gold medals.

go long—in football, sending receivers far down the field for a long pass (the farther the ball must be thrown, the less likely it is to be caught, but the more spectacular the gain if it is).

go-to guy—very dependable player in crucial parts of the game.

go to the whip—in horse racing, to hit the horse to make it go faster.

goal—in hockey and soccer, what players shoot at; basic unit of scoring.

goal posts—in football, posts on the endline through which the ball must be kicked for field goals (worth three points) and extra points (worth one) after touchdowns.

goalie/goaltender—in hockey and soccer, player who plays directly in front of his team's goal to block shots (in soccer, the goalie is the only player allowed to touch the ball with his hands).

goaltending—in basketball, blocking a shot while it is on its downward arc toward the basket (the shot is scored as if it had gone in).

Gold Glove—in baseball, award voted to the player at each position who is considered the best fielder.

good field/no hit—in baseball, player (typically an infielder) with good defensive skills but poor offensive skills; connotes someone with both strengths and weaknesses.

goose eggs—zeros on the scoreboard.

gopher ball—in baseball, pitch hit for a home run ("he served up a gopher ball").

grandstand—multiple-level seating area in a sports stadium, often at least partially covered to protect the audience from the weather.

grapefruit league—in baseball, spring training games played by teams that train in Florida.

green—in golf, well-kept turf area surrounding the hole.

green jacket—in golf, trademark jacket awarded to the winner of the Masters Tournament, signifying the best golfer in the game that year.

ground ball—in baseball, ball that bounces in the infield before being caught or going through into the outfield.

guard—in basketball, the two positions on offense and defense farthest away from the basket ("1" designates the point guard, in the lineup primarily for ball handling, "2" the guard who typically is used more as a scorer; guards are usually smaller, faster players with better ball-handling skills than forwards and the center); in football, linemen on either side of the center.

Hail Mary—in football, pass thrown in the last seconds of a half or game that seemingly can succeed only through divine intervention.

half—basic time unit in football, basketball, and soccer, which may be further divided into quarters (baseball plays nine innings, hockey three periods).

halfback—in football, running back (usually the lighter and faster of the two in the standard formation) used primarily for running around the ends of the line and as a pass receiver.

hat trick—in hockey, when one player scores three goals in the same game.

heads—in bowling, first fifteen feet of the lane, made of harder wood to absorb the shock of the thrown ball; opposite of "tails" when calling the coin toss that starts a football or soccer game.

header—in soccer, to strike the ball with your head; in other sports, to fall headfirst ("took a header into the first row").

high hard one—in baseball, fastball thrown in the upper part of the strike zone or above, where it is difficult for many players to hit.

high heat—in baseball, consistently throwing high fastballs.

hit and run—in baseball, strategic play on which a base runner starts for the next base when the ball is pitched in anticipation that the batter will hit the ball; when it succeeds, the base runner is often able to advance two bases or the batter reaches base because the defensive alignment was disrupted—when it fails, the base runner can be an easy out or a double play can result.

hit the showers—to clean up after playing the game; hitting the showers early means being taken out of the game for good before the game is over.

holding—in football and basketball, penalty called when a player from one team illegally grabs an opponent.

home—in baseball, home plate.

home field/court/ice advantage—statistically measurable competitive advantage gained by playing half of the season's games in the same stadium or arena (whose idiosyncrasies are better known and more likely to be mastered) in front of home-town fans (whose support can motivate players).

home plate—in baseball, five-sided base over which the pitcher must throw the ball to initiate play and which a player must touch to score a run.

home run—in baseball, ball hit over the outfield wall in fair territory, allowing the batter and all players on base at the time to score ("hitting a home run" connotes the ultimate offensive achievement as well as personal success).

home stretch—in horse racing, last stretch of straight track heading to the finish line; said of the last portion of any form of competition.

homer—in baseball, home run; when referring to officials and referees, someone whose calls appear to favor the home team.

424

hoops—basketball ("let's go shoot some hoops").

hot corner—in baseball, third base (so called because it is closest to right-handed batters, which most players are, leaving the defensive player positioned there the shortest reaction time to hard-hit balls).

in and out—in basketball, near-miss shot that goes partially into the basket and then spins or bounces back out.

in the hole—in golf and basketball, where the ball is supposed to go; in baseball, no-ball/two-strike count (the batter is at a disadvantage and under pressure because he must hit the next pitch if it's a strike or be out).

incompletion—in football, pass that is not caught by a player in the field of play.

ineligible—in football, the five offensive players ("linemen") who line up along the line of scrimmage are not "eligible receivers" (allowed to catch a pass); the "eligible" players are the four behind the line of scrimmage and those at each end of the line.

infield—in baseball, area between home plate and the beginning of the outfield, usually defined by a dirt area or (on artificial surfaces) a painted line; in auto and horse racing, area inside the track oval.

injured reserve (IR)—in professional football and basketball, roster category for players who are too seriously hurt to play for several games, allowing the team to assign their roster spots to replacements until they return.

inning—in baseball, the visiting team bats until it makes three outs, then the home team bats; nine such innings make up a regulation game providing the score is not tied at the end of the ninth inning (if it is, "extra innings" are played until one team wins); the home team does not bat in the bottom of the ninth if it is leading; in case of rain or weather problems, five innings must be completed for the game to count or it must be replayed.

inside track—in horse racing, position on the inside of the oval track closest to the fence or rail, where less distance must

425

be traveled; said of any situation where someone appears to have a shorter route to success than a competitor.

instant replay—television technique (made possible by video technology) of showing what just happened, allowing specific analysis and commentary; in professional football, also refers to controversial, short-lived experiment during which officials off the field reviewed the videotape of questionable plays to confirm or reverse the decision on the field before allowing play to resume.

interception—in football, pass caught by the defensive team, which takes over possession.

iron—in golf, clubs of varying weights with metal heads, used to hit the ball short and medium distances.

iron man—player who plays in almost every game.

jock-sniffer—fanatic fan who enjoys being around athletes; often a major donor to and supporter of a school's athletic program.

jockey—in horse racing, individual who rides the horse in the race; connotes competing ("jockey for position").

jump ball—in basketball, play on which the referee throws the ball straight up between two opposing players who jump when it reaches its highest point to try to tip it to a player on their team (they're not allowed to catch it themselves).

juniors—amateur hockey league for young players being groomed for professional hockey.

K—in baseball, abbreviation for strike out.

key—painted area between the foul line and the baseline under the basket (so called because it looks like a keyhole) where offensive players may remain for no longer than three seconds; also called "the paint."

knuckleball—in baseball, uncommon pitch thrown with no rotation, causing it to behave erratically and making it very difficult to hit (the grip actually involves the fingernails, not the knuckles, but the name comes from the way it looks).

lane—in basketball, the key; in bowling, what used to be called the alley (the building in which bowling "lanes" are found is a "bowling center," not a "bowling alley").

last out—in baseball, third out in an inning or the twenty-seventh out in a regular nine-inning game.

lead the league—in team sports, refers to player with the best number in a statistical category; in business, often connotes a negative ("he leads the league in sexual harassment complaints").

leg whip—in football, controversial technique in which a lineman sweeps his legs close to the ground to knock down an opposing player.

letters—in baseball, chest area on the uniform where the team's name typically appears.

lie—in golf, ball's position relative to the hole; also, what a player does to inflate his accomplishments.

line of scrimmage—in football, imaginary line that stretches sideline to sideline from the forward-most point (or "nose") of the ball; players who cross this line before the play starts are "offside" and their team is penalized five yards.

linebacker—in football, defensive player who plays behind the front line and in front of the defensive backs.

linemen—in football, very large offensive and defensive players who line up along the line of scrimmage.

line-up—players who are actually in the game.

lit up—in baseball, pitcher who is hit hard ("he got lit up in the third").

lonesome end—in football, wide receiver who lines up all alone over at the sideline.

losing streak—consecutive losses.

loss—in baseball, statistical category that keeps track of how many times a pitcher allows the eventual winning run to score.

lottery—in professional basketball, weighted system designed to build up weak teams by allowing them to pick top college players first; the eleventh worst team during the season receives one chance, the worst team eleven (the top players are called "lottery picks").

magic number—number of games a team must win and/or its closest opponent must lose to make it impossible for that opponent to win the season championship.

major league—highest competitive level (usually refers to baseball).

make book on it—to bet that it will happen.

man to man—in basketball and football, style of defense in which players guard an opposing player wherever he goes rather than stay in one assigned area (a "zone defense").

manager—in baseball, head coach.

marathon—foot-race of twenty-six miles.

mark—in bowling, a strike or spare ("she marked in the sixth and seventh frames"); in soccer, to guard an opponent ("mark a man").

measurement—in football, stoppage of play to determine whether the offensive team has advanced the ball the full ten yards required for a first down.

Mendoza Line—in baseball, pejorative term for a player unable to hit better than .200 (two base hits in every ten at bats; players who can't hit above the Mendoza Line seldom stay in the major leagues for long).

minor league—lower-level league where players train and develop their skills in hopes of someday playing at the major league level; usually refers to baseball.

momentum ("mo")—said of the team that, however momentarily, appears able to succeed at whatever it is doing (in a game, momentum may "turn," "shift," and "swing" several times); has more to do with emotion and chance than skill.

mound—in baseball, pile of dirt in the middle of the infield where the pitcher stands (sixty feet six inches from home plate).

net/nets—in hockey, the goal; in basketball, lacings attached to the basket's rim to absorb the ball's momentum when it goes through the hoop.

netminder—in hockey, goalie.

neutral zone—in hockey, area at center ice between the blue lines.

nickel—in football, formation that substitutes a fifth (hence the name) defensive back for a lineman or linebacker to protect against passing plays.

no-hitter—in baseball, rare game where one team fails to get a base hit (usually, but not always, the team without a hit loses).

0-for-(anything)—in baseball, no hits in however many attempts; connotes failure and futility ("she's 0-for-December").

offside—in football, crossing the line of scrimmage before the ball is hiked (penalty: five yards); in hockey, crossing the blue line before the puck (penalty: a face-off in the neutral zone); in soccer, playing ahead of the ball and closer to the goal than the other team's defenders (penalty: free kick by the other team).

on a roll—enjoying a series of successes, with the implication that the momentum will carry through to future competition.

on deck—in baseball, player who will bat next.

on the ropes—in boxing, fighter in trouble (the ropes limit his ability to move away or retreat from his opponent); connotes any individual or team on the verge of defeat.

one game at a time—cliché used to focus players on each day's tree instead of the forest.

one and one—in basketball, a second foul shot is awarded when a single foul shot is made as a penalty for a certain number of team fouls in a half (not awarded on two-shot fouls).

one on one—when two players from opposing teams match up individually rather than work with their teammates ("going one-on-one").

option—in football, running play on which the ball carrier can either keep the ball, lateral it to a teammate behind him, or throw a pass; in professional sports, contract provision allowing a team to move a player from its roster to that of an affiliated team at a lower level (the optioned player is "sent down").

out—in baseball, "retiring" a batter by catching a batted ball before it hits the ground, throwing the ball to the next base before the batter or a base runner gets there and tagging him or the base, or throwing three strikes past him (there are three outs to each half of the inning); in tennis, shot that lands outside the playing area of the court.

out of bounds—area along the side of a football field, basketball court, or soccer field where play is not allowed.

out of the gate—in horse racing, gated stalls open at the start of the race (one key to success is to be "fast out of the gate").

outfield—in baseball, playing area between the infield and the wall.

over/under—betting line based on the total number of points that bookmakers expect will be scored in the game (in a football game, for example, you might bet on whether the combined score will be over or under forty points).

pace car—in auto racing, car not involved in the race that leads the competing cars through one lap, allowing them to get up to speed while staying in their assigned starting positions.

pad—protective equipment worn by players in most sports; to add to a lead in the game score or an individual statistic.

paint—in basketball, area inside the key (which often is painted a different color from the rest of the floor); in baseball, to pitch on the inside or outside corners of home plate, which is edged in black ("he's really painting the black today").

par—in golf, number of shots in which a good player is expected to get the ball from the tee into the hole ("par 3"); also, total number of shots in which a good player is expected to complete an eighteen-hole course ("par 72").

parlay—bet involving the outcome of several games, usually on the same day.

pass—in football, ball thrown from behind the line of scrimmage to an eligible receiver; in basketball, hockey, and soccer, throwing the ball or hitting the puck or kicking or heading the ball to another player on your team.

penalty—in football, rule infraction for which the offending team is punished by having the ball moved closer to its own goal line and/or losing a down; in hockey, rule infraction for which the offending player must go to the penalty box for a time (two minutes for "minors," five minutes for "majors") while his team plays shorthanded; in basketball, after a team has committed six fouls in a period, the opposing team is "in the penalty," awarded an extra shot when it makes a foul shot (worth one point).

pennant—in baseball, flag awarded to the team that wins the league championship, now synonymous with that championship (the baseball season is often referred to as the "pennant race").

period—timed portion of a game; football, soccer, and professional and high school basketball have four (but college basketball games are divided into two halves), hockey has three.

pickoff—in baseball, throwing to a base, ostensibly in an attempt to catch the base runner far enough away from it to tag him out, typically to make him stay closer to the base so he doesn't have as good a chance to steal or advance on another player's hit or out; in football, pass interception.

pin—in bowling, what you try to knock down with the ball (the "head pin" is the one closest to the bowler); in golf, the hole; in wrestling, holding an opponent's shoulders to the mat for a three-count wins the match.

pinch hitter—in baseball, player who enters the game to bat for a teammate (the replaced player cannot return to the game).

pit crew—in auto racing, team of mechanics that services the car during the race; in business, connotes speed, precision, and a high level of teamwork under pressure.

pitch inside—in baseball, to throw the ball on the batter's side of home plate at the risk of hitting the batter; connotes confidence and professional courage.

place—in horse racing, to finish second (bets are taken on which horses will "win," "place," and "show").

play for a break—strategy in which one team attempts to pressure the other into making a mistake or creating a situation that can be exploited for competitive advantage; connotes an inability to win based solely on head-to-head skill and strength.

play it safe—strategy of taking no chances that might allow a competitor to get back into the contest, usually adopted when a team is comfortably ahead.

play with pain—to continue to play despite personal injuries; connotes courage and team dedication, but also masks decisions to ignore seemingly minor conditions that can lead to more serious injuries.

playground—in basketball, where many inner-city players have traditionally honed their skills; connotes strong (often spectacular) individual performance, but often at the expense of team play and success ("that's a real playground move").

plus/minus ratio—in hockey, number derived by subtracting goals scored by the opponent while a player is on the ice from goals scored by the player's team while he is playing (positive signifies a valuable team player, negative a liability).

point—in basketball and football, unit of scoring (the baseball equivalent is "runs," hockey and soccer have "goals"); in hockey, standings are determined on the basis of two points for each win, one point for each tie; in basketball and hockey, outer area in the center of the offensive zone from which plays are directed (in basketball, the guard who handles the ball most often is called the "point guard").

point spread—device that attempts to equalize a game for betting purposes by figuratively giving one team a certain number of points (if team A is favored by 4 points and beats team B 10–7, those who bet on team B win because the score for betting purposes is 11–10); the wider the point spread, the greater the disparity between the two teams.

pole position—in auto racing, first car in the first row on the inside of the track; starting on the inside of the front row is advantageous because competitors must steer through traffic to reach the front of the pack (the pole position is awarded to the car with the fastest average lap time during a qualifying period before the race).

pooch—in football, punt or kickoff deliberately kicked short, usually to prevent the opponent from running it back or letting it roll into the end zone.

pop fly—in baseball, short, weakly hit fly ball, usually caught by an infielder.

possession—in football, the offensive team is in possession of the ball ("time of possession" measures how long they have it during the game).

possession arrow—in basketball, device used to alternate who gets possession of the ball when one player from each team is holding it at the same time (formerly decided by a jump ball, which is no longer practical because players are so much taller than referees).

post—in basketball, area around the key where the center typically plays on offense ("high post" is at the foul line, "low post" is close to the baseline, to "post up" means to use a height advantage to get closer to the basket for an easier shot); in horse racing, starting point ("post time" is the time the race is scheduled to start).

power alley—in baseball, areas in the outfield between the left fielder and the center fielder, and the center fielder and the right fielder.

power game—style of play that relies on physical strength rather than speed or finesse; in baseball, it involves a reliance on homerun hitters; in basketball, on tall players who score from close to the basket; in football, on running instead of passing.

power play—in hockey, when a player is penalized for a minor infraction, he must sit out two minutes, during which his team plays shorthanded and the other team is said to be on the power play.

practice frame—in bowling, warm-up frame (two balls) that does not count against the player's score.

prayer—attempt whose main chance for success seemingly involves divine intervention ("he puts up a prayer from 25 feet").

Proposition 48—NCAA regulation that mandates certain academic achievement levels in high school before a college freshman can compete in sports; controversial because it typically affects minority athletes from poorer schools.

punt—in football, when the offensive team believes it will be unable to advance the ball to the first down marker on fourth down, it can elect to kick the ball to the opposing team in order to make it take possession farther down the field; in business, connotes giving up temporarily with the idea of getting another chance reasonably soon.

putback—in basketball, basket scored by a player who rebounds his own or a teammate's missed shot and immediately shoots and scores, usually from very close to the basket.

putt—in golf, stroke used to hit the ball short distances into the hole; requires precision and steadiness.

quality start—in baseball, game in which the starting pitcher pitches at least six full innings and gives up three or fewer runs (which, based on statistical probability, gives his team a good chance of winning).

quarter—in football and basketball, one-fourth of the game as measured by the game clock (also called "periods," although a period is not always a quarter).

quarterback—in football, player on the field who directs the actions of his team; connotes leading a team effort.

quinella—in horse racing, bet in which you must pick the horses that will finish first and second, but not their order of finish.

RBIs—in baseball, runs batted in (players who score as a result of a batter's hits, walks, and sacrifice fly balls).

rain delay—in baseball, temporary stoppage of play while it's raining, during which the infield is covered to protect it in hopes that play can be resumed when the rain stops.

rained out—in baseball, game that cannot be played because of continuing rain (football and soccer are played regardless of weather conditions).

rebound—in basketball, to catch a missed shot after it has bounced off the rim or backboard.

red card—in soccer, what the referee gives to a player who is being ejected from the game.

referee—in basketball, officials; in football and hockey, head official.

relay—in baseball, throw from an outfielder to an infielder instead of directly to a base, allowing a second throw (ideally stronger and more accurate) to attempt to get a runner out; in track, race in which several runners on the same team run in succession.

report—what a player must do (either to a referee or official scorer) before entering the game.

reps (repetitions)—number of times an action, exercise, or play is repeated in practice.

retired—in baseball, player who is out or three outs to end an inning ("the side is retired"); player who has officially ended his playing career.

ribbies—RBIs.

riding the pines—sitting on the bench instead of playing in the game.

right down the fairway—in golf, shot hit through the clear area between the tee (where the golfer starts) and the green (where the hole is located); connotes a successful project.

rim—in basketball, metal circle through which the ball must pass for a shot to be good.

road trip—traveling to play one or a series of games in the home stadiums of other teams.

rocked—in baseball, said of a pitcher who gives up a lot of hits and runs ("he got rocked," also "shelled," "pounded," "lit up").

rookie—player in his first official season in the league.

rope a dope—in boxing, strategy of forcing a slower opponent into the ropes, popularized by Muhammad Ali.

rotation—in baseball, regular order in which the team's four or five starting pitchers are used; in basketball and hockey, relatively regular pattern of substitution designed to keep players fresh and involved in the game.

rotisserie league—in baseball, fantasy league in which fans draft players and compile game scores based on how their players perform in real games.

rough—in football, to hit the quarterback harder or later than allowed (penalty for roughing: fifteen yards); in hockey, to hit a player for a reason other than keeping him away from the puck or goal (penalty: two minutes in the penalty box); in golf, higher grass along the fairways and around the green.

roundball—basketball.

rubber—in baseball, rubber strip on the pitching mound that the pitcher must be in contact with when the pitch is thrown ("toe the rubber").

rubber-band defense—in football, said of a team that gives up a lot of yards, but not many points (it stretches, but it doesn't break).

run—in baseball, unit of scoring (one run is recorded for each player who circles the bases back to home plate); in football, play on which the offense attempts to advance the ball on the ground instead of by a pass; in basketball, period in which one team scores all or most of the points ("they're on a ten-point run").

run out the clock—in football and basketball, offensive strategy of taking as much time as possible during and between plays to hasten the end of the game, typically because the team is winning.

run to daylight—in football, said of a running back able to get past the first line of defenders and into the open field.

sack—in football, to tackle the quarterback while he is attempting to throw the ball.

sacrifice—in baseball, play on which the batter hits or bunts the ball to advance another player on his team, even though he himself will be out on the play.

safety—in football, two points are awarded to the defensive team when it tackles an offensive player in his own end zone; also identifies the defensive backs who play deep and down the middle of the field (the "strong safety" is on the same side of the field as the "tight end," the "free safety" is on the opposite side).

safety valve—in football, player (usually positioned off to one side of the field and close to the line of scrimmage) to whom the quarterback can throw the ball if no receivers are open downfield.

saves—in baseball, number of games in which a pitcher has entered a game with his team leading and preserved the lead for a victory (statistically, the opposing player who represents the tying run when the pitcher enters the game must bat for the pitcher to be awarded a save); in hockey, shots on goal stopped by the goalie.

sandlot—in baseball, refers to informal practice games on simple fields (once literally sandy lots) instead of in stadiums; connotes informal, relatively unsophisticated competition.

scouting report—advance analysis of an opponent that attempts to predict its strategy and tactics, identify its strengths and weaknesses, and help prepare players for their specific roles.

seam—in football, area between two defensive zones; in baseball, raised stitching on the ball that changes the ball's aerodynamics depending on how the pitcher grips it; in stadiums with artificial surfaces, place where pieces of the turf fasten together.

second team—team made up of the highest-ranking reserves; connotes not good enough to make the first team.

send down—in baseball, to demote a player to a lower league, usually for poor performance or lack of polished skills.

set-up man—in baseball, relief pitcher who enters the game in the seventh or eighth inning, but is replaced in the ninth by the "closer" (best relief pitcher).

settle for three—in football, to attempt to kick a field goal (worth three points) instead of score a touchdown (worth six points); connotes taking what is immediately and safely available instead of risking not scoring at all.

seventh inning stretch—in baseball, tradition of standing up and stretching or moving around between the visitor's and home team's half of the seventh inning (often accompanied by singing "Take Me out to the Ball Game").

shag—in baseball, to catch or retrieve balls hit to the outfield by a batter during practice.

share—in professional sports, how the money for playoffs and championships is divided.

short-handed—in hockey, playing with fewer players than the opposing team while those players are in the penalty box for a rule infraction.

shot—statistical category that records actual scoring attempts.

shot clock—in basketball, timer that requires the team with the ball to shoot within a specific time limit (twenty-four seconds in professional games, forty-five seconds in college games); reset on change of possession or when a shot hits the rim of the basket and is rebounded by the shooting team.

show—in horse racing, to finish third (bets can be made on which horse will "win," "place," and "show").

Show, The—how players refer to Major League baseball.

shutout—game in which the opponent does not score.

sidelines—in football and basketball, lines along the sides of the field or court that mark the limits of the playing area, where coaches and reserve players wait and watch during the game.

sidewinder—in baseball, pitcher who throws the ball with a sidearm motion.

situational substitution—changing players for specific offensive or defensive reasons, not because a player is tired, injured, or ineffective.

slamdunk—in basketball, spectacular play in which a player jumps higher than the rim (which is ten-feet high) and forcefully throws the ball down through the hoop.

slipstream—in auto racing, tactic of following a car in such a way that the airflow from the preceding car reduces wind resistance, thus assisting your car.

southpaw—lefthander.

spare—in bowling, knocking down all the pins left standing after the first ball in the frame (scores ten plus the count on the bowler's first roll in the next frame).

sparring partner—in boxing, practice fighter who serves primarily as a target for a boxer's punches and realistic opponent for practicing footwork and defensive postures.

special teams—in football, players brought into the game for kickoffs, punts, and field goals; in hockey, for penalty killing and power plays.

spike—in football, to throw the ball to the ground to celebrate a touchdown; in volleyball, power shot with a downward trajectory.

spitball—in baseball, illegal pitch thrown by adding spit or another substance to one part of the ball, the added weight causing it to behave in unexpected ways, making it harder to hit.

split—in bowling, two or more pins left standing after pins between them have been knocked down (the most difficult is the 7–10 split, the two pins on the ends of the back row); in baseball, a double-header where each team wins one game.

split finger—in baseball, grip used by some pitchers to throw a fastball with more movement, making it harder to hit.

spot—to give an opponent several points in order to make the contest more even ("we'll spot you six"); in football, to officially place the ball before the next play.

spotter—someone who assists broadcasters during a game by identifying the players involved in a play.

Stanley Cup—championship trophy of the National Hockey League.

starting gate—gated stalls where horses are lined up before a race.

starting lineup—players who start a game; connotes the best players, although in reality football and basketball teams substitute fresh or specialized players constantly based on the situation, and hockey teams rotate several complete units every couple of minutes to keep fresh players on the ice.

statman—someone who keeps and can recall detailed statistics.

stay within yourself—don't try to do more than you're capable of, advice given to athletes who are prone to fail if they allow the pressure of the moment to tempt them into taking chances or neglecting their assigned roles.

steal—in baseball, to advance a base before, during, or after a play on which the ball was not hit; in basketball, statistical category that keeps track of how many times a player takes the ball away from the opposing team.

steroids—natural or synthetic hormones used, almost always illegally, to stimulate growth, muscle formation, and other physical attributes; illegal due to their long-term health hazards.

stick—in baseball, slang for the bat and a player's ability with it ("good field, no stick"); in hockey, what players hit the puck (and occasionally each other) with; in football, to hit someone forcefully.

stopper—in baseball, starting pitcher relied on to stop losing streaks; typically the most dependable pitcher, not necessarily the most talented.

stranded—in baseball, runner who does not score but is left on base when a teammate makes the third out of an inning.

strike—in baseball, pitch thrown over home plate between the letters on the batter's uniform and his knees (three strikes is a strikeout); in bowling, knocking down all ten pins with the first ball of the frame (scores ten plus the count on the bowler's next two rolls).

strike out—in baseball, out recorded when a batter fails to hit three pitches judged strikes, whether he swings at them or not.

student body right/left—in football, potentially powerful offensive play in which several blockers lead the ball carrier around the end of the defensive formation.

stuff—in baseball, relative potency of a pitcher's assortment of pitches ("he's got good stuff today"); in basketball, to dunk ("he stuffed it").

sub(stitute)—player who doesn't start but comes into the game later to allow another player to rest (football, basketball, hockey) or permanently take another player's place (baseball).

submarine—in baseball, pitcher who throws the ball with an underarm motion; in football, to go under or undercut an opposing player.

sudden death—overtime period in which the first team to score wins (which means it's actually "sudden victory").

Super Bowl—championship game of the National Football League.

sweet spot—in baseball, part of the bat where optimum contact is made.

swing away—in baseball, to try to hit the ball as far as you can instead of not swinging, or bunting, or trying to hit the ball to a particular spot on the field.

tackle—in football, to bring the player carrying the ball to the ground (when his knee touches, the play is over or "dead"); player who lines up between the guard and the end or wide receiver on each side of the ball; in fishing, the collection of lines, lures, reels, weights, bobbers, hooks and other stuff that may or may not allow someone to catch a fish; in soccer, to take possession of the ball from an opponent.

take one for the team—in baseball, when a batter allows himself to be hit by a pitch in order to get on base or a pitcher stays in the game longer than he normally would to allow other pitchers to rest for future games.

take what they give you—competitive strategy of adjusting your style of play to take advantage of opportunities instead of trying to do what you planned to do, no matter how the opponent responds.

takeaways—in football, statistical category that keeps track of how many times the team intercepts passes and recovers fumbles; the higher the number, the tougher the defense.

tale of the tape—in boxing, official measurements of the two fighters.

team player—unselfish player, usually not a star performer, who works more for team results than personal glory and statistics.

technical foul—in basketball, foul called on a player or coach for improper conduct, or arguing with or cursing at the referee.

tee it up/tee off—in golf, to put the ball on the tee prior to the first shot on the hole; in other sports, implies deliberately hitting something or someone hard.

Texas Leaguer—in baseball, base hit that falls behind the infielders and in front of the outfielders; connotes cheap hit.

three-cushion shot—in pool and billiards, difficult shot that is angled off three sides of the table to hit a specific ball; connotes any difficult action that succeeds because of the individual's skill and finesse.

three-pointer—in basketball, a shot made from behind a line either eighteen (high school and college) or twenty-one feet (professional) from the basket is awarded three points instead of two.

throw in the towel—in boxing, to concede a fight between rounds (the trainer throws the fighter's towel into the ring to signify that the fighter will not be coming out for the next round); connotes giving up before the contest is over.

timeout—stoppage of play during the game to provide a brief rest and allow coaches to plan new strategies; in football, baseball, and hockey, timeouts are limited (and thus become a part of the team's strategy); in baseball, there are no restrictions.

touchdown—in football, carrying the ball across the goal line or catching it in the end zone (value: six points).

trade—to exchange one or more players with one or more other teams.

trainer—specialist responsible for prevention and rehabilitation of injuries; individual who trains a racehorse.

trap—in football, to catch the ball just after it has hit the ground or a running play on which the offensive lineman allows the defender opposite him to come across the line of scrimmage so he can be blocked by another player, opening up a hole for the ball carrier; in basketball, defensive technique in which two or more players converge on the opponent with ball; in soccer, to control the ball by allowing it to hit your body.

traveling—in basketball, to take more than two steps without dribbling the ball (the ball is awarded to the other team); the "traveling squad" is the players on a team's roster who go on road trips.

trenches—in football, area along the line of scrimmage where linemen work.

triple—in baseball, three-base hit.

Triple Crown—in horse racing, Kentucky Derby, Preakness, and Belmont Stakes (few horses win all three); in baseball, batting average, homeruns, and RBIs (few players lead the league in all three).

triple double—in basketball, scoring ten or more points, getting ten or more rebounds, and giving out ten or more assists (passes on which a teammate scores) in a single game.

trips—in football, three wide receivers on the same side of the field.

turkey—in bowling, three consecutive strikes.

turnover—in basketball, losing control of the ball to the other team before getting a shot at the basket (a minor setback and a measure of a team's ball-handling abilities and the other team's defense); in football, losing control of the ball to the other team because of a fumble or pass interception (can be a major setback).

twin killing—in baseball, double play.

two-minute drill—in football, fast-paced offense designed to make the most of remaining time and help a team score in the last couple of minutes in a half or the game, usually when it is behind or the game is tied.

two-minute warning—in professional football, television break that occurs with exactly two minutes left in the half and the game.

umpire—in baseball, officials stationed behind home plate, along the first and third base lines, and around second base to determine balls and strikes, fair balls and foul balls, and whether players are out on a specific play.

underdog—team expected to lose.

utility man—in baseball, player who can play several positions adequately, though typically none well enough to be the regular at that position.

waive/waivers—giving up ownership rights to a player's contract, usually for purposes of releasing the player so he can be replaced by someone else; typically, other teams have the right to claim the waived player in reverse order of the current league standings.

walk—in baseball, a player who is thrown, and does not swing at, four pitches judged to be out of the "strike zone" goes to first base, even though he has not hit the ball.

wall—in football, several players moving together ("a wall of blockers"); in bowling, strip of oil laid from the heads to the 1–3 pocket that enhances scoring by guiding a ball rolled along it; for a team or individual to "hit the wall" means to be too tired to compete effectively.

warning track—in baseball, nongrassy area at the end of the outfield designed to warn a player that he is in danger of crashing into the wall.

warning track power—in baseball, implied criticism of a player unable to hit the ball out of the park; said of someone who hits fly balls but not home runs.

weigh-in—in boxing, official prefight verification that the contestants are within the weight limits of their class.

wheelhouse—in baseball, area about waist-high on the batter where swings tend to be more powerful.

whiff—in baseball, to strike out.

whitewash—shutout.

wide receiver—in football, offensive players who line up at or slightly behind each end of the offensive line and are eligible to catch a pass (also called "wideouts").

win—object of the game, whatever it is; in baseball, statistical category that tracks the number of a team's victories a pitcher is responsible for; in horse racing, one of the three bets on the outcome (see also *place* and *show*).

winger—in hockey, players to the left and right of the center on the forward line.

winning isn't everything—famous quote that ends, "It's the only thing."

winning streak—consecutive victories.

winter ball—baseball leagues set up in Central and South America during the off-season, primarily for players who need additional practice and seasoning.

wire to wire—in horse racing, to lead the race from beginning to end; can be applied to any sport where one competitor or team leads for the duration of the contest or season.

wood—in golf, clubs with wooden heads used to hit the ball for distance.

World Series—in North American professional baseball, season-concluding, best-of-seven championship series between the champions of the American and National leagues.

yellow card—in soccer, what the referee gives a player as a warning that he will be ejected for further unsportsmanlike play.

zebras—officials in football and basketball, so called because they wear black-and-white–striped shirts.

zone—in basketball, defense in which players are assigned a specific area to defend instead of working against a specific opposing player; in football, defense in which defensive backs cover players in an assigned area on the field (opposite of both is "man-to-man coverage"); slang for playing to full potential ("he's in the zone tonight").

Position Charts
BASEBALL

Left Field

Shortstop

Center Field

Second Baseman

Right Field

Third Baseman

Pitcher

First Baseman

[third base]

[second base]

[home plate]

Catcher

[first base]

FOOTBALL

Tight
End

Cornerback

Strong
Safety

Outside (Strongside)
Linebacker

Defensive
End

Free
Safety

Middle
Linebacker

Defensive
Tackle

Tackle

Defensive
Tackle

Guard

Cornerback

Outside (Weakside)
Linebacker

Defensive
End

Center

Guard

Quarterback

Halfback or
Fullback

Tackle

Wide
Receiver

Halfback

Wide
Receiver

BASKETBALL

Point (1)
Guard

Shooting (2)
Guard

Center

Small (3)
Forward

Power (4)
Forward

• [basket]

SOCCER

Winger

Forward

Midfielder
(Fullback)

Defender
(Halfback)

Forward

Midfielder
(Fullback)

Defender
(Sweeper)

Goalie

[Goal]

Winger

Midfielder
(Fullback)

Defender
(Halfback)

HOCKEY

Left Wing

Center

Right Wing

Defenseman

Defenseman

Goalie

[Goal]

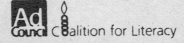
Warner Books is proud to be an active supporter of the Coalition for Literacy.